# REA's B...
## They have res...                                        e!

(a sample of the hu_____ ...REA receives each year)

" Your books are great! They are very helpful, and have upped my grade in every class. Thank you for such a great product. "

*Student, Seattle, WA*


" Your book has really helped me sharpen my skills and improve my weak areas. Definitely will buy more. "

*Student, Buffalo, NY*


" Compared to the other books that my fellow students had, your book was the most useful in helping me get a great score. "

*Student, North Hollywood, CA*


" I really appreciate the help from your excellent book. Please keep up your great work. "

*Student, Albuquerque, NM*


" Your book was such a better value and was so much more complete than anything your competition has produced (and I have them all)! "

*Teacher, Virginia Beach, VA*


*(more on next page)*

*(continued from previous page)*

" Your books have saved my GPA, and quite possibly my sanity.
My course grade is now an 'A,' and I couldn't be happier. "
*Student, Winchester, IN*

" These books are the best review books on the market.
They are fantastic! "
*Student, New Orleans, LA*

" Your book was responsible for my success on the exam. . . I
will look for REA the next time I need help. "
*Student, Chesterfield, MO*

" I think it is the greatest study guide I have ever used! "
*Student, Anchorage, AK*

" I encourage others to buy REA because of their superiority.
Please continue to produce the best quality books on the market."
*Student, San Jose, CA*

" Just a short note to say thanks for the great support your book
gave me in helping me pass the test . . . I'm on my way to a
B.S. degree because of you ! "
*Student, Orlando, FL*

# FRENCH
# VERBS

### J. Castaréde
**Professor of French**

**and the Staff of
Research & Education Association,
Carl Fuchs, Language Program Director**

*Research & Education Association*
61 Ethel Road West
Piscataway, New Jersey 08854

**Dr. M. Fogiel, Director**

# SUPER REVIEW®
# OF FRENCH VERBS

Printed in the United States of America

Library of Congress Control Number 2001097013

International Standard Book Number 0-87891-413-7

SUPER REVIEW is a registered trademark of Research & Education Association, Piscataway, New Jersey 08854

# WHAT THIS Super Review WILL DO FOR YOU

This **Super Review** provides all that you need to know to do your homework effectively and succeed on exams and quizzes.

The book focuses on the core aspects of the subject, and helps you to grasp the important elements quickly and easily.

Outstanding **Super Review** features:

- Topics are covered in logical sequence

- Topics are reviewed in a concise and comprehensive manner

- The material is presented in student-friendly language that makes it easy to follow and understand

- Individual topics can be easily located

- Provides excellent preparation for midterms, finals and in-between quizzes

- Written by professionals and experts who function as your very own tutors

In learning the French language, perhaps no area poses a more difficult challenge for students than conjugating the French verbs. This book comprises the most popular French verbs used in ordinary conversation with their English translation, so that in a compact form the student can quickly see the most appropriate endings which are required in a given case. It is a priceless aid and time-saver to the student.

The challenge of preparing this book has been to present the different conjugations in so clear and intelligible a form that they can be readily comprehended, memorized and consulted by the average student. This book is for those who may not have had the time or inclination to review their grammar. By a properly directed study of the verbs one can, in a remarkably short period, not only learn to read and understand the language, but also gain the ability to correctly speak, write and translate French.

It is the function of this **Super Review** to help the student master the verbs with the minimum expenditure of time and effort. The student will learn to apply these verbs in practical conversation and become familiar not only with their usual grammatical significance, but also with their idiomatic use.

### A Note on *"Thou"* and *"You"*

French has both an informal and a formal form of address. In French, *tu* (informal or familiar) is translated as *you* when speaking to a family member, friend, or anyone with whom you are on a first-name basis. It is also used in elevated language, like prayer and poetry. In these cases, it is translated as *thou*. *Vous* (formal) is also translated as the English *you,* but this is usually used to denote respect, such as when speaking to an employer or teacher.

To avoid confusion between the two terms, this book uses the poetic form of *tu* in its translations *(thou),* and the standard form of *vous (you)*. When *thou* is used in translation, it refers to *tu,* and when *you* is used in translation, it refers to *vous.* In your own translations of French to English, *you* can be used in both cases.

Once again, while *thou* is no longer used in conversational English, *tu,* its French equivalent, should be used when speaking to a family member or a friend. You should use *vous* (formal address) when speaking to someone of higher status or to one who is not a close friend.

Dr. Max Fogiel, Program Director
Carl Fuchs, Chief Editor

# CONTENTS

**3 VERBS WITH PECULIAR SPELLINGS**

**4 NEUTER, PASSIVE, PRONOMINAL, RECIPROCAL, AND IMPERSONAL VERBS**

## 5   IRREGULAR VERBS—FIRST CONJUGATION

# CHAPTER 1

# Auxiliary Verbs

## PRELIMINARY OBSERVATIONS ON FRENCH VERBS.

There are in French : The *auxiliary verbs*, and the *attributive verbs*.

The auxiliary verbs are :—*Avoir*, to have ; *être*, to be.  *Avoir* and *être* are called auxiliary verbs, *that is, helping verbs*, because they help to conjugate the other verbs in their compound tenses.

The *attributive verbs* have received that name because they may be considered to consist of the verbs To be—*être*, and an attribute, conjugated in the past indefinite form. This is used for actions completed in the past: *je (femme/fille) suis allée* (I went, I have gone); *vous avez compris* (You [have] understood); *ils ont dit* (They [have] said). Whereas *avoir* is conjugated and the participle is invariable, the past participle used with *être* must agree in number and gender with the subject. *There are five sorts of attributive verbs*, they are : 1. *Active or Transitive ;* 2. *Neuter or Intransitive; 3. Passive; 4. Reflective or Pronominal; 5. Unipersonal or Impersonal.*

The verbs attributive are divided in regard to their conjugation into :

*Regular, Irregular, and Defective.*

*The regular verbs* are those which follow the model conjugation.

*The irregular verbs* are those which, in some tenses or persons, deviate from the model conjugation.

*The defective verbs* are those which are lacking in some of the moods, tenses, or persons.

### CONJUGATIONS.

All the French verbs end in one or other of the following terminations : *er, ir, oir,* or *re.* Thence we get *four large groups of verbs*, which have received the name of conjugations, viz. :

| | | | | |
|---|---|---|---|---|
| Verbs ending in *er*, as *aimer*, to love, belong to the first conjugation. | | | | |
| Those | „ | *ir*, as *finir*, to finish, | „ | second „ |
| Those | „ | *oir*, as *recevoir*, to receive „ | | third „ |
| Those | „ | *re*, as *rendre*, to render | „ | fourth „ |

# CONJUGATION OF THE AUXILIARY VERB
## *AVOIR*, TO HAVE.

### INFINITIVE MOOD.

| PRESENT. | | PAST. | |
|---|---|---|---|
| Avoir. | *to have.* | Avoir eu. | *to have had.* |

| PARTICIPLE PRESENT. | | COMPOUND OF PARTICIPLE PRESENT. | |
|---|---|---|---|
| Ay*ant*. | *having.* | Ayant eu. | *having had.* |

PARTICIPLE PAST.

Eu (m.s.) (1).—Eue (f.s.)—Eus (m.pl.)—Eues (f.pl.) *had.*

### INDICATIVE MOOD.

| SIMPLE TENSES. | COMPOUND TENSES. |
|---|---|

#### PRESENT.

*Singular. Plural.*

| J'ai (2). | *I have.* |
|---|---|
| Tu as. | *thou hast.* |
| Il a (3). | *he has.* |
| Elle a. (3) | *she has.* |
| Nous avons. | *we have.* |
| Vous avez. | *you have.* |
| Ils ont. | *they have.* |
| Elles ont. | *they have.* |

#### PAST INDEFINITE.

*Singular. Plural.*

| J'ai eu. | *I have had.* |
|---|---|
| Tu as eu. | *thou hast had.* |
| Il a eu. | *he has had.* |
| Elle a eu. | *she has had.* |
| Nous avons eu. | *we have had.* |
| Vous avez eu. | *you have had.* |
| Ils ont eu. | *they have had.* |
| Elles ont eu. | *they have had.* |

#### IMPERFECT.

| J'av*ais*. | *I had* or *used* |
|---|---|
| Tu av*ais*. | *thou hadst* or *usedst* |
| Il av*ait*. | *he had* or *used* |
| Nous avi*ons*. | *we had* or *used* |
| Vous avi*ez*. | *you had* or *used* |
| Ils av*aient*. | *they had* or *used* |

*to have.*

#### PLUPERFECT.

| J'avais eu. | *I had had.* |
|---|---|
| Tu avais eu. | *thou hadst had.* |
| Il avait eu. | *he had had.* |
| Nous avions eu. | *we had had.* |
| Vous aviez eu. | *you had had.* |
| Ils avaient eu. | *they had had.* |

#### PAST DEFINITE.

| J'eus. | *I had.* |
|---|---|
| Tu eus. | *thou hadst.* |
| Il eut. | *he had.* |
| Nous eûmes. | *we had.* |
| Vous eûtes. | *you had.* |
| Ils eurent. | *they had.* |

#### PAST ANTERIOR.

| J'eus eu. | *I had had.* |
|---|---|
| Tu eus eu. | *thou hadst had.* |
| Il eut eu. | *he had had.* |
| Nous eûmes eu. | *we had had.* |
| Vous eûtes eu. | *you had had.* |
| Ils eurent eu. | *they had had.* |

#### FUTURE.

| J'au*rai*. | *I shall* or *will have.* |
|---|---|
| Tu au*ras*. | *thou shalt* or *wilt have.* |
| Il au*ra*. | *he shall* or *will have.* |
| Nous au*rons*. | *we shall* or *will have.* |
| Vous au*rez*. | *you shall* or *will have.* |
| Ils au*ront*. | *they shall or will have.* |

#### FUTURE ANTERIOR.

| J'aurai eu. | *I shall* or *will have* |
|---|---|
| Tu auras eu. | *thou shalt* or *wilt have* |
| Il aura eu. | *he shall* or *will have* |
| Nous aurons eu. | *we shall* or *will have* |
| Vous aurez eu. | *you shall* or *will have* |
| Ils auront eu. | *they shall* or *will have* |

*had.*

N.B.—(1) m.s. stands for *masculine singular.*—f.s. for *feminine singular.*
m.p. „ *masculine plural.* f.pl. for *feminine plural.*
(2) *Je*, loses the *e*, which is replaced by an apostrophe ('), when the verb begins with *a vowel* or silent *h*. as *j'ai*, *j'obéis*, I obey ; *j'habite*, I live in.
(3) As in French there is no *neuter gender*, *il, elle*, (he, she) are also rendered by *it*, in English.

# CONDITIONAL MOOD.

| SIMPLE TENSES. | | COMPOUND TENSES. | |
|---|---|---|---|
| **PRESENT.** | | **PAST.** | |
| J'au*rais*. | *I should* or *would have.* | J'aurais eu. | *I should* or *would have* |
| Tu au*rais*. | *thou shouldst* or *wouldst have.* | Tu aurais eu. | *thou shouldst* or *wouldst have* |
| Il au*rait*. | *he should* or *would have.* | Il aurait eu. | *he should* or *would have* |
| Nous au*rions*. | *we should* or *would have.* | Nous aurions eu. | *we should* or *would have* |
| Vous au*riez*. | *you should* or *would have.* | Vous auriez eu. | *you should* or *would have* |
| Ils au*raient*. | *they should* or *would have.* | Ils auraient eu. | *they should* or *would have* |

*had.*

# IMPERATIVE MOOD.

### PRESENT OR FUTURE.

| | |
|---|---|
| Aie. | *Have (thou).* |
| Qu'il ait. | *let him have.* |
| Qu'elle ait. | *let her have.* |
| Ayons. | *let us have.* |
| Ayez. | *have (ye or you).* |
| Qu'ils aient. | *let them have.* |
| Qu'elles aient. | *let them have.* |

# SUBJUNCTIVE MOOD.

| PRESENT. | | PAST. | |
|---|---|---|---|
| Que j'aie. | *That I may have.* | Que j'aie eu.* | *That I may have* |
| Que tu aies. | *that thou mayest have.* | Que tu aies eu. | *that thou mayest have* |
| Qu'il ait. | *that he may have.* | Qu'il ait eu. | *that he may have* |
| Que nous ayons. | *that we may have.* | Que nous ayons eu. | *that we may have* |
| Que vous ayez. | *that you may have.* | Que vous ayez eu. | *that you may have* |
| Qu'ils aient. | *that they may have.* | Qu'ils aient eu. | *that they may have* |

*had.*

| IMPERFECT. | | PLUPERFECT.* | |
|---|---|---|---|
| Que j'eusse. | *That I might have.* | Que j'eusse eu. | *That I might have* |
| Que tu eusses. | *that thou mightest have.* | Que tu eusses eu. | *that thou mightest have* |
| Qu'il eût. | *that he might have.* | Qu'il eût eu. | *that he might have* |
| Que nous eussions. | *that we might have.* | Que nous eussions eu. | *that we might have* |
| Que vous eussiez. | *that you might have.* | Que vous eussiez eu. | *that you might have* |
| Qu'ils eussent. | *that they might have.* | Qu'ils eussent eu. | *that they might have* |

*had.*

\* By suppressing *que*, the Pluperfect of the Subj. is also used for the Conditional Past.

### IMPORTANT REMARK.

The following Tenses have the same termination in all French verbs.

*The Participle Present* ends always in *ant.*

| | 1st Person. | 2nd Pers. | 3rd Pers. | 1st Pers. | 2nd Pers. | 3rd Pers. |
|---|---|---|---|---|---|---|
| | *Singular :* | | | *Plural :* | | |
| | JE. | TU. | IL-ELLE. | NOUS. | VOUS. | ILS-ELLES. |
| The *Imperfect* (Ind.) by | ais. | ais. | ait. | ions. | iez. | aient. |
| „ *Future* . . by | rai. | ras. | ra. | rons. | rez. | ront. |
| „ *Conditional* . by | rais. | rais. | rait. | rions. | riez. | raient. |
| „ *Imperfect* (Sub.) by | sse. | sses. | t. | ssions. | ssiez. | ssent. |

N.B.—The terminations of the *Imperfect of the Indicative* for instance being known, the *learner* is already master of the terminations of the Imperfect in all French verbs (regular or irregular). What we say of the *Imperfect* applies to the other tenses.

# REMARKS ON VERBS CONJUGATED INTERROGATIVELY.

1.—Verbs can be conjugated interrogatively only in the tenses of the *Indicative and Conditional Moods.*

2.—The interrogation is made in French by placing *the pronoun, which is the subject or nominative, after the verb in simple tenses;* in compound tenses *it is placed after the auxiliary* and is joined to the verb by a hyphen.

> Ex.: *Avons-nous?* Have we?  |  *Avez-vous eu?* Have you had?

When *the third person* of a verb ends with a vowel a *t* is inserted between the pronoun and the verb. This is done for the sake of euphony.

> Ex.: *A-t-il?* Has he?  |  *Aura-t-il?* Will he have?
> *Aime-t-il?* Does he love?  |  *Finira-t-il?* Will he finish?

3.—When the verb has a noun for its nominative, the noun comes first and one of the pronouns *il-elle, ils-elles,* according to the gender and number of the subject or nominative, is placed after the verb.

> Ex.: *Les enfants ont-ils?* Have the children?

4.—If the *first person* of a tense conjugated interrogatively ends by *e* mute, an acute accent is put over that *e* (for the sake of euphony) in sentences *interrogative* or exclamative.

> Ex.: *Parlé-je?* Do I speak?  |  *Puissé-je le voir!* May I see him!

5.—Another form of interrogation, sometimes employed, is in using the expression:—*Est-ce que,* then the *nominative precedes the verb.*

That form of interrogation marks: doubt, surprise, etc. Nevertheless *est-ce que* is used before monosyllabic verbs, in the first person of the Indicative present, principally to avoid *hard sounds* (as in : *Cours-je?* Do I run?) or *ambiguity* (as in : *Mens-je?* Do I lie? sounds as *mange,* eat); we therefore use : *Est-ce que je cours? Est-ce que je mens?* However, we say (because there is no hard sound or ambiguity):

| | | | | | |
|---|---|---|---|---|---|
| *Ai-je?* | Have I? | *Fais-je?* | Do I make? | *Vais-je?* | Do I go? |
| *Suis-je?* | Am I? | *Sais-je?* | Do I know? | *Dis-je?* | Do I say? |
| *Dois-je?* | Do I owe? | *Vois-je?* | Do I see? | *Puis-je?* | Can I? |

N.B.—An auxiliary verb (*do, did,* etc.) is generally used in English, when a question is asked, and the nominative is placed after that auxiliary; in French, the nominative pronoun follows the verb, and *do* or *did is not expressed.*

> Do we speak? *Parlons-nous?*

## 5

# VERB.—*AVOIR*, to have.

## INTERROGATIVELY.

## INDICATIVE MOOD.

### SIMPLE TENSES.

#### PRESENT.

| | |
|---|---|
| Ai-je ? | Have I ? |
| As-tu ? | hast thou ? |
| A-t-il ? (1) | has he ? |
| A-t-elle ? | has she ? |
| Avons-nous ? | have we ? |
| Avez-vous ? | have you ? |
| Ont-ils ? | have they ? |
| Ont-elles ? | have they ? |

#### IMPERFECT.

| | |
|---|---|
| Avais-je ? | Had I ? |
| Avais-tu ? | hadst thou ? |
| Avait-il ? | had he ? |
| Avions-nous ? | had we ? |
| Aviez-vous ? | had you ? |
| Avaient-il ? | had they ? |

#### PAST DEFINITE.

| | |
|---|---|
| Eus-je ? | Had I ? |
| Eus-tu ? | hadst thou ? |
| Eut-il ? | had he ? |
| Eûmes-nous? | had we ? |
| Eûtes-vous ? | had you ? |
| Eurent-ils ? | had they ? |

#### FUTURE.

| | |
|---|---|
| Aurai-je ? | Shall I have ? |
| Auras-tu ? | wilt thou have ? |
| Aura-t-il ? (1) | will he have ? |
| Aurons-nous ? | shall we have ? |
| Aurez-vous ? | will you have ? |
| Auront-ils ? | will they have ? |

### COMPOUND TENSES.

#### PAST INDEFINITE.

| | |
|---|---|
| Ai-je eu ? | Have I had ? |
| As-tu eu ? | hast thou had? |
| A-t-il eu ? (1) | has he had ? |
| A-t-elle eu ? | has she had ? |
| Avons-nous eu ? | have we had ? |
| Avez-vous eu ? | have you had ? |
| Ont-ils eu ? | have they had ? |
| Ont-elles eu? | have they had ? |

#### PLUPERFECT.

| | |
|---|---|
| Avais-je eu ? | Had I had ? |
| Avais-tu eu ? | hadst thou had ? |
| Avait-il eu ? | had he had ? |
| Avions-nous eu ? | had we had ? |
| Aviez-vous eu ? | had you had ? |
| Avaient-ils eu ? | had they had ? |

#### PAST ANTERIOR.

| | |
|---|---|
| Eus-je eu ? | Had I had ? |
| Eus-tu eu ? | hadst thou had ? |
| Eut-il eu ! | had he had ? |
| Eûmes-nous eu ? | had we had ? |
| Eûtes-vous eu ? | had you had ? |
| Eurent-ils eu ? | had they had ? |

#### FUTURE ANTERIOR.

| | |
|---|---|
| Aurai-je eu ? | Shall I have had ? |
| Auras-tu eu ? | wilt thou have had ? |
| Aura-t-il eu ? | will he have had ? |
| Aurons-nous eu ? | shall we have had ? |
| Aurez-vous eu ? | will you have had ? |
| Auront-ils eu ? | will they have had? |

## CONDITIONAL MOOD.

### PRESENT.

| | |
|---|---|
| Aurais-je ? | Should I have ? |
| Aurais-tu ? | wouldst thou have ? |
| Aurait-il ? | would he have ? |
| Aurions-nous ? | should we have ? |
| Auriez-vous ? | would you have ? |
| Auraient-ils ? | would they have ? |

### PAST.

| | |
|---|---|
| Aurais-je eu? | Should I have had ? |
| Aurais-tu eu ? | wouldst thou have had? |
| Aurait-il eu ? | would he have had ? |
| Aurions-nous eu ? | should we have had ? |
| Auriez-vous eu ? | would you have had ? |
| Auraient-ils eu ? | would they have had ? |

(1) *A-t-*, is used before *il, elle,* for the sake of euphony. See page 4, No. 2.

# CONJUGATION OF A VERB WITH A NEGATIVE.

The adverb *not*, renders an English verb negative ; it is translated in French generally by two words : *ne* and *pas*, or *ne* and *point*.

1.—To conjugate a *French verb* negatively, in simple tenses, *ne* or *n'* is placed before the verb and *pas* or *point* after it. (See N.B.—3, page 7.)

Ex. :—Je *n'*ai *pas*, I have not.

2.—In compound tenses *ne* or *n'* comes before the auxiliary and *pas* or *point* after it.

Ex. :—Je *n'*ai *pas* eu, I have not had.

3.—When the verb is in the Infinitive (present), *ne* is not generally separated from *pas*, but it is optional to place *pas* before or after the verb.

Ex. :—*Ne pas* avoir
or
*N'*avoir pas. } Not to have.

If the verb is in the Perfect or Past of the Infinitive, it is also optional to place *ne* and *pas* together before the verb or to separate them.

Ex. :—*N'*avoir *pas* eu
or
*Ne pas* avoir eu. } Not to have had.

4.—The words do or did, which generally precede an English verb conjugated negatively, are not expressed in French. Ex. :—Je *ne* parle *pas*, I do not speak.

## VERB.—*AVOIR*, TO HAVE.
## CONJUGATED NEGATIVELY.

### INFINITIVE MOOD.

**PRESENT.**

Ne pas avoir. *Not to have.*

**PARTICIPLE PRESENT.**

N'ayant pas. *Not having.*

**PAST.**

N'avoir pas eu. *Not having had.*

**COMPOUND OF PARTICIPLE PRESENT.**

N'ayant pas eu. *Not having had.*

### INDICATIVE MOOD.

**SIMPLE TENSES.**

**PRESENT.**

*Singular.*
Je n'ai pas. *I have not.*
Tu n'as pas. *thou hast not.*
Il n'a pas. { *he has not.*
Elle n'a pas. { *she has not.*
*Plural.*
Nous n'avons pas. *we have not.*
Vous n'avez pas. *you have not.*
Ils n'ont pas. { *they have not.*
Elles n'ont pas. { *they have not.*

**IMPERFECT.**

Je n'avais pas. *I had not.*
Tu n'avais pas. *thou hadst not.*
Il n'avait pas. *he had not.*
Nous n'avions pas. *we had not.*
Vous n'aviez pas. *you had not.*
Ils n'avaient pas. *they had not.*

**PAST DEFINITE.**

Je n'eus pas. *I had not.*
Tu n'eus pas. *thou hadst not.*
Il n'eut pas. *he had not.*
Nous n'eûmes pas. *we had not.*
Vous n'eûtes pas. *you had not.*
Ils n'eurent pas. *they had not.*

**COMPOUND TENSES.**

**PAST INDEFINITE.**

*Singular.*
Je n'ai pas eu. *I have not had.*
Tu n'as pas eu. *thou hast not had.*
Il n'a pas eu. { *he has not had.*
Elle n'a pas eu. { *she has not had.*
*Plural.*
Nous n'avons pas eu. *we have not had.*
Vous n'avez pas eu. *you have not had.*
Ils n'ont pas eu. { *they have not had.*
Elles n'ont pas eu. { *they have not had.*

**PLUPERFECT.**

Je n'avais pas eu. *I had not had.*
Tu n'avais pas eu. *thou hadst not had.*
Il n'avait pas eu. *he had not had.*
Nous n'avions pas eu. *we had not had.*
Vous n'aviez pas eu. *you had not had.*
Ils n'avaient pas eu. *they had not had.*

**PAST ANTERIOR.**

Je n'eus pas eu. *I had not had.*
Tu n'eus pas eu. *thou hadst not had.*
Il n'eut pas eu. *he had not had.*
Nous n'eûmes pas eu. *we had not had.*
Vous n'eûtes pas eu. *you had not had.*
Ils n'eurent pas eu. *they had not had.*

| SIMPLE TENSES. | | COMPOUND TENSES. | |
|---|---|---|---|
| **FUTURE.** | | **FUTURE ANTERIOR.** | |

| | | | |
|---|---|---|---|
| Je n'aurai pas. | *I shall not have.* | Je n'aurai pas eu. | *I shall not have* ⎫ |
| Tu n'auras pas. | *thou wilt not have.* | Tu n'auras pas eu. | *thou wilt not have* ⎪ |
| Il n'aura pas. | *he will not have.* | Il n'aura pas eu. | *he will not have* ⎪ |
| Nous n'aurons pas. | *we shall not have.* | Nous n'aurons pas eu. | *we shall not have* ⎬ *had.* |
| Vous n'aurez pas. | *you will not have.* | Vous n'aurez pas eu | *you will not have* ⎪ |
| Ils n'auront pas. | *they will not have.* | Ils n'auront pas eu. | *they will not have* ⎭ |

## CONDITIONAL MOOD.

| PRESENT. | | PAST. | |
|---|---|---|---|
| Je n'aurais pas. | *I should not have.* | Je n'aurais pas eu. | *I should not have* ⎫ |
| Tu n'aurais pas. | *thou wouldst not have.* | Tu n'aurais pas eu. | *thou wouldst not have* ⎪ |
| Il n'aurait pas. | *he would not have* | Il n'aurait pas eu. | *he would not have* ⎪ |
| Nous n'aurions pas. | *we should not have.* | Nous n'aurions pas eu. | *we should not have* ⎬ *had.* |
| Vous n'auriez pas. | *you would not have.* | Vous n'auriez pas eu. | *you would not have* ⎪ |
| Ils n'auraient pas. | *they would not have.* | Ils n'auraient pas eu. | *they would not have* ⎭ |

## IMPERATIVE.

### PRESENT OR FUTURE.

| | |
|---|---|
| N'aie pas. | *Have not (thou).* |
| Qu'il n'ait pas. | *let him not have.* |
| N'ayons pas. | *let us not have.* |
| N'ayez pas. | *have not (ye or you.)* |
| Qu'ils n'aient pas. | *let them not have.* |

## SUBJUNCTIVE.

| PRESENT. | | PAST. | |
|---|---|---|---|
| Que je n'aie pas. | *That I may not have.* | Que je n'aie pas eu. | *That I may not have* ⎫ |
| Que tu n'aies pas. | *that thou mayest not have.* | Que tu n'aies pas eu. | *that thou mayest not have* ⎪ |
| Qu'il n'ait pas. | *that he may not have.* | Qu'il n'ait pas eu. | *that he may not have* ⎪ |
| Que nous n'ayons pas. | *that we may not have.* | Que nous n'ayons pas eu. | *that we may not have* ⎬ *had.* |
| Que vous n'ayez pas. | *that you may not have.* | Que vous n'ayez pas eu. | *that you may not have* ⎪ |
| Qu'ils n'aient pas. | *that they may not have.* | Qu'ils n'aient pas eu. | *that they may not have* ⎭ |

| IMPERFECT. | | PLUPERFECT. | |
|---|---|---|---|
| Que je n'eusse pas. | *That I might not have.* | Que je n eusse pas eu. | *That I might not have* ⎫ |
| Que tu n'eusses pas. | *that thou mightest not have.* | Que tu n'eusses pas eu. | *that thou mightest not have* ⎪ |
| Qu'il n'eût pas. | *that he might not have.* | Qu'il n'eût pas eu. | *that he might not have* ⎪ |
| Que nous n'eussions pas. | *that we might not have.* | Que nous n'eussions pas eu | *that we might not have* ⎬ *had.* |
| Que vous n'eussiez pas. | *that you might not have.* | Que vous n'eussiez pas eu. | *that you might not have* ⎪ |
| Qu'ils n'eussent pas. | *that they might not have.* | Qu'ils n'eussent pas eu. | *that they might not have* ⎭ |

---

N.B.—1. *Ne.* or *N'* is used without *pas*, if there is in the sentence, *a negative expression*, such as :

| *Not at all* | ne. . . point. | *Never* | ne. . . jamais. |
|---|---|---|---|
| *Nobody* | ne. . . personne | *Nothing* | ne. . . rien, etc. |

Ex. :

| | | | |
|---|---|---|---|
| Je n'ai point. | *I have not at all.* | Nous n'avons personne. | *We have nobody.* |
| *Point* is a stronger negative than *pas*. | | Ils n'ont jamais. | *They have never.* |

2. *N'* is used instead of *ne*, before a vowel or silent h, so instead of writing Je *ne ai* pas, je ne hésite pas, we write *je n'ai pas, je n'hésite pas.*

3. In simple tenses and compound ones, *ne* precedes *the personal pronoun or pronouns*, used objectively, if any.

| | |
|---|---|
| Ex. : Je ne *me* flatte pas, | I do not flatter myself. |
| Je ne *me* suis pas flatté, | I have not flattered myself. |

# REMARKS ON VERBS CONJUGATED NEGATIVELY AND INTERROGATIVELY.

When a verb is conjugated *Negatively* and *Interrogatively*, *ne* always stands before the verb in simple tenses,* and *pas* or *point*, etc., after the pronouns nominative. In compound tenses, *ne* is placed before the auxiliary, and *pas* or *point*, etc., after the pronouns nominative.

## VERB *AVOIR*—TO HAVE.
## NEGATIVELY AND INTERROGATIVELY.

### INDICATIVE MOOD.

| SIMPLE TENSES. | | COMPOUND TENSES. | |
|---|---|---|---|
| **PRESENT.** | | **PAST INDEFINITE.** | |
| N'ai-je pas? | Have I not? | N'ai-je pas eu? | Have I not had? |
| N'as-tu pas? | hast thou not? | N'as-tu pas eu? | hast thou not had? |
| N'a-t-il pas? | has he not? | N'a-t-il pas eu? | has he not had? |
| N'a-t-elle pas? | has she not? | N'a-t-elle pas eu? | has she not had? |
| N'avons-nous pas? | have we not? | N'avons-nous pas eu? | have we not had? |
| N'avez-vous pas? | have you not? | N'avez-vous pas eu? | have you not had? |
| N'ont-ils pas? | have they not? | N'ont-ils pas eu? | have they not had? |
| N'ont-elles pas? | have they not? | N'ont-elles pas eu? | have they not had? |
| **IMPERFECT.** | | **PLUPERFECT.** | |
| N'avais-je pas? | Had I not? | N'avais-je pas eu? | Had I not had? |
| N'avais-tu pas? | hadst thou not? | N'avais-tu pas eu? | hadst thou not had? |
| N'avait-il pas? | had he not? | N'avait-il pas eu? | had he not had? |
| N'avions-nous pas? | had we not? | N'avions-nous pas eu? | had we not had? |
| N'aviez-vous pas? | had you not? | N'aviez-vous pas eu? | had you not had? |
| N'avaient-ils pas? | had they not? | N'avaient-ils pas eu? | had they not had? |
| **PAST DEFINITE.** | | **PAST ANTERIOR.** | |
| N'eus-je pas? | Had I not? | N'eus-je pas eu? | Had I not had? |
| N'eus-tu pas? | hadst thou not? | N'eus tu pas eu? | hadst thou not had? |
| N'eut-il pas? | had he not? | N'eut-il pas eu? | had he not had? |
| N'eûmes-nous pas? | had we not? | N'eûmes-nous pas eu? | had we not had? |
| N'eûtes-vous pas? | had you not? | N'eûtes-vous pas eu? | had you not had? |
| N'eurent-ils pas? | had they not? | N'eurent-ils pas eu? | had they not had? |
| **FUTURE.** | | **FUTURE ANTERIOR.** | |
| N'aurai-je pas? | Shall I not have? | N'aurai-je pas eu? | Shall I not have had? |
| N'auras-tu pas? | wilt thou not have? | N'auras-tu pas eu? | wilt thou not have had? |
| N'aura-t-il pas? | will he not have? | Naura-t-il pas eu? | will he not have had? |
| N'aurons-nous pas? | shall we not have? | N'aurons-nous pas eu? | shall we not have had? |
| N'aurez-vous pas? | will you not have? | N'aurez-vous pas eu? | will you not have had? |
| N'auront-ils pas? | will they not have? | N'auront-ils pas eu? | will they not have had? |

### CONDITIONAL MOOD.

| PRESENT. | | PAST. | |
|---|---|---|---|
| N'aurais-je pas? | Should I not have? | N'aurais-je pas eu? | Should I not have had? |
| N'aurais-tu pas? | wouldst thou not have? | N'aurais-tu pas eu? | wouldst thou not have had? |
| N'aurait-il-pas? | would he not have? | N'aurait-il pas eu? | would he not have had? |
| N'aurions-nous pas? | should we not have? | N'aurions-vous pas eu? | should we not have had? |
| N'auriez-vous pas? | would you not have? | N'auriez-vous pas eu? | would you not have had? |
| N'auraient-ils pas? | would they not have? | N'auraient-ils pas eu? | would they not have had? |

* And before *the personal pronoun or pronouns*, used objectively, if any. Ex.: Ne *me* flatté-je pas? Do I not flatter myself?

# CONJUGATION OF THE AUXILIARY VERB
## *Être*—TO BE.

---

### INFINITIVE MOOD.

| PRESENT. | | PAST. |
|---|---|---|
| Être. | *to be.* | Avoir été. | *to have been.* |

| PARTICIPLE PRESENT. | | COMPOUND OF PARTICIPLE PRESENT. |
|---|---|---|
| Étant. | *being.* | Ayant été. | *having been.* |

PARTICIPLE PAST.

Été   (invariable)   *been.*

### INDICATIVE MOOD.

| SIMPLE TENSES. | COMPOUND TENSES. |
|---|---|

**PRESENT.**

| | |
|---|---|
| Je suis. | *I am.* |
| Tu es. | *thou art.* |
| Il est. | *he is.* |
| Elle est. | *she is.* |
| Nous sommes. | *we are.* |
| Vous êtes. | *you are.* |
| Ils sont. | *they are.* |
| Elles sont. | *they are.* |

*Singular. Plural.*

**PAST INDEFINITE.**

| | |
|---|---|
| J'ai été. | *I have been.* |
| Tu as été. | *thou hast been.* |
| Il a été. | *he has been.* |
| Elle a été. | *she has been.* |
| Nous avons été. | *we have been.* |
| Vous avez été. | *you have been.* |
| Ils ont été. | *they have been.* |
| Elles ont été. | *they have been.* |

**IMPERFECT.**

| | |
|---|---|
| J'étais. | *I was* or *used* |
| Tu étais. | *thou wast* or *usedst* |
| Il était. | *he was* or *used* |
| Nous étions. | *we were* or *used* |
| Vous étiez. | *you were* or *used* |
| Ils étaient. | *they were* or *used* |

*to be.*

**PLUPERFECT.**

| | |
|---|---|
| J'avais été. | *I had been.* |
| Tu avais été. | *thou hadst been.* |
| Il avait été. | *he had been.* |
| Nous avions été. | *we had been.* |
| Vous aviez été. | *you had been.* |
| Ils avaient été. | *they had been* |

**PAST DEFINITE.**

| | |
|---|---|
| Je fus. | *I was.* |
| Tu fus. | *thou wast.* |
| Il fut. | *he was.* |
| Nous fûmes. | *we were.* |
| Vous fûtes. | *you were.* |
| Ils furent. | *they were.* |

**PAST ANTERIOR.**

| | |
|---|---|
| J'eus été. | *I had been.* |
| Tu eus été. | *thou hadst been.* |
| Il eut été. | *he had been.* |
| Nous eûmes été. | *we had been.* |
| Vous eûtes été. | *you had been.* |
| Ils eurent été. | *they had been.* |

| SIMPLE TENSES. | | COMPOUND TENSES. | |
|---|---|---|---|
| **FUTURE.** | | **FUTURE ANTERIOR.** | |
| Je serai. | I shall or will be. | J'aurai été. | I shall or will have |
| Tu seras. | thou shalt or wilt be. | Tu auras été. | thou shalt or wilt have |
| Il sera. | he shall or will be. | Il aura été. | he shall or will have |
| Nous serons. | we shall or will be. | Nous aurons été. | we shall or will have |
| Vous serez. | you shall or will be. | Vous aurez été. | you shall or will have |
| Ils seront. | they shall or will be. | Ils auront été. | they shall or will have |

*been.* (braced after the compound tenses)

## CONDITIONAL MOOD.

| **PRESENT.** | | **PAST.** | |
|---|---|---|---|
| Je serais. | I should or would be. | J'aurais été. | I should or would have |
| Tu serais. | thou shouldst or wouldst be. | Tu aurais été. | thou shouldst or wouldst have |
| Il serait. | he should or would be. | Il aurait été. | he should or would have |
| Nous serions. | we should or would be. | Nous aurions été. | we should or would have |
| Vous seriez. | you should or would be. | Vous auriez été. | you should or would have |
| Ils seraient. | they should or would be. | Ils auraient été. | they should or would have |

*been.*

## IMPERATIVE MOOD.

### PRESENT OR FUTURE.

| Sois. | Be (thou). |
|---|---|
| Qu'il soit. | let him be. |
| Soyons. | let us be. |
| Soyez. | be (you). |
| Qu'ils soient. | let them be. |

## SUBJUNCTIVE MOOD.

| **PRESENT.** | | **PAST.** | |
|---|---|---|---|
| Que je sois. | That I may be. | Que j'aie été. | That I may have |
| Que tu sois. | that thou mayest be. | Que tu aies été. | that thou mayest have |
| Qu'il soit. | that he may be. | Qu'il ait été. | that he may have |
| Que nous soyons. | that we may be. | Que nous ayons été | that we may have |
| Que vous soyez. | that you may be. | Que vous ayez été. | that you may have |
| Qu'ils soient. | that they may be. | Qu'ils aient été. | that they may have |

*been.*

| **IMPERFECT.** | | **PLUPERFECT.*** | |
|---|---|---|---|
| Que je fusse. | That I might be. | Que j'eusse été. | That I might have |
| Que tu fusses. | that thou mightest be. | Que tu eusses été. | that thou mightest have |
| Qu'il fût. | that he might be. | Qu'il eût été. | that he might have |
| Que nous fussions. | that we might be. | Que nous eussions été. | that we might have |
| Que vous fussiez. | that you might be. | Que vous eussiez été | that you might have |
| Qu'ils fussent. | that they might be. | Qu'ils eussent été. | that they might have |

*been.*

N.B.—The student will remark that the terminations of the *Imperfect of the Indicative, Future, Conditional, Imperfect of Subjunctive,* and *Participle Present* of the verb *être*, are similar to those of the verb *avoir*, in the same tenses.

* By suppressing *que*, the Pluperfect of the Subjunctive, is also used for the Conditional Past.

# VERB *ÊTRE*—TO BE.—CONJUGATED.

## NEGATIVELY.
### INFINITIVE MOOD.

*Present.*
N'être pas.    *Not to be.*
        *Past.*
N'avoir pas été.   *Not to have been.*
### PARTICIPLES.
*Present.*
N'étant pas.    *Not being.*
        *Compound.*
N'ayant pas été.   *Not having been.*

### INDICATIVE MOOD.
#### SIMPLE TENSES.
*Present.*
Je ne suis pas, etc.   *I am not, etc.*
*Imperfect.*
Je n'étais pas, etc.   *I was not, etc.*
*Past Definite.*
Je ne fus pas, etc.   *I was not, etc.*
*Future.*
Je ne serai pas, etc.   *I shall not be, etc.*

### CONDITIONAL MOOD.
*Present.*
Je ne serais pas, etc.   *I should not be, etc.*

### IMPERATIVE MOOD.
#### PRESENT OR FUTURE.
Ne sois pas.    *Be not.*
Qu'il ne soit pas.   *let him not be.*
Ne soyons pas.   *let us not be.*
Ne soyez pas.   *be not.*
Qu'ils ne soient pas.   *let them not be.*

### SUBJUNCTIVE MOOD.
*Present.*
Que je ne sois pas, etc. *That I may not be, etc.*
*Imperfect.*
Que je ne fusse pas,etc. *That I might not be,etc.*
#### COMPOUND TENSES.
*Past Indefinite.*
Je n'ai pas été, etc.   *I have not been etc.*
*Past Anterior.*
Je n'eus pas été, etc.   *I had not been, etc.*
*Pluperfect.*
Je n'avais pas été, etc. *I had not been, etc.*
*Future Anterior.*
Je n'aurai pas été, etc. *I shall not have been,etc.*
*Conditional Past.*
Je n'aurais pas été, etc. *I should not have been,etc.*
*Subjunctive Past.*
Que je n'aie pas été, *That I may not have*
   etc.        *been, etc.*
*Pluperfect.*
Que je n'eusse pas été, *That I might not have*
   etc.        *been, etc.*

## INTERROGATIVELY.
### INDICATIVE MOOD.

*Present.*
Suis-je ? etc.   *Am I ? etc.*
*Imperfect.*
Étais-je ? etc.   *Was I ? etc.*
*Past Definite.*
Fus-je ? etc.   *Was I ? etc.*
*Future.*
Serai-je ? etc.   *Shall I be ? etc.*
*Conditional.*
Serais-je ? etc.   *Should I be ? etc.*

#### COMPOUND TENSES.
*Past Indefinite.*
Ai-je été ? etc.   *Have I been ? etc.*
*Past Anterior.*
Eus-je été ? etc.   *had I been ? etc.*
*Pluperfect.*
Avais-je été ? etc.   *Had I been ? etc.*
*Future Anterior.*
Aurai-je été ? etc.   *Shall I have been ? etc.*
*Conditional Past.*
Aurais-je été? etc.   *Should I have been? etc.*

## NEGATIVELY AND INTERROGATIVELY.

#### SIMPLE TENSES.
*Indicative Present.*
Ne suis-je pas ? etc.   *Am I not ? etc.*
*Imperfect.*
N'étais-je pas ? etc.   *Was I not ? etc.*
*Past Definite.*
Ne fus-je pas ? etc.   *Was I not ? etc.*
*Future.*
Ne serai-je pas ? etc.   *Shall I not be ? etc.*
*Conditional Present.*
Ne serais-je pas ? etc.   *Should I not be ? etc.*

#### COMPOUND TENSES.
*Past Indefinite.*
N'ai-je pas été ? etc.   *Have I not been ? etc.*
*Past Anterior.*
N'eus-je pas été ? etc. *Had I not been ? etc.*
*Pluperfect.*
N'avais-je pas été? etc. *Had I not been ? etc.*
*Future Anterior.*
N'aurai-je pas été ?   *Shall I not have been ?*
   etc.       *etc.*
*Conditional Past.*
N'aurais-je pas été ?   *Should I not have been?*
   etc.       *etc.*

N.B.—1. Verb *To be* (être) when conjugated *Interrogatively, Negatively,* and *Interrogatively and Negatively,* follows the model verb *avoir,* as it may be seen above.
2. We have given only the first person of *Simple and Compound Tenses,* thinking it sufficient to guide the learner through the verb negatively, etc.

# CHAPTER 2

# Active and Regular Verbs

## FIRST, SECOND, THIRD, AND FOURTH CONJUGATIONS.

An active verb expresses *action*, passing from an *actor, called in grammar the nominative or subject*, to an object *named in grammar the accusative or the direct regimen*.

Ex. :

James strikes the table. | *Jacques frappe la table.*

*Jacques* : is the nominative or the subject.

*frappe* : the verb active, and

*table* : the accusative or direct regimen.

### CONJUGATION OF ACTIVE VERBS :

1.—*To easily conjugate a French verb*, it is necessary to observe that in each verb there are the *radical* and the *termination*. The *radical*, which contains the meaning of the verb, never changes in regular verbs.*

*The termination* varies according to the persons and tenses.

2.—To conjugate, for example, a verb of the first conjugation, the terminations being known, it is necessary only to add the radical to the terminations.

3.—Thus, suppose we want to conjugate *parler*, of which the radical is *parl*. If we add the terminations of the different persons of the *Indicative of the first conjugation* (see next page) we have : *Je parl-e, tu parl-es, il parl-e, nous parl-ons, vous parl-ez, ils parl-ent*, and so on, for the other tenses, and the other conjugations.

N.B.—The pupil, before learning a conjugation, would do well to master the different terminations of it.

---

* The radical of a verb is obtained by cutting off the ending *er*, *ir*, *oir*, or *re*. So in *aimer*, the radical is *aim* (cutting off the termination *er*) ; in *finir*, the radical is *fin*, etc.

# REGULAR VERBS.

## TERMINATIONS OF THE FOUR CONJUGATIONS.

*Plural. Singular.*

**CONJUGATIONS:**

**INFINITIVE.**

| | 1 | 2 | 3 | 4 |
|---|---|---|---|---|
| | er | ir | evoir | re |

**PARTICIPLE PRESENT.**

| | 1 | 2 | 3 | 4 |
|---|---|---|---|---|
| | ant | issant | evant | ant |

**PARTICIPLE PAST.**

| | 1 | 2 | 3 | 4 |
|---|---|---|---|---|
| | é | i | u | u |

**INDICATIVE PRESENT.**

| | 1 | 2 | 3 | 4 |
|---|---|---|---|---|
| Je | e | is | ois | s |
| Tu | es | is | ois | s |
| Il | e | it | oit | d |
| Nous | ons | issons | evons | ons |
| Vous | ez | issez | evez | ez |
| Ils | ent | issent | oivent | ent |

**IMPERFECT.**

| | 1 | 2 | 3 | 4 |
|---|---|---|---|---|
| Je | ais | issais | evais | ais |
| Tu | ais | issais | evais | ais |
| Il | ait | issait | evait | ait |
| Nous | ions | issions | evions | ions |
| Vous | iez | issiez | eviez | iez |
| Ils | aient | issaient | evaient | aient |

**PAST DEFINITE.**

| | 1 | 2 | 3 | 4 |
|---|---|---|---|---|
| Je | ai | is | us | is |
| Tu | as | is | us | is |
| Il | a | it | ut | it |
| Nous | âmes | îmes | ûmes | îmes |
| Vous | âtes | îtes | ûtes | îtes |
| Ils | èrent | irent | urent | irent |

**FUTURE.**

| | 1 | 2 | 3 | 4 |
|---|---|---|---|---|
| Je | erai | irai | evrai | rai |
| Tu | eras | iras | evras | ras |
| Il | era | ira | evra | ra |
| Nous | erons | irons | evrons | rons |
| Vous | erez | irez | evrez | rez |
| Ils | eront | iront | evront | ront |

**CONJUGATIONS:**

**CONDITIONAL.**

| | 1 | 2 | 3 | 4 |
|---|---|---|---|---|
| Je | erais | irais | evrais | rais |
| Tu | erais | irais | evrais | rais |
| Il | erait | irait | evrait | rait |
| Nous | erions | irions | evrions | rions |
| Vous | eriez | iriez | evriez | riez |
| Ils | eraient | iraient | evraient | raient |

**IMPERATIVE.**

| 1 | 2 | 3 | 4 |
|---|---|---|---|
| e | is | ois | s |
| e | isse | oive | e |
| ons | issons | evons | ons |
| ez | issez | evez | ez |
| ent | issent | oivent | ent |

**SUBJUNCTIVE PRESENT.**

| | 1 | 2 | 3 | 4 |
|---|---|---|---|---|
| Je | e | isse | oive | e |
| Tu | es | isses | oives | es |
| Il | e | isse | oive | e |
| Nous | ions | issions | evions | ions |
| Vous | iez | issiez | eviez | iez |
| Ils | ent | issent | oivent | ent |

**IMPERFECT.**

| | 1 | 2 | 3 | 4 |
|---|---|---|---|---|
| Je | asse | isse | usse | isse |
| Tu | asses | isses | usses | isses |
| Il | ât | ît | ût | ît |
| Nous | assions | issions | ussions | issions |
| Vous | assiez | issiez | ussiez | issiez |
| Ils | assent | issent | ussent | issent |

**RADICALS OF THE MODEL VERBS**

**OF THE FOUR CONJUGATIONS.**

| 1 | 2 | 3 | 4 |
|---|---|---|---|
| Parl-er | Fin-ir | Recev-oir | Vend-re |
| *to speak* | *to finish* | *to receive* | *to sell* |

**N.B.**—Another way, to learn easily the regular verbs, is to know the formation of the tenses of a verb
(see next page).

# FORMATION OF THE TENSES OF A VERB.

There are amongst the *simple tenses* of a French verb, two sorts called *Primitive* and *Derivative*.

From the *Primitive Tenses* the derivative are formed.

There are five Primitive Tenses :—

1. The Present of the Infinitive. | 3. The Participle Past.
2. The Participle Present. | 4. The Present of the Indicative.
5. The Past Definite.

1.—THE PRESENT OF THE INFINITIVE FORMS TWO TENSES, viz. : *The Future and the Present of the Conditional.*

I.  *The Future* by changing *r, oir,* or *re,* into : *rai, ras, ra, rons, rez, ront.*
1st. conjugation.—Aime-*r* : Future, j'aime-*rai,* tu aime-*ras,* etc.
2nd conjugation.—Fini-*r* : Future, je fini-*rai,* tu fini-*ras,* etc.
3rd conjugation.—Recev-*oir* : Future, je recev-*rai,* tu recev-*ras,* etc.
4th conjugation.—Rend-*re* : Future, je rend-*rai,* tu rend-*ras,* etc.

II.  *The Present of the Conditional* in changing *r, oir,* or *re* into : *rais, rais, rait, rions, riez, raient.*

Aime-*r* Conditional j'aime-*rais,* tu aime-*rais,* etc.
Fini-*r*      ,,     je fini-*rais,* tu fini-*rais,* etc.
Recev-*oir,* ,,    je recev-*rais,* tu recev-*rais,* etc.
Rend-*re*      ,,    je rend-*rais,* tu rend-*rais,* etc.

2.—THE PARTICIPLE PRESENT FORMS :—
I. The plural of the *Present of the Indicative* by changing *ant* into : *ons, ez, ent.*

Aim-*ant,* nous aim-*ons,* vous aim-*ez,* ils aim-*ent.*
Finiss-*ant,* nous finiss-*ons,* vous finiss-*ez,* ils finiss-*ent.*
Recev-*ant,* nous recev-*ons,* vous recev-*ez,* ils reçoiv-*ent.*
Rend-*ant,* nous rend-*ons,* vous rend-*ez,* ils rend-*ent.*

II.  *The Imperfect of the Indicative* by changing *ant* into : *ais, ais ait, ions, iez, aient.*

Aim-*ant,* j'aim-*ais,* tu aim-*ais,* etc.
Finiss-*ant,* je finiss-*ais,* tu finiss-*ais,* etc.
Recev-*ant,* je recev-*ais,* tu recev-*ais,* etc.
Rend-*ant,* je rend-*ais,* tu rend-*ais,* etc.

III.—The Present of the Subjunctive by changing *ant* into : *e, es, e, ions, iez, ent.*

Aim-*ant* :  Que j'aim-*e*,  que tu aim-*es*, etc.
Finiss-*ant* :  Que je finiss-*e*,  que tu finiss-*es*, etc.
Recev-*ant* :
Rend-*ant* :  Que je rend-*e*,  que tu rend-*es*, etc.

3. THE PARTICIPLE PAST FORMS ALL THE COMPOUND TENSES *with the help of the auxiliary verbs :* Avoir *or* être.

The compound tenses are the following :

| | | | |
|---|---|---|---|
| *Past indefinite* | - - - | - J'ai, etc. | }
| *Past anterior* | - - - | - J'eus, etc. | *Aimé.* |
| *Pluperfect* - | - - - | - J'avais, etc. | |
| *Future anterior* - | - - | - J'aurai, etc. | *Fini.* |
| *Conditional past* - | - - | - J'aurais, etc. | |
| *Past of the subjunctive* | - | - Que j'aie, etc. | *Reçu.* |
| *Pluperfect of the subjunctive* | - | Que j'eusse, etc. | |
| *Infinitive past* | - - - | - Avoir. | *Rendu.* |
| *Compound of participle present* | - | Ayant. | }

4. THE PRESENT OF THE INDICATIVE FORMS *the Imperative by the suppression of the pronouns :* Je, nous, vous.*

*Present of the Indicative.*
J'aime,  *nous* aimons.  *vous* aimez.
Je finis,  *nous* finissons,  *vous* finissez.
Je reçois,  *nous* recevons,  *vous* recevez.
Je rends,  *nous* rendons,  *vous* rendez.

*Imperative.*
Aime,  aimons,  aimez.
Finis,  finissons,  finissez.
Reçois,  recevons,  recevez.
Rends,  rendons,  rendez.

5. THE PAST DEFINITE FORMS *the Imperfect of the Subjunctive,* by changing *s* of the second person singular into : *sse, sses, t, ssions, ssiez, ssent.*

Tu aima-*s* :  Que j'aima-*sse*, etc.
Tu fini-*s* :  Que je fini-*sse*, etc.
Tu reçu-*s* :  Que je reçu-*sse*, etc.
Tu rendi-*s* :  Que je rendi-*sse*, etc.

* Exceptions: *j'ai,* Imperative, *aie ; je sais,* Imp. *sache ; je suis,* Imp. *sois ; je vais.* Imp. *va.*
*Remarks :*—1st. In the third conjugation the third person plural of the Indicative present being : *reçoivent* is irregular.
2nd. In the Present of the Subjunctive (third conjugation) the two persons plural are the only regular, *que nous recevions, que vous receviez.*
3rd. The rules for the formation of the tenses are only for the regular verbs.

# REGULAR VERBS.

## FIRST CONJUGATION ENDING IN *ER.*

### MODEL VERB.

### *PARLER*, TO SPEAK.

#### INFINITIVE MOOD.

|  | *Present.* |  | *Past.* |
|---|---|---|---|
| Parler. | *to speak.* | Avoir parlé. | *to have spoken.* |
|  | *Participle Present.* |  | *Comp. of Part. Present.* |
| Parlant. | *speaking.* | Ayant parlé. | *having spoken.* |

*Participle past.*—Parlé (m.s.), parlée (f.s.), parlés (m.pl.), parlées (f.pl.), *spoken.*

#### INDICATIVE MOOD.

**SIMPLE TENSES.**

**COMPOUND TENSES.**

##### PRESENT.

| | | |
|---|---|---|
| Je parle. | *I speak* or *I am* | |
| Tu parles. | *thou speakest* or *thou art* | |
| Il parle. | *he speaks* or *he is* | *speaking.* |
| Elle parle. | *she speaks* or *she is* | |
| Nous parlons. | *we speak* or *we are* | |
| Vous parlez. | *you speak* or *you are* | |
| Ils parlent. | *they speak* or *they are* | |
| Elles parlent | *they speak* or *they are* | |

##### PAST INDEFINITE.

| | | |
|---|---|---|
| J'ai parlé. | *I have* | |
| Tu as parlé. | *thou hast* | |
| Il a parlé. | *he has* | *spoken.* |
| Elle a parlé. | *she has* | |
| Nous avons parlé. | *we have* | |
| Vous avez parlé. | *you have* | |
| Ils ont parlé. | *they have* | |
| Elles ont parlé. | *they have* | |

##### IMPERFECT.

| | |
|---|---|
| Je parlais. | *I was speaking, I used* |
| Tu parlais. | *thou wast speaking, thou usedst* |
| Il parlait. | *he was speaking, he used* |
| Nous parlions. | *we were speaking, we used* |
| Vous parliez. | *you were speaking, you used* |
| Ils parlaient. | *they were speaking, they used* |

*to speak.*

##### PLUPERFECT.

| | |
|---|---|
| J'avais parlé. | *I had* |
| Tu avais parlé. | *thou hadst* |
| Il avait parlé. | *he had* |
| Nous avions parlé. | *we had* |
| Vous aviez parlé. | *you had* |
| Ils avaient parlé. | *they had* |

*spoken.*

##### PAST DEFINITE.

| | |
|---|---|
| Je parlai. | *I spoke.* |
| Tu parlas. | *thou spokest.* |
| Il parla. | *he spoke.* |
| Nous parlâmes. | *we spoke.* |
| Vous parlâtes. | *you spoke.* |
| Ils parlèrent. | *they spoke.* |

##### PAST ANTERIOR.

| | |
|---|---|
| J'eus parlé. | *I had* |
| Tu eus parlé. | *thou hadst* |
| Il eut parlé. | *he had* |
| Nous eûmes parlé. | *we had* |
| Vous eûtes parlé. | *you had* |
| Ils eurent parlé. | *they had* |

*spoken.*

---

**N.B.—1st.** All verbs ending in *er* belong to the first conjugation, and are conjugated like *parler.* There are very few exceptions.

The English form: *I do speak, thou dost speak, he does speak, we do speak, you do speak, they do speak.* is rendered in French by *je parle, tu parles,* etc.

So translate the Indicative Present: *I speak, I do speak, I am speaking,* by simply, *je parle, thou speakest, thou dost speak, thou art speaking,* by *tu parles.* And the Imperfect *I was speaking, I used to speak,* etc., by *je parlais,* not *j'étais parlant.*

---

### CONJUGATE LIKE *PARLER.*

| | | | | | |
|---|---|---|---|---|---|
| Accuser - | - *To accuse.* | Chanter - | - *To sing.* | Écouter | - *To listen to.* |
| Admirer - | - *— admire.* | Conter - | - *— relate.* | Entrer | *— enter, go in.* |
| Aider - | - *— help.* | Danser - | - *— dance.* | Éviter | *— avoid.* |
| Brûler - | - *— burn.* | Déjeûner | *— breakfast.* | Flatter | *— flatter.* |
| Cacher - | - *— hide.* | Dessiner | *— draw.* | Former | *— form.* |

## SIMPLE TENSES.

### FUTURE.

| | |
|---|---|
| Je parlerai. | I shall or will speak. |
| Tu parleras. | thou shalt or wilt speak. |
| Il parlera. | he shall or will speak. |
| Nous parlerons. | we shall or will speak. |
| Vous parlerez. | you shall or will speak. |
| Ils parleront. | they shall or will speak. |

## COMPOUND TENSES.

### FUTURE ANTERIOR.

| | |
|---|---|
| J'aurai parlé. | I shall or will have |
| Tu auras parlé | thou shalt or wilt have |
| Il aura parlé. | he shall or will have |
| Nous aurons parlé. | we shall or will have |
| Vous aurez parlé. | you shall or will have |
| Ils auront parlé. | they shall or will have |

*spoken.*

## CONDITIONAL MOOD.

### PRESENT.

| | |
|---|---|
| Je parlerais. | I should or would speak. |
| Tu parlerais. | thou shouldst or wouldst speak. |
| Il parlerait. | he should or would speak. |
| Nous parlerions. | we should or would speak. |
| Vous parleriez. | you should or would speak. |
| Ils parleraient. | they should or would speak. |

### PAST.

| | |
|---|---|
| J'aurais parlé. | I should or would have spoken. |
| Tu aurais parlé. | thou shouldst or wouldst have spoken. |
| Il aurait parlé. | he should or would have spoken. |
| Nous aurions parlé. | we should or would have spoken. |
| Vous auriez parlé. | you should or would have spoken. |
| Ils auraient parlé. | they should or would have spoken. |

## IMPERATIVE MOOD.

### PRESENT OR FUTURE.

| | |
|---|---|
| Parle. | Speak (thou). |
| Qu'il parle. | let him speak. |
| Parlons. | Let us speak. |
| Parlez. | Speak (you). |
| Qu'ils parlent. | let them speak. |

## SUBJUNCTIVE.

### PRESENT.

| | |
|---|---|
| Que je parle. | That I may speak. |
| Que tu parles. | that thou mayest speak. |
| Qu'il parle. | that he may speak. |
| Que nous parlions. | that we may speak. |
| Que vous parliez. | that you may speak. |
| Qu'ils parlent. | that they may speak. |

### PAST.

| | |
|---|---|
| Que j'aie parlé. | That I may have spoken. |
| Que tu aies parlé. | that thou mayest have spoken. |
| Qu'il ait parlé. | that he may have spoken. |
| Que nous ayons parlé. | that we may have spoken. |
| Que vous ayez parlé. | that you may have spoken. |
| Qu'ils aient parlé. | that they may have spoken. |

### IMPERFECT.

| | |
|---|---|
| Que je parlasse. | That I might speak. |
| Que tu parlasses. | that thou mightest speak. |
| Qu'il parlât. | that he might speak. |
| Que nous parlassions. | that we might speak. |
| Que vous parlassiez. | that you might speak |
| Qu'ils parlassent. | that they might speak. |

### PLUPERFECT.*

| | |
|---|---|
| Que j'eusse parlé. | That I might have spoken. |
| Que tu eusses parlé. | that thou mightest have spoken. |
| Qu'il eût parlé. | that he might have spoken. |
| Que nous eussions parlé. | that we might have spoken. |
| Que vous eussiez parlé. | that you might have spoken. |
| Qu'ils eussent parlé. | that they might have spoken. |

---

N.B.—Each of the three persons plural of the *Past definite* take an accent on the vowel beginning the termination. The third person singular of the *Imperfect of the Subjunctive* has a circumflex accent, on the vowel preceding the t *final*, in all verbs.

### CONJUGATE LIKE *PARLER.*

| | | | | | | | |
|---|---|---|---|---|---|---|---|
| Fumer | . | *To smoke.* | Habiller | . | *To dress.* | Laver . . . | *To wash.* |
| Garder | . | *— keep.* | Imprimer | . | *— print.* | Livrer . . . | *— deliver.* |
| Griser | . | *— make tipsy.* | Irriter | . | *— irritate.* | Marquer . . . | *— mark.* |

* The Pluperfect of the Subjunctive of each verb, may be used, in suppressing *que*, to replace the *Conditional Past.* Ex.: J'aurais parlé *or* j'eusse parlé. Tu aurais parlé *or* tu eusses parlé, etc.

VERSAILLES, THE ORANGERIE

CHATEAU DE LUSSE ON THE RIVER

# VERB *PARLER*, TO SPEAK.

## CONJUGATED NEGATIVELY.

---

### INFINITIVE MOOD.

| PRESENT. | | PAST. |
|---|---|---|

Ne pas parler.    *Not to speak.*      N'avoir pas parl*é*.    *Not to have spoken.*

**PARTICIPLE PRESENT.**      COMPOUND OF PARTICIPLE PRESENT.

Ne parlant pas.    *Not speaking.*      N'ayant pas parl*é*.    *Not having spoken.*

---

### INDICATIVE MOOD.

#### SIMPLE TENSES.

##### PRESENT.

| | | |
|---|---|---|
| Je ne parle pas. | *I do not speak.* | *I am not speaking.* |
| Tu ne parles pas. | *thou dost not speak.* | *thou art not speaking.* |
| Il ne parle pas. | *he does not speak.* | *he is not speaking.* |
| Nous ne parlons pas. | *we do not speak.* | *we are not speaking.* |
| Vous ne parlez pas. | *you do not speak.* | *you are not speaking.* |
| Ils ne parlent pas. | *they do not speak.* | *they are not speaking.* |

##### IMPERFECT.

| | | |
|---|---|---|
| Je ne parlais pas. | *I was not speaking.* | *I used not to speak.* |
| Tu ne parlais pas. | *thou wast not speaking.* | *thou usedst not to speak.* |
| Il ne parlait pas. | *he was not speaking.* | *he used not to speak.* |
| Nous ne parlions pas. | *we were not speaking.* | *we used not to speak.* |
| Vous ne parliez pas. | *you were not speaking.* | *you used not to speak.* |
| Ils ne parlaient pas. | *they were not speaking.* | *they used not to speak.* |

##### PAST DEFINITE.

| | |
|---|---|
| Je ne parlais pas. | *I did not speak.* |
| Tu ne parlas pas. | *thou didst not speak.* |
| Il ne parla pas. | *he did not speak.* |
| Nous ne parlâmes pas. | *we did not speak.* |
| Vous ne parlâtes pas. | *you did not speak.* |
| Ils ne parlèrent pas. | *they did not speak.* |

##### FUTURE.

| | |
|---|---|
| Je ne parlerai pas. | *I shall not speak.* |
| Tu ne parleras pas. | *thou wilt not speak.* |
| Il ne parlera pas. | *he will not speak.* |
| Nous ne parlerons pas. | *we shall not speak.* |
| Vous ne parlerez pas. | *you will not speak.* |
| Ils ne parleront pas. | *they will not speak.* |

# INDICATIVE MOOD *(continued)*.

―――

## COMPOUND TENSES.

### PAST INDEFINITE.

| | |
|---|---|
| Je n'ai pas parlé. | *I have not spoken.* |
| Tu n'as pas parlé. | *thou hast not spoken.* |
| Il n'a pas parlé. | *he has not spoken.* |
| Nous n'avons pas parlé. | *we have not spoken.* |
| Vous n'avez pas parlé. | *you have not spoken.* |
| Ils n'ont pas parlé. | *they have not spoken.* |

### PLUPERFECT.

| | |
|---|---|
| Je n'avais pas parlé. | *I had not spoken.* |
| Tu n'avais pas parlé. | *thou hadst not spoken.* |
| Il n'avait pas parlé. | *he had not spoken.* |
| Nous n'avions pas parlé. | *we had not spoken.* |
| Vous n'aviez pas parlé. | *you had not spoken.* |
| Ils n'avaient pas parlé. | *they had not spoken.* |

### PAST ANTERIOR.

| | |
|---|---|
| Je n'eus pas parlé. | *I had not spoken.* |
| Tu n'eus pas parlé. | *thou hadst not spoken.* |
| Il n'eut pas parlé. | *he had not spoken.* |
| Nous n'eûmes pas parlé. | *we had not spoken.* |
| Vous n'eûtes pas parlé. | *you had not spoken.* |
| Ils n'eurent pas parlé. | *they had not spoken.* |

### FUTURE ANTERIOR.

| | |
|---|---|
| Je n'aurai pas parlé. | *I shall not have spoken.* |
| Tu n'auras pas parlé. | *thou wilt not have spoken.* |
| Il n'aura pas parlé. | *he will not have spoken.* |
| Nous n'aurons pas parlé. | *we shall not have spoken.* |
| Vous n'aurez pas parlé. | *you will not have spoken.* |
| Ils n'auront pas parlé. | *they will not have spoken.* |

―――

## CONJUGATE NEGATIVELY.

| | | | | |
|---|---|---|---|---|
| Marcher | - - - - - | *To walk.* | Oser - - - - - | *To dare.* |
| Montrer | - - - - - | *— show.* | Ôter - - - - - | *— take off.* |
| Nommer | - - - - - | *— name.* | Pardonner - - - - | *— pardon.* |
| Observer | - - - - - | *— observe.* | Patiner - - - - | *— skate.* |

# CONDITIONAL MOOD.

| SIMPLE TENSES. | | COMPOUND TENSES. | |
|---|---|---|---|
| **PRESENT.** | | **PAST.** | |
| Je ne parlerais pas. | *I should not speak.* | Je n'aurais pas parlé. | *I should not have spoken.* |
| Tu ne parlerais pas. | *thou wouldst not speak.* | Tu n'aurais pas parlé. | *thou wouldst not have spoken.* |
| Il ne parlerait pas. | *he would not speak.* | Il n'aurait pas parlé. | *he would not have spoken.* |
| Nous ne parlerions pas. | *we should not speak.* | Nous n'aurions pas parlé. | *we should not have spoken.* |
| Vous ne parleriez pas. | *you would not speak.* | Vous n'auriez pas parlé. | *you would not have spoken.* |
| Ils ne parleraient pas. | *they would not speak.* | Ils n'auraient pas parlé. | *they would not have spoken.* |

## IMPERATIVE MOOD.
### PRESENT OR FUTURE.

| | |
|---|---|
| Ne parle pas - - - - - | *Do not speak (thou).* |
| Qu'il ne parle pas - - - . | *Let him not speak.* |
| Ne parlons pas - - - - | *Let us not speak.* |
| Ne parlez pas - - - - | *Do not speak (you).* |
| Qu'ils ne parlent pas - - - | *Let them not speak.* |

## SUBJUNCTIVE MOOD.

| PRESENT. | | PAST. | |
|---|---|---|---|
| Que je ne parle pas. | *That I may not speak.* | Que je n'aie pas parlé. | *That I may not have spoken.* |
| Que tu ne parles pas. | *that thou mayest not speak.* | Que tu n'aies pas parlé. | *that thou mayest not have spoken.* |
| Qu'il ne parle pas. | *that he may not speak.* | Qu'il n'ait pas parlé. | *that he may not have spoken.* |
| Que nous ne parlions pas. | *that we may not speak.* | Que nous n'ayons pas parlé. | *that we may not have spoken.* |
| Que vous ne parliez pas. | *that you may not speak.* | Que vous n'ayez pas parlé. | *that you may not have spoken.* |
| Qu'ils ne parlent pas. | *that they may not speak.* | Qu'ils n'aient pas parlé. | *that they may not have spoken.* |

| IMPERFECT. | | PLUPERFECT. | |
|---|---|---|---|
| Que je ne parlasse pas. | *That I might not speak.* | Que je n'eusse pas parlé. | *That I might not have spoken.* |
| Que tu ne parlasses pas. | *that thou mightest not speak.* | Que tu n'eusses pas parlé. | *that thou mightest not have spoken.* |
| Qu'il ne parlât pas. | *that he might not speak.* | Qu'il n'eût pas parlé. | *that he might not have spoken.* |
| Que nous ne parlassions pas. | *that we might not speak.* | Que nous n'eussions pas parlé. | *that we might not have spoken.* |
| Que vous ne parlassiez pas | *that you might not speak.* | Que vous n'eussiez pas parlé. | *that you might not have spoken.* |
| Qu'ils ne parlassent pas. | *that they might not speak.* | Qu'ils n'eussent pas parlé. | *that they might not have spoken.* |

## LIST OF THE FRENCH NEGATIONS.

| | | | | | |
|---|---|---|---|---|---|
| Ne—pas - | *not.* | Ne—personne - | {*nobody.* / *not anybody.*} | Ne—aucunement | *not at all.* |
| Ne—point - | *not (at all).* | Ne—rien - | *nothing.* | Ne—nulle part - | *nowhere.* |
| Ne—plus - | *no more, no longer.* | Ne—nul - | *no, not any.* | Ne—ni, ni - | *neither, nor.* |
| Ne—jamais - | *never.* | Ne—aucun - | *no, not any.* | Ne—pas encore - | *not yet.* |
| Ne—guère - | {*scarcely.* / *not often.*} | Ne—nullement - | *not at all.* | Ne—pas un, une, | *none, not one.* |

As we have already said (p. 6), the *French negation* is expressed by two words, *ne* and *pas, point, plus, jamais,* etc. *Ne* is placed before the verb, *in simple tenses,* and *pas, point, plus,* etc., after it; and *in compound tenses,* ne, stands before the auxiliary, and *pas, point, plus,* etc., between the auxiliary and the *past participle.*
N.B.—Personne, aucun, nul, nulle part, *in compound tenses,* follow the participle. Ex.: Je n'ai parlé à personne.

# VERB *PARLER*, TO SPEAK.

## CONJUGATED INTERROGATIVELY.

---

### INDICATIVE MOOD.

| SIMPLE TENSES. | | COMPOUND TENSES. | |
|---|---|---|---|
| **PRESENT.** | | **PAST INDEFINITE.** | |
| Parlé-je ? | *Do I speak?* | Ai-je parlé ? | *Have I spoken?* |
| Parles-tu ? | *dost thou speak?* | As-tu parlé ? | *hast thou spoken?* |
| Parle-t-il ? | *does he speak?* | A-t-il parlé ? | *has he spoken?* |
| Parlons-nous ? | *do we speak?* | Avons-nous parlé ? | *have we spoken?* |
| Parlez-vous ? | *do you speak?* | Avez-vous parlé ? | *have you spoken?* |
| Parlent-ils ? | *do they speak?* | Ont-ils parlé ? | *have they spoken?* |
| **IMPERFECT.** | | **PLUPERFECT.** | |
| Parlais-je ? | *Was I speaking?* | Avais-je parlé ? | *Had I spoken?* |
| Parlais-tu ? | *wast thou speaking?* | Avais-tu parlé ? | *hadst thou spoken?* |
| Parlait-il ? | *was he speaking?* | Avait-il parlé ? | *had he spoken?* |
| Parlions-nous ? | *were we speaking?* | Avions-nous parlé ? | *had we spoken?* |
| Parliez-vous ? | *were you speaking?* | Aviez-vous parlé ? | *had you spoken?* |
| Parlaient-ils ? | *were they speaking?* | Avaient-ils parlé ? | *had they spoken?* |
| **PAST DEFINITE.** | | **PAST ANTERIOR.** | |
| Parlai-je ? | *Did I speak?* | Eus-je parlé ? | *Had I spoken?* |
| Parlas-tu ? | *didst thou speak?* | Eus-tu parlé ? | *hadst thou spoken?* |
| Parla-t-il ? | *did he speak?* | Eut-il parlé ? | *had he spoken?* |
| Parlâmes-nous ? | *did we speak?* | Eûmes-nous parlé ? | *had we spoken?* |
| Parlâtes-vous ? | *did you speak?* | Eûtes-vous parlé ? | *had you spoken?* |
| Parlèrent-ils ? | *did they speak?* | Eurent-ils parlé ? | *had they spoken?* |
| **FUTURE.** | | **FUTURE ANTERIOR.** | |
| Parlerai-je ? | *Shall I speak?* | Aurai-je parlé ? | *Shall I have spoken?* |
| Parleras-tu ? | *wilt thou speak?* | Auras-tu parlé ? | *wilt thou have spoken?* |
| Parlera-t-il ? | *will he speak?* | Aura-t-il parlé ? | *will he have spoken?* |
| Parlerons-nous ? | *shall we speak?* | Aurons-nous parlé ? | *shall we have spoken?* |
| Parlerez-vous ? | *will you speak?* | Aurez-vous parlé ? | *will you have spoken?* |
| Parleront-ils ? | *will they speak?* | Auront-ils parlé ? | *will they have spoken?* |

### CONDITIONAL MOOD.

| PRESENT. | | PAST. | |
|---|---|---|---|
| Parlerais-je? | *Should I speak?* | Aurais-je parlé ? | *Should I have spoken?* |
| Parlerais-tu ? | *wouldst thou speak?* | Aurais-tu parlé ? | *wouldst thou have spoken?* |
| Parlerait-il ? | *would he speak?* | Aurait-il parlé ? | *would he have spoken?* |
| Parlerions-nous ? | *should we speak?* | Aurions-nous parlé ? | *should we have spoken?* |
| Parleriez-vous ? | *would you speak?* | Auriez-vous parlé ? | *would you have spoken?* |
| Parleraient-ils ? | *would they speak?* | Auraient-ils parlé ? | *would they have spoken?* |

N.B.—I. In *parlé-je?* (first person of the Present Indicative) an acute accent is employed over the *e*, for the sake of euphony ; and in all verbs of the first conjugation used interrogatively in the same person.

II. *A-t-*, for the same reason (euphony), is inserted between the verb and the pronoun after the third person singular of the Indicative Present, *Parle-t-il;* Past Definite; *Parla-t-il;* and Future, *Parlera-t-il.*

### CONJUGATE INTERROGATIVELY.

| | | | | | | | | | | |
|---|---|---|---|---|---|---|---|---|---|---|
| Prêter | . | . | . | . | *To lend.* | Ramasser | . | . | . | *To pick up.* |
| Quereller | . | . | . | . | *— quarrel.* | Rester | . | . | . | *— remain.* |
| Raconter | . | . | . | . | *— relate.* | Sauter | . | . | . | *— jump.* |

# VERB *PARLER*, TO SPEAK.

## USED INTERROGATIVELY AND NEGATIVELY.

### INDICATIVE MOOD.

**SIMPLE TENSES.**

#### PRESENT.

| | |
|---|---|
| Ne parle-je pas ? | *Do I not speak?* |
| Ne parles-tu pas ? | *dost thou not speak?* |
| Ne parle-t-il pas ? | *does he not speak?* |
| Ne parlons-nous pas ? | *do we not speak?* |
| Ne parlez-vous pas ? | *do you not speak?* |
| Ne parlent-ils pas ? | *do they not speak?* |

#### IMPERFECT.

| | | |
|---|---|---|
| Ne parlais-je pas ? | *Was I not* | |
| Ne parlais-tu pas ? | *wast thou not* | |
| Ne parlait-il pas ? | *was he not* | *speaking?* |
| Ne parlions-nous pas ? | *were we not* | |
| Ne parliez-vous pas ? | *were you not* | |
| Ne parlaient-ils pas ? | *were they not* | |

#### PAST DEFINITE.

| | |
|---|---|
| Ne parlai-je pas ? | *Did I not speak?* |
| Ne parlas-tu pas ? | *didst thou not speak?* |
| Ne parla-t-il pas ? | *did he not speak?* |
| Ne parlâmes-nous pas ? | *did we not speak?* |
| Ne parlâtes-vous pas ? | *did you not speak?* |
| Ne parlèrent-ils pas ? | *did they not speak?* |

#### FUTURE.

| | |
|---|---|
| Ne parlerai-je pas ? | *Shall I not speak?* |
| Ne parleras-tu pas ? | *wilt thou not speak?* |
| Ne parlera-t-il pas ? | *will he not speak?* |
| Ne parlerons-nous pas ? | *shall we not speak?* |
| Ne parlerez-vous pas ? | *will you not speak?* |
| Ne parleront-ils pas ? | *will they not speak?* |

**COMPOUND TENSES.**

#### PAST INDEFINITE.

| | | |
|---|---|---|
| N'ai-je pas parlé ? | *Have I not* | |
| N'as-tu pas parlé ? | *hast thou not* | |
| N'a-t-il pas parlé ? | *has he not* | *spoken?* |
| N'avons-nous pas parlé ? | *have we not* | |
| N'avez-vous pas parlé ? | *have you not* | |
| N'ont-ils pas parlé ? | *have they not* | |

#### PLUPERFECT.

| | | |
|---|---|---|
| N'avais-je pas parlé ? | *Had I not* | |
| N'avais-tu pas parlé ? | *hadst thou not* | |
| N'avait-il pas parlé ? | *had he not* | *spoken?* |
| N'avions-nous pas parlé? | *had we not* | |
| N'aviez-vous pas parlé ? | *had you not* | |
| N'avaient-ils pas parlé ? | *had they not* | |

#### PAST ANTERIOR.

| | | |
|---|---|---|
| N'eus-je pas parlé ? | *Had I not* | |
| N'eus-tu pas parlé ? | *hadst thou not* | |
| N'eut-il pas parlé ? | *had he not* | *spoken?* |
| N'eûmes-nous pas parlé ? | *had we not* | |
| N'eûtes-vous pas parlé ? | *had you not* | |
| N'eurent-ils pas parlé ? | *had they not* | |

#### FUTURE ANTERIOR.

| | | |
|---|---|---|
| N'aurai-je pas parlé ? | *Shall I not have* | |
| N'auras-tu pas parlé ? | *wilt thou not have* | |
| N'aura-t-il pas parlé ? | *will he not have* | *spoken?* |
| N'aurons-nous pas parlé? | *shall we not have* | |
| N'aurez-vous pas parlé ? | *will you not have* | |
| N'auront-ils pas parlé ? | *will they not have* | |

### CONDITIONAL MOOD.

#### PRESENT.

| | |
|---|---|
| Ne parlerais-je pas ? | *Should I not speak?* |
| Ne parlerais-tu pas ? | *wouldst thou not speak?* |
| Ne parlerait-il pas ? | *would he not speak?* |
| Ne parlerions-nous pas? | *should we not speak?* |
| Ne parleriez-vous pas ? | *would you not speak?* |
| Ne parleraient-ils pas ? | *would they not speak?* |

#### PAST.

| | | |
|---|---|---|
| N'aurais-je pas parlé ? | *Should I not have* | |
| N'aurais-tu pas parlé ? | *wouldst thou not have* | |
| N'aurait-il pas parlé ? | *would he not have* | *spoken?* |
| N'aurions-nous pas parlé? | *should we not have* | |
| N'auriez-vous pas parlé ? | *would you not have* | |
| N'auraient-ils pas parlé ? | *would they not have* | |

#### CONJUGATE INTERROGATIVELY AND NEGATIVELY.

| | | | | |
|---|---|---|---|---|
| Souhaiter | - - - - | *To wish.* | Tomber | - - - - *To fall.* |
| Supposer | - - - - | *— suppose.* | Tousser | - - - - *— cough.* |
| Souper | - - - - | *— sup.* | Travailler | - - - - *— work.* |
| Soupirer | - - - - | *— sigh.* | Trouver | - - - - *— find.* |

# REGULAR VERBS. (*Continued.*)
## SECOND CONJUGATION ENDING IN *IR.*\*

### MODEL VERB.

### *FINIR*, TO FINISH.

### INFINITIVE MOOD.

| PRESENT. | | PAST. | |
|---|---|---|---|
| Fin*ir*. | *To finish.* | Avoir fin*i*. | *To have finished.* |
| **PARTICIPLE PRESENT.** | | **COMP. OF PART. PRESENT.** | |
| Fin*issant*. | *Finishing.* | Ayant fin*i*. | *Having finished.* |

### PARTICIPLE PAST.

Fin*i* (m.s.), fin*ie* (f.s.), fin*is* (m.pl.), fin*ies* (f.pl.), *finished.*

---

## INDICATIVE MOOD.

### SIMPLE TENSES.

#### PRESENT.

| | | |
|---|---|---|
| Je fin*is*. | *I finish* or *I am* | |
| Tu fin*is*. | *thou finishest* or *thou art* | |
| Il fin*it*. | *he finishes* or *he is* | |
| Elle fin*it*. | *she finishes* or *she is* | *finishing.* |
| Nous fin*issons*. | *we finish* or *we are* | |
| Vous fin*issez*. | *you finish* or *you are* | |
| Ils fin*issent*. | *they finish* or *they are* | |
| Elles fin*issent*. | *they finish* or *they are* | |

#### IMPERFECT.

| Je fin*issais*. | *I was finishing* or *I used to finish.* |
|---|---|
| Tu fin*issais*. | *thou wast finishing* or *thou usedst to finish.* |
| Il fin*issait*. | *he was finishing* or *he used to finish.* |
| Nous fin*issions*. | *we were finishing* or *we used to finish.* |
| Vous fin*issiez*. | *you were finishing* or *you used to finish.* |
| Ils fin*issaient*. | *they were finishing* or *they used to finish.* |

#### PAST DEFINITE.

| Je fin*is*. | *I finished.* |
|---|---|
| Tu fin*is*. | *thou finishedst.* |
| Il fin*it*. | *he finished.* |
| Nous fin*îmes*. | *we finished.* |
| Vous fin*îtes*. | *you finished.* |
| Ils fin*irent*. | *they finished.* |

### COMPOUND TENSES.

#### PAST INDEFINITE.

| | | |
|---|---|---|
| J'ai fin*i*. | *I have finished.* | |
| Tu as fin*i*. | *thou hast finished.* | |
| Il a fin*i*. | *he has finished.* | |
| Elle a fin*i*. | *she has finished.* | |
| Nous avons fin*i*. | *we have finished.* | |
| Vous avez fin*i*. | *you have finished.* | |
| Ils ont fin*i*. | *they have finished.* | |
| Elles ont fin*i*. | *they have finished.* | |

#### PLUPERFECT.

| J'avais fin*i*. | *I had finished.* |
|---|---|
| Tu avais fin*i*. | *thou hadst finished.* |
| Il avait fin*i*. | *he had finished.* |
| Nous avions fin*i*. | *we had finished.* |
| Vous aviez fin*i*. | *you had finished.* |
| Ils avaient fin*i*. | *they had finished.* |

#### PAST ANTERIOR.

| J'eus fin*i*. | *I had finished.* |
|---|---|
| Tu eus fin*i*. | *thou hadst finished.* |
| Il eut fin*i*. | *he had finished.* |
| Nous eûmes fin*i*. | *we had finished.* |
| Vous eûtes fin*i*. | *you had finished.* |
| Ils eurent fin*i*. | *they had finished.* |

---

\* Verbs ending in *ir*, are conjugated like *finir*, except the irregular ones.

### CONJUGATE LIKE *FINIR* :

| | | | | | | | | | | | | |
|---|---|---|---|---|---|---|---|---|---|---|---|---|
| Abolir | - | - | - | - | - | *To abolish.* | Fournir | - | - | - | - | *To furnish.* |
| Adoucir | - | - | - | - | - | *— soften.* | Frémir | - | - | - | - | *— shudder.* |
| Agir | - | - | - | - | - | *— act.* | Guérir | - | - | - | - | *— cure.* |
| Bâtir | - | - | - | - | - | *— build.* | Noircir | - | - | - | - | *— blacken.* |
| Blanchir | - | - | - | - | - | *— whiten.* | Nourrir | - | - | - | - | *— feed.* |
| Choisir | - | - | - | - | - | *— choose.* | Obéir | - | - | - | - | *— obey.* |
| Démolir | - | - | - | - | - | *— demolish.* | Obscurcir | - | - | - | - | *— darken.* |
| Embellir | - | - | - | - | - | *— embellish.* | Périr | - | - | - | - | *— perish.* |

# VERB FIN*IR* (*continued.*)

| SIMPLE TENSES. | | COMPOUND TENSES. | |
|---|---|---|---|

### FUTURE.

| | | | |
|---|---|---|---|
| Je fin*irai*. | *I shall* or *will finish.* | J'aurai fin*i*. | *I shall* or *will* |
| Tu fin*iras*. | *thou shalt* or *wilt finish* | Tu auras fin*i*. | *thou shalt* or *wilt* |
| Il fin*ira*. | *he shall* or *will finish.* | Il aura fin*i*. | *he shall* or *will* |
| Nous fin*irons*. | *we shall* or *will finish.* | Nous aurons fin*i*. | *we shall* or *will* |
| Vous fin*irez*. | *you shall* or *will finish.* | Vous aurez fin*i*. | *you shall* or *will* |
| Ils fin*iront*. | *they shall* or *will finish.* | Ils auront fin*i*. | *they shall* or *will* |

### FUTURE ANTERIOR.

*have finished.*

## CONDITIONAL MOOD.

| PRESENT. | | PAST. | |
|---|---|---|---|
| Je fin*irais*. | *I should* or *would finish.* | J'aurais fin*i*. | *I should* or *would* |
| Tu fin*irais*. | *thou shouldst* or *wouldst finish.* | Tu aurais fin*i*. | *thou shouldst* or *wouldst* |
| Il fin*irait*. | *he should* or *would finish.* | Il aurait fin*i*. | *he should* or *would* |
| Nous fin*irions*. | *we should* or *would finish.* | Nous aurions fin*i*. | *we should* or *would* |
| Vous fin*iriez*. | *you should* or *would finish.* | Vous auriez fin*i*. | *you should* or *would* |
| Ils fin*iraient*. | *they should* or *would finish.* | Ils auraient fin*i*. | *they should* or *would* |

*have finished.*

## IMPERATIVE MOOD.

### PRESENT OR FUTURE.

| | |
|---|---|
| Fin*is*. | *Finish* (*thou*). |
| Qu'il fin*isse*. | *let him finish.* |
| Fin*issons*. | *let us finish.* |
| Fin*issez*. | *finish* (*you*). |
| Qu'ils fin*issent*. | *let them finish.* |

## SUBJUNCTIVE MOOD.

| PRESENT. | | PAST. | |
|---|---|---|---|
| Que je fin*isse*. | *That I may finish.* | Que j'aie fin*i*. | *That I may* |
| Que tu fin*isses*. | *that thou mayest finish.* | Que tu aies fin*i*. | *that thou mayest* |
| Qu'il fin*isse*. | *that he may finish.* | Qu'il ait fin*i*. | *that he may* |
| Que nous fin*issions*. | *that we may finish.* | Que nous ayons fin*i*. | *that we may* |
| Que vous fin*issiez*. | *that you may finish.* | Que vous ayez fin*i*. | *that you may* |
| Qu'ils fin*issent*. | *that they may finish.* | Qu'ils aient fin*i*. | *that they may* |

*have finished.*

| IMPERFECT. | | PLUPERFECT. | |
|---|---|---|---|
| Que je fin*isse*. | *That I might finish.* | Que j'eusse fin*i*. | *That I might* |
| Que tu fin*isses*. | *that thou mightest finish.* | Que tu eusses fin*i*. | *that thou mightest* |
| Qu'il fin*ît*. | *that he might finish.* | Qu'il eût fin*i*. | *that he might* |
| Que nous fin*issions*. | *that we might finish.* | Que nous eussions fin*i*. | *that we might* |
| Que vous fin*issiez*. | *that you might finish.* | Que vous eussiez fin*i*. | *that you might* |
| Qu'ils fin*issent*. | *that they might finish.* | Qu'ils eussent fin*i*. | *that they might* |

*have finished.*

### COUJUGATE LIKE *FINIR*:

| | | | |
|---|---|---|---|
| Punir | *To punish.* | Trahir | *To betray.* |
| Remplir | *— fill.* | Travestir | *— disguise.* |
| Rougir | *— blush.* | Unir | *— unite.* |
| Salir | *— soil.* | Vernir | *— varnish.* |
| Saisir | *— seize.* | Vieillir | *— grow old.* |

To conjugate *Finir* Negatively, see p. 18; Interrogatively, p. 21; and Negatively and Interrogatively, p. 22.

# REGULAR VERBS (*Continued*).

## THIRD CONJUGATION, ENDING IN *OIR* (*EVOIR*).

### MODEL VERB.

### *RECEVOIR*, TO RECEIVE.

### INFINITIVE MOOD.

| PRESENT. | | PAST. | |
|---|---|---|---|
| Rec*evoir* | *To receive.* | Avoir reç*u* | *To have received.* |
| **PARTICIPLE PRESENT.** | | **COMPOUND OF PARTICIPLE PRESENT.** | |
| Rec*evant* | *Receiving.* | Ayant reç*u* | *Having received.* |

### PARTICIPLE PAST.

Reç*u* (m.s.)—reç*ue* (f.s.)—reç*us* (m.pl.)—reç*ues* (f.pl.) *received.*

### INDICATIVE MOOD.

SIMPLE TENSES. | COMPOUND TENSES.

#### PRESENT. — PAST INDEFINITE.

| *Singular.* | | |
|---|---|---|
| Je reç*ois.* | *I receive* or *I am receiving.* | |
| Tu reç*ois.* | *thou receivest* or *thou art receiving.* | |
| Il reç*oit.* | *he receives* or *he is receiving.* | |
| Elle reç*oit.* | *she receives* or *she is receiving.* | |

| *Plural.* | | |
|---|---|---|
| Nous rec*evons.* | *we receive* or *we are receiving.* | |
| Vous rec*evez.* | *you receive* or *you are receiving.* | |
| Ils reç*oivent.* | *they receive* or *they are receiving.* | |
| Elles reç*oivent.* | *they receive* or *they are receiving.* | |

| *Singular.* | | |
|---|---|---|
| J'ai reç*u.* | *I have received.* | |
| Tu as reç*u.* | *thou hast received.* | |
| Il a reç*u.* | *he has received.* | |
| Elle a reç*u.* | *she has received.* | |

| *Plural.* | | |
|---|---|---|
| Nous avons reç*u.* | *we have received.* | |
| Vous avez reç*u.* | *you have received.* | |
| Ils ont reç*u.* | *they have received.* | |
| Elles ont reç*u.* | *they have received.* | |

#### IMPERFECT. — PLUPERFECT.

| Je rec*evais.* | *I was receiving* | | J'avais reç*u.* | *I had received.* |
|---|---|---|---|---|
| Tu rec*evais.* | *thou wast receiving* | or *I used to re-ceive, etc.* | Tu avais reç*u.* | *thou hadst received.* |
| Il rec*evait.* | *he was receiving* | | Il avait reç*u.* | *he had received.* |
| Nous rec*evions.* | *we were receiving* | | Nous avions reç*u.* | *we had received.* |
| Vous rec*eviez.* | *you were receiving* | | Vous aviez reç*u.* | *you had received.* |
| Ils rec*evaient.* | *they were receiving* | | Ils avaient reç*u.* | *they had received.* |

#### PAST DEFINITE. — PAST ANTERIOR.

| Je reç*us.* | *I received.* | J'eus reç*u.* | *I had received.* |
|---|---|---|---|
| Tu reç*us.* | *thou receivedst.* | Tu eus reç*u.* | *thou hadst received.* |
| Il reç*ut.* | *he received.* | Il eut reç*u.* | *he had received.* |
| Nous reç*ûmes.* | *we received.* | Nous eûmes reç*u.* | *we had received.* |
| Vous reç*ûtes.* | *you received.* | Vous eûtes reç*u.* | *you had received.* |
| Ils reç*urent.* | *they received.* | Ils eurent reç*u.* | *they had received.* |

REMARKS:—

I.—This Conjugation has only seven verbs, which are :

| Aper*cevoir* - | - | - | - | *To perceive.* |
|---|---|---|---|---|
| Con*cevoir* - | - | - | - | — *conceive.* |
| Dé*cevoir* - | - | - | - | — *deceive.* |
| *Devoir* - | - | - | - | — *owe.* |

{ Re*cevoir* - - - *To receive.* (given as model)

Re*devoir* - - - { — *remain in debt.* / — *owe still.*

Per*cevoir* - - - — *collect.*

II.—The verbs of the Conjugation ending in *cevoir* as *recevoir*, etc., take a cedilla (ç) under the c coming before *o, u,* to preserve the soft sound of *s,* which it has in the Infinitive Present, (c with a cedilla is sounded soft, i.e., as *s*).

III.—The other verbs ending in *oir* are irregular.

# VERB REC*E*V*OIR* (*Continued*).

## SIMPLE TENSES.

### FUTURE.

| | |
|---|---|
| Je rec*e*vrai. | *I shall* or *will receive.* |
| Tu rec*e*vras. | *thou shalt* or *wilt receive.* |
| Il rec*e*vra. | *he shall* or *will receive.* |
| Nous rec*e*vrons. | *we shall* or *will receive.* |
| Vous rec*e*vrez. | *you shall* or *will receive.* |
| Ils rec*e*vront. | *they shall* or *will receive.* |

## COMPOUND TENSES.

### FUTURE ANTERIOR.

| | | |
|---|---|---|
| J'aurai reç*u*. | *I shall* or *will* | *have received.* |
| Tu auras reç*u*. | *thou shalt* or *wilt* | |
| Il aura reç*u*. | *he shall* or *will* | |
| Nous aurons reç*u*. | *we shall* or *will* | |
| Vous aurez reç*u*. | *you shall* or *will* | |
| Ils auront reç*u*. | *they shall* or *will* | |

## CONDITIONAL MOOD.

### PRESENT.

| | |
|---|---|
| Je rec*e*vrais. | *I should* or *would receive.* |
| Tu rec*e*vrais. | *thou shouldst* or *wouldst receive.* |
| Il rec*e*vrait. | *he should* or *would receive.* |
| Nous rec*e*vrions. | *we should* or *would receive.* |
| Vous rec*e*vriez. | *you should* or *would receive.* |
| Ils rec*e*vraient. | *they should* or *would receive.* |

### PAST.

| | |
|---|---|
| J'aurais reç*u*. | *I should* or *would have received.* |
| Tu aurais reç*u*. | *thou shouldst* or *wouldst have received.* |
| Il aurait reç*u*. | *he should* or *would have received.* |
| Nous aurions reç*u*. | *we should* or *would have received.* |
| Vous auriez reç*u*. | *you should* or *would have received.* |
| Ils auraient reç*u*. | *they should* or *would have received.* |

## IMPERATIVE MOOD.

### PRESENT or FUTURE.

| | |
|---|---|
| Reçois - - - - | *Receive* (*thou*). |
| Qu'il reç*o*ive | *let him receive.* |
| Rec*e*vons . - - | *let us receive.* |
| Rec*e*vez - - - | *receive* (*you*). |
| Qu'ils reç*o*ivent - - | *let them receive.* |

## SUBJUNCTIVE MOOD.

### PRESENT.

| | |
|---|---|
| Que je reç*o*ive. | *That I may receive.* |
| Que tu reç*o*ives. | *that thou mayest receive.* |
| Qu'il reç*o*ive. | *that he may receive.* |
| Que nous rec*e*vions. | *that we may receive.* |
| Que vous rec*e*viez. | *that you may receive.* |
| Qu'ils reç*o*ivent. | *that they may receive.* |

### IMPERFECT.

| | |
|---|---|
| Que je reç*u*sse. | *that I might receive.* |
| Que tu reç*u*sses. | *that thou mightest receive.* |
| Qu'il reç*û*t. | *that he might receive.* |
| Que nous reç*u*ssions. | *that we might receive.* |
| Que vous reç*u*ssiez. | *that you might receive.* |
| Qu'ils reç*u*ssent. | *that they might receive.* |

### PAST.

| | |
|---|---|
| Que j'aie reç*u*. | *That I may* |
| Que tu aies reç*u*. | *that thou mayest* |
| Qu'il ait reç*u*. | *that he may* |
| Que nous ayons reç*u*. | *that we may* |
| Que vous ayez reç*u*. | *that you may* |
| Qu'ils aient reç*u*. | *that they may* |

(have received.)

### PLUPERFECT.

| | |
|---|---|
| Que j'eusse reç*u*. | *That I might* |
| Que tu eusses reç*u*. | *that thou mightest* |
| Qu'il eût reç*u*. | *that he might* |
| Que nous eussions reç*u*. | *that we might* |
| Que vous eussiez reç*u*. | *that you might* |
| Qu'ils eussent reç*u*. | *that they might* |

(have received.)

N.B.—The verbs *Devoir* and *Redevoir* take a circumflex accent in the Past Participle (mas. sing.), *dû*, *redû*. In the feminine and in the plural they are written without an accent: *due* (f.), *redue* (f.), *dus* (m.pl.), *redus* (m.pl.)

# REGULAR VERBS *(Continued).*

## FOURTH CONJUGATION, ENDING IN *RE.*\*

### MODEL VERB.

### *VENDRE*, TO SELL.

---

## INFINITIVE MOOD.

| PRESENT. | | PAST. | |
|---|---|---|---|
| Vend*re*. | *To sell.* | Avoir vend*u*. | *To have sold.* |
| **PARTICIPLE PRESENT.** | | **COMPOUND OF PARTICIPLE PRESENT.** | |
| Vend*ant*. | *Selling.* | Ayant vend*u*. | *Having sold.* |

### PARTICIPLE PAST.

Vend*u* (m. s.), vend*ue* (f. s.), vend*us* (m. p.), vend*ues* (f. p.) *sold.*

## INDICATIVE MOOD.

### SIMPLE TENSES. — COMPOUND TENSES.

#### PRESENT.

| | | | |
|---|---|---|---|
| Je vend*s*. | *I sell* or *I am* | J'ai vend*u*. | *I have sold.* |
| Tu vend*s*. | *thou sellest* or *thou art* | Tu as vend*u*. | *thou hast sold.* |
| Il vend. | *he sells* or *he is* | Il a vend*u*. | *he has sold.* |
| Elle vend. | *she sells* or *she is* | Elle a vend*u*. | *she has sold.* |
| Nous vend*ons*. | *we sell* or *we are* | Nous avons vend*u*. | *we have sold.* |
| Vous vend*ez*. | *you sell* or *you are* | Vous avez vend*u*. | *you have sold.* |
| Ils vend*ent*. | *they sell* or *they are* | Ils ont vend*u*. | *they have sold.* |
| Elles vend*ent*. | *they sell* or *they are* | Elles ont vend*u*. | *they have sold.* |

(selling.)

#### IMPERFECT. — PLUPERFECT.

| | | | |
|---|---|---|---|
| Je vend*ais*. | *I was selling* | J'avais vend*u*. | *I had sold.* |
| Tu vend*ais*. | *thou wast selling* | Tu avais vend*u*. | *thou hadst sold.* |
| Il vend*ait*. | *he was selling* | Il avait vend*u*. | *he had sold.* |
| Nous vend*ions*. | *we were selling* | Nous avions vend*u*. | *we had sold.* |
| Vous vend*iez*. | *you were selling* | Vous aviez vend*u*. | *you had sold.* |
| Ils vend*aient*. | *they were selling* | Ils avaient vend*u*. | *they had sold.* |

(or, I sell, &c.)

#### PAST DEFINITE. — PAST ANTERIOR.

| | | | |
|---|---|---|---|
| Je vend*is*. | *I sold.* | J'eus vend*u*. | *I had sold.* |
| Tu vend*is*. | *thou soldst.* | Tu eus vend*u*. | *thou hadst sold.* |
| Il vend*it*. | *he sold.* | Il eut vend*u*. | *he had sold.* |
| Nous vend*îmes*. | *we sold.* | Nous eûmes vend*u*. | *we had sold.* |
| Vous vend*îtes*. | *you sold.* | Vous eûtes vend*u*. | *you had sold.* |
| Ils vend*irent*. | *they sold.* | Ils eurent vend*u*. | *they had sold.* |

---

\* Verbs ending in *re* are conjugated like *Vendre*, except the Irregular ones.

### CONJUGATE LIKE *VENDRE.*

| | | |
|---|---|---|
| Attendre | *To wait for.* | Mordre | *To bite.* |
| Confondre | *— confound.* | Pendre | *— hang.* |
| Correspondre | *— correspond.* | Perdre | *— lose.* |
| Défendre | *— defend.* | Prétendre | *— pretend.* |
| Descendre | *— come or go down.* | Rendre | *— render.* |
| Entendre | *— hear.* | Répandre | *— spread.* |
| Fendre | *— split.* | Reperdre | *— lose again.* |
| Fondre | *— melt.* | Répondre | *— answer.* |

## VERB VEND*RE* *(continued)*.

| SIMPLE TENSES. | | COMPOUND TENSES. | |
|---|---|---|---|
| **FUTURE.** | | **FUTURE ANTERIOR.** | |

| | | | |
|---|---|---|---|
| Je vend*rai*. | *I shall* or *will sell.* | J'aurai vend*u*. | *I shall* or *will* |
| Tu vend*ras*. | *thou shalt* or *wilt sell.* | Tu auras vend*u*. | *thou shalt* or *wilt* |
| Il vend*ra*. | *he shall* or *will sell.* | Il aura vend*u*. | *he shall* or *will* |
| Nous vend*rons*. | *we shall* or *will sell,* | Nous aurons vend*u*. | *we shall* or *will* |
| Vous vend*rez*. | *you shall* or *will sell.* | Vous aurez vend*u*. | *you shall* or *will* |
| Ils vend*ront*. | *they shall* or *will sell.* | Ils auront vend*u*. | *they shall* or *will* |

*have sold.*

### CONDITIONAL MOOD.

| PRESENT. | | PAST. | |
|---|---|---|---|
| Je vend*rais*. | *I should* or *would sell.* | J'aurais vend*u*. | *I should* or *would* |
| Tu vend*rais*. | *thou shouldst* or *wouldst sell.* | Tu aurais vend*u*. | *thou shouldst* or *wouldst* |
| Il vend*rait*. | *he should* or *would sell.* | Il aurait vend*u*. | *he should* or *would* |
| Nous vend*rions*. | *we should* or *would sell.* | Nous aurions vend*u*. | *we should* or *would* |
| Vous vend*riez*. | *you should* or *would sell.* | Vous auriez vend*u*. | *you should* or *would* |
| Ils vend*raient*. | *they should* or *would sell.* | Ils auraient vend*u*. | *they should* or *would* |

*have sold.*

### IMPERATIVE MOOD.

#### PRESENT OR FUTURE.

| | | |
|---|---|---|
| Vend*s* | - - - - | *Sell (thou).* |
| Qu'il vend*e* | - - - | *let him sell.* |
| Vend*ons* | - - - | *let us sell.* |
| Vend*ez* | - - - - | *sell (you).* |
| Qu'ils vend*ent* | - - - | *let them sell.* |

### SUBJUNCTIVE MOOD.

| PRESENT. | | PAST. | |
|---|---|---|---|
| Que je vend*e*. | *That I may sell.* | Que j'aie vend*u*. | *That I may* |
| Que tu vend*es*. | *that thou mayest sell.* | Que tu aies vend*u*. | *that thou mayest* |
| Qu'il vend*e*. | *that he may sell.* | Qu'il ait vend*u*. | *that he may* |
| Que nous vend*ions*. | *that we may sell.* | Que nous ayons vend*u*. | *that we may* |
| Que vous vend*iez*. | *that you may sell.* | Que vous ayez vend*u*. | *that you may* |
| Qu'ils vend*ent*. | *that they may sell.* | Qu'ils aient vend*u*. | *that they may* |

*have sold.*

| IMPERFECT. | | PLUPERFECT. | |
|---|---|---|---|
| Que je vend*isse*. | *That I might sell.* | Que j'eusse vend*u*. | *That I might* |
| Que tu vend*isses*. | *that thou mightest sell.* | Que tu eusses vend*u*. | *that thou mightest* |
| Qu'il vend*ît*. | *that he might sell.* | Qu'il eût vend*u*. | *that he might* |
| Que nous vend*issions*. | *that we might sell.* | Que nous eussions vend*u* | *that we might* |
| Que vous vend*issiez*. | *that you might sell.* | Que vous eussiez vend*u* | *that you might* |
| Qu'ils vend*issent*. | *that they might sell.* | Qu'ils eussent vend*u*. | *that they might* |

*have sold.*

---

| | | | | |
|---|---|---|---|---|
| Revendre | - - - - | *To sell again.* | Suspendre - - - - | *To suspend* |
| Survendre | - - - | *— overcharge.* | Tordre - - - - | *— twist.* |

# CHAPTER 3

# Verbs With Peculiar Spellings

1.—The verbs conjugated in this chapter are not *Irregular*. They have the same terminations as the regular ones — but they offer some peculiarities, in their spelling, in some persons.

Instead of giving a rule to conjugate them, with one or two examples, we have fully conjugated those verbs, and put, *in italic letters*, the persons in which some peculiarities occur ; in that way, we enable the pupil to see, *at a glance*, in which persons a different spelling is used.

2.—The verbs conjugated in this chapter are the following, those ending in :—

| | | | | | |
|---|---|---|---|---|---|
| cer | *as* | Avan*cer*, | *to advance*, | page 30. | |
| ger | — | Man*ger*, | — *eat*, | — 31. | |
| eler | — | App*eler*, | — *call*, | — 32. | |
| eter | — | J*eter*, | — *throw* | — 33. | |
| yer | — | Emplo*yer*, | — *employ*, | — 34. | |
| ayer | — | Pa*yer*, | — *pay*, | — 35. | |
| ier | — | Pr*ier*, | — *pray*, | — 36. | |
| éer | — | Cr*éer*, | — *create*, | — 37. | |
| ener | — | M*ener*, | — *lead*, | — 38. | *Or verbs having* an E |

MUTE *at the last syllable of the radical.*

| | | | | | |
|---|---|---|---|---|---|
| érer | — | Rév*érer*, | — *revere*, | — 39. | *Or verbs having* an É |

WITH AN ACUTE ACCENT *at the last syllable of the radical.*

---

N.B.—The following verbs also present slight irregularities (see pages 41 and 42).

| | | | | | |
|---|---|---|---|---|---|
| Arguer | · | · | · | · | *To argue.* |
| Jouer | · | · | · | · | — *play.* |
| Bénir | · | · | · | · | — *bless.* |
| Fleurir | · | · | · | · | { — *blossom.* <br> { — *be prosperous.* |

| | | | | | |
|---|---|---|---|---|---|
| Refleurir · | · | · | · | · | *To blossom again* |
| Haïr | · | · | · | · | — *hate.* |
| Battre | · | · | · | · | — *beat.* |
| Rompre · | · | · | · | · | — *break.* |

## VERB *AVANCER*, TO ADVANCE.[*]

### INFINITIVE MOOD.

| PRESENT. | | PAST. | |
|---|---|---|---|
| Avancer. | *To advance.* | Avoir avancé. | *To have advanced.* |

| PARTICIPLE PRESENT. | | COMP. OF PART PRESENT. | |
|---|---|---|---|
| Avançant. | *Advancing.* | Ayant avancé. | *Having advanced.* |

### PARTICIPLE PRESENT.

Avancé (m.s.) avancée (f.s.), avaneés (m.pl.), avancées (f.pl.), *advanced.*

### INDICATIVE MOOD.

#### PRESENT.

| J'avance. | *I advance.* |
|---|---|
| Tu avances. | *thou advancest.* |
| Il avance. | *he advances.* |
| Nous *avançons.* | *we advance.* |
| Vous avancez. | *you advance.* |
| Ils avancent. | *they advance.* |

#### IMPERFECT.

| J'*avançais.* | *I was advancing.* |
|---|---|
| Tu *avançais.* | *thou wast advancing.* |
| Il *avançait.* | *he was advancing.* |
| Nous avancions. | *we were advancing.* |
| Vous avanciez. | *you were advancing.* |
| Ils *avançaient.* | *they were advancing.* |

#### PAST DEFINITE.

| J'*avançai.* | *I advanced.* |
|---|---|
| Tu *avanças.* | *thou advancedst.* |
| Il *avança.* | *he advanced.* |
| Nous *avançâmes.* | *we advanced.* |
| Vous *avançâtes.* | *you advanced.* |
| Ils avancèrent. | *they advanced.* |

#### FUTURE.

| J'avancerai. | *I shall advance.* |
|---|---|
| Tu avanceras. | *thou wilt advance.* |
| Il avancera. | *he will advance.* |
| Nous avancerons. | *we shall advance.* |
| Vous avancerez. | *you will advance.* |
| Ils avonceront. | *they will advance.* |

---

### COMPOUND TENSES.

*Past ind.* J'ai avancé, *I have advanced, etc.* etc.

*Plup.* J'avais avancé, *I had advanced, etc.* etc.

*Past ant.* J'eus avancé,*I had advanced, etc.* etc.

*Fut. ant.* J'aurai avancé, etc. *I shall have advanced. etc.*

### CONDITIONAL MOOD.

#### PRESENT.

| J'avancerais. | *I should advance.* |
|---|---|
| Tu avancerais. | *thou wouldst advance.* |
| Il avancerait. | *he would advance.* |
| Nous avancerions. | *we should advance.* |
| Vous avanceriez. | *you would advance.* |
| Ils avanceraient. | *they would advance.* |

### IMPERATIVE MOOD.

#### PRESENT OR FUTURE.

| Avance. | *Advance (thou).* |
|---|---|
| Qu'il avance. | *let him advance.* |
| Avançons. | *let us advance.* |
| Avancez. | *advance (you).* |
| Qu'ils avancent. | *let them advance.* |

### SUBJUNCTIVE MOOD.

#### PRESENT.

| Que j'avance. | *That I may* | |
|---|---|---|
| Que tu avances. | *that thou mayest* | |
| Qu'il avance. | *that he may* | *advance.* |
| Que nous avancions. | *that we may* | |
| Que vous avanciez. | *that you may* | |
| Qu'ils avancent. | *that they may* | |

#### IMPERFECT.

| Que j'*avançasse.* | *That I might* | |
|---|---|---|
| Que tu *avançasses.* | *that thou mightest* | |
| Qu'il *avançât.* | *that he might* | *advance.* |
| Que nous *avançassions.* | *that we might.* | |
| Que vous *avançassiez.* | *that you might.* | |
| Qu'ils *avançassent.* | *that they might.* | |

---

### COMPOUND TENSES.

*Cond. past.* J'aurais avancé, etc. *I should have advanced, etc.*

*Sub. past.* Que j'aie avancé, etc. *that I may have advanced, etc.*

*Sub. plup.* Que j'eusse avancé, etc. *that I might have advanced, etc.*

---

* Rule.—In verbs ending in *cer* a cedilla (ç) is put under the *c*, when it comes before *a* or *o*; because the *c* must be kept soft throughout the verb; *c* with a cedilla (ç) is sounded soft, i.e., like *s* in *same*; and *c* before *a* or *o* is sounded hard, like *k* in *king*.

The *learner* may at a glance know in which persons, the *c* takes the cedilla, viz., *those persons printed in italics.*

### CONJUGATE LIKE *AVANCER.*

| | | | | | | | |
|---|---|---|---|---|---|---|---|
| Commencer - | - *To commence.* | Forcer - | - *To force.* | Policer - | - *To civilize.* |
| Délacer - | - *— unlace.* | Grimacer - | - *— make grimaces.* | Prononcer - | - *—pronounce.* |
| Devancer - | - *— precede.* | Lacer - | - *— lace.* | Rincer - | - *— rinse.* |
| Exaucer - | - *— grant.* | Percer - | - *— pierce.* | Sucer - | - *— suck.* |

# VERB *MANGER*, TO EAT,*

## INFINITIVE MOOD.

| PRESENT. | | PAST. | |
|---|---|---|---|
| Manger. | *to eat.* | Avoir mangé, | *To have eaten.* |
| **PARTICIPLE PRESENT.** | | **COMPOUND OF PARTICIPLE PRESENT.** | |
| *Mangeant.* | *Eating.* | Ayant mangé. | *Having eaten.* |

### PARTICIPLE PAST.

Mangé (m.s.), mangée (f.s.), mangés (m.pl.), mangées (f.pl.), *eaten.*

## INDICATIVE MOOD.

### PRESENT.

| Je mange. | *I eat.* |
|---|---|
| Tu manges. | *thou eatest.* |
| Il mange. | *he eats.* |
| Nous *mangeons.* | *we eat.* |
| Vous mangez. | *you eat.* |
| Ils mangent. | *they eat.* |

### IMPERFECT.

| Je *mangeais.* | *I was eating.* |
|---|---|
| Tu *mangeais.* | *thou wast eating.* |
| Il *mangeait.* | *he was eating.* |
| Nous mangions. | *we were eating.* |
| Vous mangiez. | *you were eating.* |
| Ils *mangeaient.* | *they were eating.* |

### PAST DEFINITE.

| Je *mangeai.* | *I ate.* |
|---|---|
| Tu *mangeas.* | *thou atest.* |
| Il *mangea.* | *he ate.* |
| Nous *mangeâmes.* | *we ate.* |
| Vous *mangeâtes.* | *you ate.* |
| Ils mangèrent. | *they ate.* |

### FUTURE.

| Je mangerai. | *I shall eat.* |
|---|---|
| Tu mangeras. | *thou wilt eat.* |
| Il mangera. | *he will eat.* |
| Nous mangerons. | *we shall eat.* |
| Vous mangerez. | *you will eat.* |
| Ils mangeront. | *they will eat.* |

## COMPOUND TENSES.

| *Past ind.* | J'ai mangé, | *I have eaten, etc.* |
|---|---|---|
| | etc. | |
| *Pluperf.* | J'avais mangé, | *I had eaten, etc.* |
| | etc. | |
| *Past ant.* | J'eus mangé | *I had eaten, etc.* |
| | etc. | |
| *Fut. ant.* | J'aurai mangé, | *I shall have eaten,* |
| | etc. | *etc.* |

## CONDITIONAL MOOD.

### PRESENT.

| Je mangerais. | *I should eat.* |
|---|---|
| Tu mangerais. | *thou wouldst eat.* |
| Il mangerait. | *he would eat.* |
| Nous mangerions. | *we should eat.* |
| Vous mangeriez. | *you would eat.* |
| Ils mangeraient. | *they would eat.* |

## IMPERATIVE MOOD.

### PRESENT or FUTURE.

| Mange. | *Eat (thou).* |
|---|---|
| Qu'il mange. | *let him eat.* |
| *Mangeons.* | *let us eat.* |
| Mangez. | *eat (you).* |
| Qu'ils mangent. | *let them eat.* |

## SUBJUNCTIVE MOOD.

### PRESENT.

| Que je mange. | *That I may eat.* |
|---|---|
| Que tu manges. | *that thou mayest eat.* |
| Qu'il mange. | *that he may eat.* |
| Que nous mangions. | *that we may eat.* |
| Que vous mangiez. | *that you may eat.* |
| Qu'ils mangent. | *that they may eat.* |

### IMPERFECT.

| Que je *mangeasse.* | *That I might eat.* |
|---|---|
| Que tu *mangeasses.* | *that thou mightest eat.* |
| Qu'il *mangeât.* | *that he might eat.* |
| Que nous *mangeassions.* | *that we might eat.* |
| Que vous *mangeassiez.* | *that you might eat.* |
| Qu'ils *mangeassent.* | *that they might eat.* |

## COMPOUND TENSES.

| *Cond. past.* | J'aurais | *I should have eaten,* |
|---|---|---|
| | mangé, etc. | *etc.* |
| *Sub. past.* | Que j'aie | *that I may have eaten,* |
| | mangé, etc. | *etc.* |
| *Sub. plup.* | Que j'eusse | *that I might have* |
| | mangé, etc. | *eaten, etc.* |

---

* Rule.—In verbs ending in *ger*, like *manger*, an *e* mute is placed after the *g*, when the *g* is followed by *a* or *o*. EX.: *Nous mangeons; Je mangeais;* because the *g* must be kept soft throughout the verb and *g* followed by *a* or *o* sounds hard.

Persons, in which the *g* is followed by *e* mute, are printed in italic letters.

### CONJUGATE LIKE *MANGER:*

| | | | | | | | | |
|---|---|---|---|---|---|---|---|---|
| Arranger - | - | *To arrange.* | Gager | - | - *To bet.* | Songer | - - | *To dream.* |
| Déranger - | - | *— derange.* | Juger | - | - *—judge.* | Soulager | - - | *— relieve.* |
| Engager - | - | *— engage.* | Nager | - | - *— swim.* | Voyager | - - | *— travel.* |
| Ériger - | - | *— erect.* | Singer | - | - *— mimic.* | | | |

# VERB.—*APPELER*, to call.*

## INFINITIVE MOOD.

| PRESENT. | | PAST. | |
|---|---|---|---|
| Appeler. | *To call.* | Avoir appelé. | *To have called.* |

| PARTICIPLE PRESENT. | | COMP. OF PART. PRESENT. | |
|---|---|---|---|
| Appelant. | *Calling.* | Ayant appelé. | *Having called.* |

PARTICIPLE PAST.

Appelé (m. s.)—Appelée (f. s.)—Appelés (m. pl.)—Appelées (f. pl.)—*called.*

## INDICATIVE MOOD.

### PRESENT.

| J'*appelle.* | *I call.* |
|---|---|
| Tu *appelles.* | *thou callest.* |
| Il *appelle.* | *he calls.* |
| Nous appelons. | *we call.* |
| Vous appelez. | *you call.* |
| Ils *appellent.* | *they call.* |

### IMPERFECT.

| J'appelais. | *I was calling.* |
|---|---|
| Tu appelais. | *thou wast calling.* |
| Il appelait. | *he was calling.* |
| Nous appelions. | *we were calling.* |
| Vous appeliez. | *you were calling.* |
| Ils appelaient. | *they were calling.* |

### PAST DEFINITE.

| J'appelai. | *I called.* |
|---|---|
| Tu appelas. | *thou calledst.* |
| Il appela. | *he called.* |
| Nous appelâmes. | *we called.* |
| Vous appelâtes. | *you called.* |
| Ils appelèrent. | *they called.* |

### FUTURE.

| J'*appellerai.* | *I shall call.* |
|---|---|
| Tu *appelleras.* | *thou wilt call.* |
| Il *appellera.* | *he will call.* |
| Nous *appellerons.* | *we shall call.* |
| Vous *appellerez.* | *you will call.* |
| Ils *appelleront.* | *they will call.* |

### COMPOUND TENSES.

| *Past ind.* | J'ai appelé, etc. | *I have called, etc.* |
|---|---|---|
| *Plup.* | J'avais appelé, etc. | *I had called, etc.* |
| *Past ant.* | J'eus appelé, etc. | *I had called, etc.* |
| *Fut. ant.* | J'aurai appelé, etc. | *I shall have called, etc.* |

## CONDITIONAL MOOD.

### PRESENT.

| J'*appellerais.* | *I should call.* |
|---|---|
| Tu *appellerais.* | *thou wouldst call.* |
| Il *appellerait.* | *he would call.* |
| Nous *appellerions.* | *we should call.* |
| Vous *appelleriez.* | *you would call.* |
| Ils *appelleraient.* | *they would call.* |

## IMPERATIVE MOOD.

### PRESENT OR FUTURE.

| *Appelle.* | *Call (thou).* |
|---|---|
| Qu'il *appelle.* | *let him call.* |
| Appelons. | *let us call.* |
| Appelez. | *call (you).* |
| Qu'ils *appellent.* | *let them call.* |

## SUBJUNCTIVE MOOD.

### PRESENT.

| Que j'*appelle.* | *That I may call.* |
|---|---|
| Que tu *appelles.* | *that thou mayest call.* |
| Qu'il *appelle.* | *that he may call.* |
| Que nous appelions. | *that we may call.* |
| Que vous appeliez. | *that you may call.* |
| Qu'ils *appellent.* | *that they may call* |

### IMPERFECT.

| Que j'appelasse. | *That I might call.* |
|---|---|
| Que tu appelasses. | *that thou mightest call.* |
| Qu'il appelât. | *that he might call.* |
| Que nous appelassions. | *that we might call.* |
| Que vous appelassiez. | *that you might call.* |
| Qu'ils appelassent. | *that they might call.* |

### COMPOUND TENSES.

| *Cond. past.* | J'aurais appelé, etc. | *I should have called, etc.* |
|---|---|---|
| *Sub. past.* | Que j'aie appelé, etc. | *that I may have called, etc.* |
| ,, *plup.* | Que j'eusse appelé, etc. | *that I might have called, etc.* |

---

* **Rule.**—Verbs ending in *eler*, like *appeler*, take two *l*'s before a syllable mute. *The following verbs are exceptions to the preceding rule:*—

| Bourreler | - | - | - | *To torment.* | Dégeler | - | - | - | *To thaw.* | Harceler | - | - | - | *To harass.* |
|---|---|---|---|---|---|---|---|---|---|---|---|---|---|---|
| Celer | - | - | - | *— conceal.* | Ecarteler | - | - | - | *— quarter.* | Marteler | - | - | - | *— hammer.* |
| Déceler | - | - | - | *— disclose.* | Geler | - | - | - | *— freeze.* | Modeler | - | - | - | *— model.* |
| | | | | | | | | | | Peler | - | - | - | *— peel.* |

Those verbs, instead of doubling *l* before a mute syllable, take a grave accent on the *e* preceding it.
Ex.: Je pèle (*I peal*), instead of (Je *pelle*), etc.

The persons having two *l*'s are in italic letters.

### CONJUGATE LIKE *APPELER:*

| Botteler | - | - | - | *To bottle.* | Morceler | - | - | *To parcel out.* | Râteler | - | - | *To rake.* |
|---|---|---|---|---|---|---|---|---|---|---|---|---|
| Chanceler | - | - | - | *— totter.* | Niveler | - | - | *— level.* | Renouveler | - | - | *— renew.* |
| Etinceler | - | - | - | *— sparkle.* | Rappeler | - | - | *— call again.* | Ressemeler | - | - | *— new-sole (shoes or boots.)* |

# 33

# VERB *JETER*, TO THROW.*

## INFINITIVE MOOD.

| PRESENT. | | PAST. | |
|---|---|---|---|
| Jeter. | *To throw.* | Avoir jeté. | *To have thrown.* |
| PARTICIPLE PRESENT. | | COMP. OF PART. PRESENT. | |
| Jetant. | *Throwing.* | Ayant jeté. | *Having thrown.* |

PARTICIPLE PAST.
Jeté (m.s.), jetée (f.s.), jetés (m.pl.), jetées (f.pl.), *thrown.*

## INDICATIVE MOOD.

### PRESENT.
Je *jette.* (1) — *I throw.*
Tu *jettes.* — *thou throwest.*
Il *jette.* — *he throws.*
Nous jetons. — *we throw.*
Vous jetez. — *you throw.*
Ils *jettent.* — *they throw.*

### IMPERFECT.
Je jetais. — *I was throwing.*
Tu jetais. — *thou wast throwing.*
Il jetait. — *he was throwing.*
Nous jetions. — *we were throwing.*
Vous jetiez. — *you were throwing.*
Ils jetaient. — *they were throwing.*

### PAST DEFINITE.
Je jetai. — *I threw.*
Tu jetas. — *thou threwest.*
Il jeta. — *he threw.*
Nous jetâmes. — *we threw.*
Vous jetâtes. — *you threw.*
Ils jetèrent. — *they threw.*

### FUTURE.
Je *jetterai.* — *I shall throw.*
Tu *jetteras.* — *thou wilt throw.*
Il *jettera.* — *he will throw.*
Nous *jetterons.* — *we shall throw.*
Vous *jetterez.* — *you will throw.*
Ils *jetteront.* — *they will throw.*

### COMPOUND TENSES.
*Past Ind.* J'ai jeté, etc. — *I have thrown, etc.*
*Plup.* J'avais jeté, etc. — *I had thrown, etc.*
*Past Ant.* J'eus jeté, etc. — *I had thrown, etc.*
*Fut. Ant.* J'aurai jeté, etc. — *I shall have thrown, etc.*

## CONDITIONAL MOOD.

### PRESENT.
Je *jetterais.* — *I should throw.*
Tu *jetterais.* — *thou wouldst throw.*
Il *jetterait.* — *he would throw.*
Nous *jetterions.* — *we should throw.*
Vous *jetteriez.* — *you would throw.*
Ils *jetteraient.* — *they would throw.*

## IMPERATIVE MOOD.
### PRESENT OR FUTURE.
*Jette.* — *Throw (thou).*
Qu'il *jette.* — *let him throw.*
Jetons. — *let us throw.*
Jetez. — *throw (you).*
Qu'ils *jettent.* — *let them throw.*

## SUBJUNCTIVE MOOD.
### PRESENT.
Que je *jette.* — *That I may throw.*
Que tu *jettes.* — *that thou mayest throw.*
Qu'il *jette.* — *that he may throw.*
Que nous jetions. — *that we may throw.*
Que vous jetiez. — *that you may throw.*
Qu'ils *jettent.* — *that they may throw.*

### IMPERFECT.
Que je jetasse. — *That I might throw.*
Que tu jetasses. — *that thou mightest throw.*
Qu'il jetât. — *that he might throw.*
Que nous jetassions. — *that we might throw.*
Que vous jetassiez. — *that you might throw.*
Qu'ils jetassent. — *that they might throw.*

### COMPOUND TENSES.
*Cond. past.* J'aurais jeté, etc. — *I should have thrown, etc.*
*Sub. past.* Que j'aie jeté, etc. — *that I may have thrown, etc.*
*Sub. Plup.* Que j'eusse jeté, etc. — *that I might have thrown, etc.*

---

* Verbs ending in *eter* usually take two *t*'s before an *e* mute, such as: *jeter*, to throw, etc. The following verbs do not take two *t*'s, but a grave accent is put over the *e*, preceding the *t*, when it is followed by an *e* mute:

| | | |
|---|---|---|
| Acheter - - - | *To buy.* | |
| Becqueter *or* Béqueter | *—peck.* | |
| Craqueter - - - | *—crackle.* | |
| Étiqueter - - , | *To label.* | |
| Racheter - - - | *— redeem.* | |

Ex.: *j'achète, tu achètes,* etc., instead of: *j'achette, tu achettes,* etc.

### CONJUGATE LIKE *JETER:*
Billeter - - - *To ticket.* | Empaqueter - - - *To pack.* | Projeter - - - *To project.*
Cacheter - - - *— seal.* | Parqueter - - - *—floor.* | Voleter - - - *—flutter.*

(1) Persons in which two *t*'s are used are printed in italics.

# VERB *EMPLOYER*, TO EMPLOY.*

## INFINITIVE MOOD.

| PRESENT. | | PAST. | |
|---|---|---|---|
| Employer. | *To employ.* | Avoir employé. | *To have employed.* |

| PARTICIPLE PRESENT. | | COMP. OF PART. PRESENT. | |
|---|---|---|---|
| Employant. | *Employing.* | Ayant employé. | *Having employed.* |

PARTICIPLE PAST.

Employé (m.s.), employée (f.s.), employés (m.pl.), employées (f.pl.), *employed.*

### INDICATIVE MOOD.
#### PRESENT.

| J'emploie.(1) | *I employ.* |
|---|---|
| Tu *emploies.* | *thou employest.* |
| Il *emploie.* | *he employs.* |
| Nous employons. | *we employ.* |
| Vous employez. | *you employ.* |
| Ils *emploient.* | *they employ.* |

#### IMPERFECT.

| J'employais. | *I was employing.* |
|---|---|
| Tu employais. | *thou wast employing.* |
| Il employait. | *he was employing.* |
| Nous employions. | *we were employing.* |
| Vous employiez. | *you were employing.* |
| Ils employaient. | *they were employing.* |

#### PAST DEFINITE.

| J'employai. | *I employed.* |
|---|---|
| Tu employas. | *thou employedst.* |
| Il employa. | *he employed.* |
| Nous employâmes. | *we employed.* |
| Vous employâtes. | *you employed.* |
| Ils employèrent. | *they employed.* |

#### FUTURE.

| J'*emploierai.* | *I shall employ.* |
|---|---|
| Tu *emploieras.* | *thou wilt employ.* |
| Il *emploiera.* | *he will employ.* |
| Nous *emploierons.* | *we shall employ.* |
| Vous *emploierez.* | *you will employ.* |
| Ils *emploieront.* | *they will employ.* |

### CONDITIONAL MOOD.
#### PRESENT.

| J'*emploierais.* | *I should employ.* |
|---|---|
| Tu *emploierais.* | *thou wouldst employ.* |
| Il *emploierait.* | *he would employ.* |
| Nous *emploierions.* | *we should employ.* |
| Vous *emploieriez.* | *you would employ.* |
| Ils *emploieraient.* | *they would employ.* |

### IMPERATIVE MOOD.
#### PRESENT OR FUTURE.

| Emploie. | *Employ (thou).* |
|---|---|
| Qu'il *emploie.* | *let him employ.* |
| Employons. | *let us employ.* |
| Employez. | *employ (you).* |
| Qu'ils *emploient.* | *let them employ.* |

### SUBJUNCTIVE MOOD.
#### PRESENT.

| Que j'*emploie.* | *That I may* |
|---|---|
| Que tu *emploies.* | *that thou mayest* |
| Qu'il *emploie.* | *that he may* |
| Que nous employions. | *that we may* |
| Que vous employiez. | *that you may* |
| Qu'ils *emploient.* | *that they may* |

employ.

#### IMPERFECT.

| Que j'employasse. | *That I might* |
|---|---|
| Que tu employasses. | *that thou mightest* |
| Qu'il employât. | *that he might* |
| Que nous employassions | *that we might* |
| Que vous employassiez. | *that you might* |
| Qu'ils employassent. | *that they might* |

employ.

### COMPOUND TENSES.

| Past ind. | J'ai employé, etc. | *I have* |
|---|---|---|
| Plup. | J'avais employé, etc. | *I had* |
| Past ant. | J'eus employé, etc. | *I had* |
| Fut. ant. | J'aurai employé, etc. | *I shall have* |

employed, etc.

| Cond. past. | J'aurais employé, etc. | *I should have* |
|---|---|---|
| Sub. past. | Que j'aie employé, etc. | *that I may have* |
| Sub. Plup. | Que j'eusse employé, etc. | *that I might have.* |

employed, etc.

---

* Rule.—Verbs ending in *yer* change *y* to *i* before an *e* mute, excepting the verbs *grasseyer, langueyer,* and verbs in which the *y* is preceded by an *a* as in *payer.* (See next page.)

N.B.—In all verbs ending in *yer* the *y* in the *Imperfect of the Indicative* (first and second person plural), and in the same persons of the Present of Subjunctive is followed by *i*. Ex.:

*Imperfect:* Nous employions.   Vous employiez.
*Sub. pres.:* Nous employions.   Vous employiez.

(1) Persons in which *y* is changed into *i* are printed in italic letters.

## CONJUGATE LIKE *EMPLOYER:*

| Appuyer | - *To support, to lean (against).* | Ennuyer | - *To weary, to bore.* | Noyer | - - - *To drown.* |
|---|---|---|---|---|---|
| Côtoyer - | - - - *To coast.* | Envoyer | - *— send.* | Ondoyer | - - *— undulate.* |
| | | Nettoyer | - *— clean.* | Ployer | - - *— bend.* |

# VERB *PAYER*—TO PAY.*

## INFINITIVE MOOD.

| PRESENT. | | PAST. | |
|---|---|---|---|
| Payer. | *To pay.* | Avoir payé. | *To have paid.* |
| **PARTICIPLE PRESENT.** | | **COMPOUND OF PARTICIPLE PRESENT.** | |
| Payant. | *Paying.* | Ayant payé. | *Having paid.* |

**PARTICIPLE PAST.**

Payé (m.s.), payée (f.s.), payés (m.pl.), payées (f.pl.), *paid.*

## INDICATIVE MOOD.

### PRESENT.

| | |
|---|---|
| Je paye. | *I pay.* |
| Tu payes. | *thou payest.* |
| Il paye. | *he pays.* |
| Nous payons. | *we pay.* |
| Vous payez. | *you pay.* |
| Ils payent. | *they pay.* |

### IMPERFECT.

| | |
|---|---|
| Je payais. | *I was paying.* |
| Tu payais. | *thou wast paying.* |
| Il payait. | *he was paying.* |
| Nous payions. | *we were paying.* |
| Vous payiez. | *you were paying.* |
| Ils payaient. | *they were paying.* |

### PAST DEFINITE.

| | |
|---|---|
| Je payai. | *I paid.* |
| Tu payas. | *thou paidst.* |
| Il paya. | *he paid.* |
| Nous payâmes. | *we paid.* |
| Vous payâtes. | *you paid.* |
| Ils payèrent. | *they paid.* |

### FUTURE.

| | |
|---|---|
| Je payerai. | *I shall* |
| Tu payeras. | *thou wilt* |
| Il payera. | *he will* |
| Nous payerons. | *we shall* |
| Vous payerez. | *you will* |
| Ils payeront. | *they will* |

*} pay.*

## CONDITIONAL MOOD.

### PRESENT.

| | |
|---|---|
| Je payerais. | *I should* |
| Tu payerais. | *thou wouldst* |
| Il payerait. | *he would* |
| Nous payerions. | *we should* |
| Vous payeriez. | *you would* |
| Ils payeraient. | *they would* |

*} pay.*

## IMPERATIVE MOOD.

### PRESENT.

| | |
|---|---|
| Paye | *Pay (thou).* |
| Qu'il paye. | *let him pay,* |
| Payons. | *let us pay.* |
| Payez. | *pay (you).* |
| Qu'ils payent. | *let them pay.* |

## SUBJUNCTIVE MOOD.

### PRESENT.

| | |
|---|---|
| Que je paye. | *That I may pay.* |
| Que tu payes. | *that thou mayest pay.* |
| Qu'il paye. | *that he may pay.* |
| Que nous payions. | *that we may pay.* |
| Que vous payiez. | *that you may pay.* |
| Qu'ils payent. | *that they may pay.* |

### IMPERFECT.

| | |
|---|---|
| Que je payasse. | *That I might pay.* |
| Que tu payasses. | *that thou mightest pay.* |
| Qu'il payât. | *that he might pay.* |
| Que nous payassions. | *that we might pay.* |
| Que vous payassiez. | *that you might pay.* |
| Qu'ils payassent. | *that they might pay.* |

## COMPOUND TENSES.

| | | | |
|---|---|---|---|
| *Past. Ind.*—J'ai payé, etc. | *I have paid, etc.* | *Cond. Past.*—J'aurais payé, etc. | *I should have paid, etc.* |
| *Plup.* —J'avais payé, etc. | *I had paid, etc.* | *Sub. Past.*—Que j'aie payé, etc. | *that I may have paid, etc.* |
| *Past. ant.*—J'eus payé, etc. | *I had paid, etc.* | *Sub. Plup.*—Que j'eusse payé, etc. | *that I might have paid, etc.* |
| *Fut. ant.*—J'aurai payé, etc. | *I shall have paid, etc.* | | |

**RULE.**—Verbs ending in *ayer* preserve the *y* throughout.

*Conjugate like Payer* all verbs ending in *ayer.*

N.B.—Verb *Grasseyer*, to speak thick (by articulating the *r* imperfectly) preserves *y* throughout the verb.
Ex. : Je grasseye, je grasseyerai, etc ; *instead of*: Je grasseie, je grasseierai, *and Langueyer* also (*to examine the tongue*).

## CONJUGATE LIKE *PAYER.*

| | | | | | |
|---|---|---|---|---|---|
| Balayer - - - *To sweep.* | Déblayer - - *To clear away.* | Effrayer - - *To frighten.* |
| Bayer - - - - *— gape.* | Délayer - - *— dilute (liquid).* | Essayer - - *— try.* |

**ARLES, THE ROMAN ARENA**

CHATEAU AZAY-LE-RIDEAU

# VERB *PRIER*, to pray.*

## INFINITIVE MOOD.

| | | | |
|---|---|---|---|
| **PRESENT.** | | **PAST.** | |
| Prier. | *To pray.* | Avoir prié. | *To have prayed.* |
| **PARTICIPLE PRESENT.** | | **COMPOUND OF PARTICIPLE PRESENT.** | |
| Priant | *Praying.* | Ayant prié. | *Having prayed.* |

### PARTICIPLE PAST.

Prié (m.s.), priée (f.s.), priés (m.pl.), priées (f.pl.), *prayed.*

| INDICATIVE MOOD. | | CONDITIONAL MOOD. | |
|---|---|---|---|
| **PRESENT.** | | **PRESENT.** | |
| Je prie. | *I pray.* | Je prierais. | *I should pray.* |
| Tu pries. | *thou prayest.* | Tu prierais. | *thou wouldst pray.* |
| Il prie. | *he prays.* | Il prierait. | *he would pray.* |
| Nous prions. | *we pray.* | Nous prierions. | *we should pray.* |
| Vous priez. | *you pray.* | Vous prieriez. | *you would pray.* |
| Ils prient. | *they pray.* | Ils prieraient. | *they would pray.* |
| **IMPERFECT.** | | **IMPERATIVE MOOD.** | |
| Je priais. | *I was praying.* | **PRESENT OR FUTURE.** | |
| Tu priais. | *thou wast praying.* | Prie. | *Pray (thou).* |
| Il priait. | *he was praying.* | Qu'il prie. | *let him pray.* |
| Nous *priions.* | *we were praying.* | Prions. | *let us pray.* |
| Vous *priiez.* | *you were praying.* | Priez. | *pray (you).* |
| Ils priaient. | *they were praying.* | Qu'ils prient. | *let them pray.* |
| **PAST DEFINITE.** | | **SUBJUNCTIVE MOOD.** | |
| Je priai. | *I prayed.* | **PRESENT.** | |
| Tu prias. | *thou prayedst.* | Que je prie. | *That I may pray.* |
| Il pria. | *he prayed.* | Que tu pries. | *that thou mayest pray.* |
| Nous priâmes. | *we prayed.* | Qu'il prie. | *that he may pray.* |
| Vous priâtes. | *you prayed.* | Que nous *priions.* | *that we may pray.* |
| Ils prièrent. | *they prayed.* | Que vous *priiez.* | *that you may pray.* |
| | | Qu'ils prient. | *that they may pray.* |
| **FUTURE.** | | **IMPERFECT.** | |
| Je prierai. | *I shall pray.* | Que je priasse. | *That I might pray.* |
| Tu prieras. | *thou wilt pray.* | Que tu priasses. | *that thou mightest pray.* |
| Ils priera. | *he will pray.* | Qu'il priât. | *that he might pray.* |
| Nous prierons. | *we shall pray.* | Que nous priassions. | *that we might pray.* |
| Vous prierez. | *you will pray.* | Que vous priassiez. | *that you might pray.* |
| Ils prieront. | *they will pray.* | Qu'ils priassent. | *that they might pray.* |

### COMPOUND TENSES.

| | | | |
|---|---|---|---|
| *Past ind.* J'ai prié, etc. | *I have prayed, etc.* | *Cond. past.* J'aurais prié, etc. | *I should have prayed, etc.* |
| *Plup.* J'avais prié etc. | *I had prayed, etc.* | | |
| *Past ant.* J'eus prié, etc. | *I had prayed, etc.* | *Sub. past.* Que j'aie prié, etc. | *That I may have prayed, etc.* |
| *Fut. ant.* J'aurai prié, etc. | *I shall have prayed, etc.* | *Imp.* Que j'eusse prié, etc. | *That I might have prayed, etc.* |

*N.B.—The Verbs ending in *ier*, such as *prier*, to pray ; *crier*, to cry, have two *i*'s in the following tenses :
*Imperfect of the Indicative*: first and second person plural. *Nous priions. Vous priiez.*
*Subjunctive Present*: first and second person plural. *Que nous priions. Que vous priiez.*
The reason is, the radical in those verbs ends by *i*, and the terminations in the Imperfect of the Indicative and the Present of the Subjunctive, first and second person plural, are : *ions, iez.* thence two *i*'s.

*Indicative Imperfect* { Nous pri-ions.
Vous pri-iez.

*Subjunctive Present* { Que nous pri-ions.
Que vous pri-iez.

### CONJUGATE LIKE *PRIER*:

| | | | | | |
|---|---|---|---|---|---|
| Certifier | *To certify.* | Lier | *To tie.* | Oublier | *To forget.* |
| Crier | *— cry.* | Manier | *— handle.* | Plier | *— bend.* |
| Étudier | *— study.* | Nier | *— deny.* | Remercier | *— thank.* |

# VERB *CRÉER*, TO CREATE.*

## INFINITIVE MOOD.

| PRESENT. | | PAST. | |
|---|---|---|---|
| Créer. | To create. | Avoir créé. | To have created. |

| PARTICIPLE PRESENT. | | COMP. OF PARTICIPLE PRESENT. | |
|---|---|---|---|
| Créant. | Creating. | Ayant créé. | Having created. |

PARTICIPLE PAST.
Créé (m. s.), créée (f.s.) créés (m.pl.), créées (f.pl.), created. (1)

<table>
<tr><td colspan="2">INDICATIVE MOOD.</td><td colspan="2">CONDITIONAL MOOD.</td></tr>
<tr><td colspan="2">PRESENT.</td><td colspan="2">PRESENT.</td></tr>
<tr><td>Je crée. (2)</td><td>I create.</td><td>Je créerais.</td><td>I should create.</td></tr>
<tr><td>Tu crées.</td><td>thou createst.</td><td>Tu créerais.</td><td>thou wouldst create.</td></tr>
<tr><td>Il crée.</td><td>he creates.</td><td>Il créerait.</td><td>he would create.</td></tr>
<tr><td>Nous créons.</td><td>we create.</td><td>Nous créerions.</td><td>we should create.</td></tr>
<tr><td>Vous créez.</td><td>you create.</td><td>Vous créeriez.</td><td>you would create.</td></tr>
<tr><td>Ils créent.</td><td>they create.</td><td>Ils créeraient.</td><td>they would create.</td></tr>
<tr><td colspan="2">IMPERFECT.</td><td colspan="2">IMPERATIVE MOOD.</td></tr>
<tr><td>Je créais.</td><td>I was creating.</td><td colspan="2">PRESENT OR FUTURE.</td></tr>
<tr><td>Tu créais.</td><td>thou wast creating.</td><td>Crée.</td><td>Create (thou).</td></tr>
<tr><td>Il créait.</td><td>he was creating.</td><td>Qu'il crée.</td><td>let him create.</td></tr>
<tr><td>Nous créions.</td><td>we were creating.</td><td>Créons.</td><td>let us create.</td></tr>
<tr><td>Vous créiez.</td><td>you were creating.</td><td>Créez.</td><td>create (you).</td></tr>
<tr><td>Ils créaient.</td><td>they were creating.</td><td>Qu'ils créent.</td><td>let them create.</td></tr>
<tr><td colspan="2">PAST DEFINITE.</td><td colspan="2">SUBJUNCTIVE MOOD.</td></tr>
<tr><td>Je créai.</td><td>I created.</td><td colspan="2">PRESENT.</td></tr>
<tr><td>Tu créas.</td><td>thou createdst.</td><td>Que je crée.</td><td>That I may create.</td></tr>
<tr><td>Il créa.</td><td>he created.</td><td>Que tu crées.</td><td>that thou mayest create.</td></tr>
<tr><td>Nous créâmes.</td><td>we created.</td><td>Qu'il crée.</td><td>that he may create.</td></tr>
<tr><td>Vous créâtes.</td><td>you created.</td><td>Que nous créions.</td><td>that we may create.</td></tr>
<tr><td>Ils créèrent.</td><td>they created.</td><td>Que vous créiez.</td><td>that you may create.</td></tr>
<tr><td colspan="2"></td><td>Qu'ils créent.</td><td>that they may create.</td></tr>
<tr><td colspan="2">FUTURE. (3)</td><td colspan="2">IMPERFECT.</td></tr>
<tr><td>Je créerai.</td><td>I shall create.</td><td>Que je créasse.</td><td>That I might create.</td></tr>
<tr><td>Tu créeras.</td><td>thou wilt create.</td><td>Que tu créasses.</td><td>that thou mightest create.</td></tr>
<tr><td>Il créera.</td><td>he will create.</td><td>Qu'il créât.</td><td>that he might create.</td></tr>
<tr><td>Nous créerons.</td><td>we shall create.</td><td>Que nous créassions.</td><td>that we might create.</td></tr>
<tr><td>Vous créerez.</td><td>you will create.</td><td>Que vous créassiez.</td><td>that you might create.</td></tr>
<tr><td>Ils créeront.</td><td>they will create.</td><td>Qu'ils créassent.</td><td>that they might create.</td></tr>
</table>

## COMPOUND TENSES.

| | | | | | | |
|---|---|---|---|---|---|---|
| Past Ind. | J'ai créé, etc. | I have created, etc. | Cond.Past. | J'aurais créé, etc. | I should have created, etc. |
| Plup. | J'avais créé, etc. | I had created, etc. | | | |
| Past Ant. | J'eus créé, etc | I had created, etc. | Sub. Past. | Que j'aie créé, etc. | that I may have created, etc. |
| Fut. Ant. | J'aurai créé, etc. | I shall have created, etc. | Sub. Plup. | Que j'eusse créé, etc. | that I might have created, etc. |

* Verbs ending in *éer* are regular, but they have two *e*'s in some tenses. The reason is, the radical part ends by *é*, and some terminations are *e*, or begin by *e*.
(1) The Past Participle of verbs in *éer* has two *e*'s, with an acute accent, as *créé*; an additional *e* is added to form the feminine: *créé* (masc. sing.), *créée* (fem. sing.)
(2) Persons having two *e*'s are printed in italic letters, in the above conjugation.

## LIST OF VERBS ENDING IN *ÉER*.

| | | | | | | | | |
|---|---|---|---|---|---|---|---|---|
| Agréer | - | - | To accept of. | Féer | - | - | To enchant. | Ragréer - - - To finish off. |
| Créer | - | - | — create. | Gréer | - | - | — rig. | Récréer - - - — divert. |
| Dégréer | - | - | — unrig. | Guéer | - | - | — ford (a river). | Regréer - - - —fresh rig. |
| Désagréer | - | - | — displease. | Maugréer | - | - | — rage. | Suppléer - - - — supply. |
| | | | | Procréer | - | - | — procreate. | |

(3) In the Future and Conditional of verbs ending in *éer*, poets generally suppress the second *e*: "Nos hôtes *agréront* les soins," etc. (*La Fontaine*), instead of *agréeront*. In prose, the suppression of an *e* would be an error.

# VERB *MENER*, TO LEAD.*

## INFINITIVE MOOD.

| | PRESENT. | | PAST. |
|---|---|---|---|
| Mener. | *To lead.* | Avoir mené. | *To have led.* |

| | PARTICIPLE PRESENT. | | COMPOUND OF PARTICIPLE PRESENT |
|---|---|---|---|
| Menant. | *Leading.* | Ayant mené. | *Having led.* |

### PARTICIPLE PAST.

Mené (m.s.), menée (f.s.), menés (m.pl.), menées (f.pl.), *led.*

## INDICATIVE MOOD.

### PRESENT.

| Je mène. (1) | *I lead.* |
|---|---|
| Tu *mènes.* | *thou leadest.* |
| Il *mène.* | *he leads.* |
| Nous menons. | *we lead.* |
| Vous menez. | *you lead.* |
| Ils *mènent.* | *they lead.* |

### IMPERFECT.

| Je menais. | *I was leading.* |
|---|---|
| Tu menais. | *thou wast leading.* |
| Il menait. | *he was leading.* |
| Nous menions. | *we were leading.* |
| Vous meniez. | *you were leading.* |
| Ils menaient. | *they were leading.* |

### PAST DEFINITE.

| Je menai. | *I led.* |
|---|---|
| Tu menas. | *thou ledst.* |
| Il mena. | *he led.* |
| Nous menâmes. | *we led.* |
| Vous menâtes. | *you led.* |
| Ils menèrent. | *they led.* |

### FUTURE.

| Je *mènerai.* | *I shall lead.* |
|---|---|
| Tu *mèneras.* | *thou wilt lead.* |
| Il *mènera.* | *he will lead.* |
| Nous *mènerons.* | *we shall lead.* |
| Vous *mènerez.* | *you will lead.* |
| Ils *mèneront.* | *they will lead.* |

## CONDITIONAL MOOD.

### PRESENT.

| Je *mènerais.* | *I should lead.* |
|---|---|
| Tu *mènerais.* | *thou wouldst lead.* |
| Il *mènerait.* | *he would lead.* |
| Nous *mènerions.* | *we should lead.* |
| Vous *mèneriez.* | *you would lead.* |
| Ils *mèneraient.* | *they would lead.* |

## IMPERATIVE MOOD.

### PRESENT OR FUTURE.

| *Mène.* | *Lead (thou).* |
|---|---|
| Qu'il *mène.* | *let him lead.* |
| Menons. | *let us lead.* |
| Menez. | *lead (you).* |
| Qu'ils *mènent.* | *let them lead.* |

## SUBJUNCTIVE MOOD.

### PRESENT.

| Que je *mène.* | *That I may lead.* |
|---|---|
| Que tu *mènes.* | *that thou mayest lead.* |
| Qu'il *mène.* | *that he may lead.* |
| Que nous menions. | *that we may lead.* |
| Que vous meniez. | *that you may lead.* |
| Qu'ils *mènent.* | *that they may lead.* |

### IMPERFECT.

| Que je menasse. | *That I might lead.* |
|---|---|
| Que tu menasses. | *that thou mightest lead.* |
| Qu'il menât. | *that he might lead.* |
| Que nous menassions. | *that we might lead.* |
| Que vous menassiez. | *that you might lead.* |
| Qu'ils menassent. | *that they might lead.* |

## COMPOUND TENSES.

| Past ind. | J'ai mené, etc. | *I have led, etc.* | Cond. past. | J'aurais mené, etc. | *I should have led, etc.* |
|---|---|---|---|---|---|
| Plup. | J'avais mené, etc. | *I had led, etc.* | Sub. past. | Que j'aie mené, | *that I may have led, etc.* |
| Past ant. | J'eus mené, etc. | *I had led, etc.* | Imp. | Que j'eusse mené, etc. | *that I might have led, etc.* |
| Fut. ant. | J'aurai mené, etc. | *I shall have led, etc.* | | | |

* RULE.—For the sake of euphony, verbs having an e mute, *at the last syllable of the radical,* take a grave accent over that *e,* before a mute syllable.

(1) *Persons having the grave accent are printed in italic letters.*

### CONJUGATE LIKE *MENER:*

| Achever | To finish. | Enlever | To carry away. | Peser | To weigh. |
|---|---|---|---|---|---|
| Amener | — bring. | Lever | — lift up. | Semer | — sow. |
| Élever | — bring up. | Parsemer | — strew. | Soulever | — raise. |

# VERB *RÉVÉRER*, TO REVERE.*

## INFINITIVE MOOD.

| PRESENT. | | PAST. | |
|---|---|---|---|
| Révérer. | *To revere.* | Avoir révéré. | *To have revered.* |
| PARTICIPLE PRESENT. | | COMPOUND OF PARTICIPLE PRESENT. | |
| Révérant. | *Revering.* | Ayant révéré. | *Having revered.* |

PARTICIPLE PAST.
Révéré (m.s.), révérée (f.s.), révérés (m.pl.), révérées (f.pl.), *revered.*

## INDICATIVE MOOD.
### PRESENT.
Je *révère.* (1)   *I revere.*
Tu *révères.*   *thou reverest.*
Il *révère.*   *he reveres.*
Nous révérons.   *we revere.*
Vous révérez.   *you revere.*
Ils *révèrent.*   *they revere.*

### IMPERFECT.
Je révérais.   *I was revering.*
Tu révérais.   *thou wast revering.*
Il révérait.   *he was revering.*
Nous révérions.   *we were revering.*
Vous révériez.   *you were revering.*
Ils révéraient.   *they were revering.*

### PAST DEFINITE.
Je révérai.   *I revered.*
Tu révéras.   *thou reveredst.*
Il révéra.   *he revered.*
Nous révérâmes.   *we revered.*
Vous révérâtes.   *you revered.*
Ils révérèrent.   *they revered.*

### FUTURE.
Je révérerai.   *I shall revere.*
Tu révéreras.   *thou wilt revere.*
Il révérera.   *he will revere.*
Nous révérerons.   *we shall revere.*
Vous révérerez.   *you will revere.*
Ils révéreront.   *they will revere.*

## CONDITIONAL MOOD.
### PRESENT.
Je révérerais.   *I should revere.*
Tu révérerais.   *thou wouldst revere.*
Il révérerait.   *he would revere.*
Nous révérerions.   *we should revere.*
Vous révéreriez.   *you would revere.*
Ils révéreraient.   *they would revere.*

## IMPERATIVE MOOD.
### PRESENT.
Révère.   *Revere (thou).*
Qu'il *révère.*   *let him revere.*
Révérons.   *let us revere.*
Révérez.   *revere (you).*
Qu'ils *révèrent.*   *let them revere.*

## SUBJUNCTIVE MOOD.
### PRESENT.
Que je *révère.*   *That I may revere.*
Que tu *révères.*   *that thou mayest revere.*
Qu'il *révère.*   *that he may revere.*
Que nous révérions.   *that we may revere.*
Que vous révériez.   *that you may revere.*
Qu'ils *révèrent.*   *that they may revere.*

### IMPERFECT.
Que je révérasse.   *That I might* \
Que tu révérasses.   *that thou mightest* \
Qu'il révérât.   *that he might* \
Que nous révérassions. *that we might* } *revere.* \
Que vous révérassiez.   *that you might* \
Qu'ils révérassent.   *that they might*

## COMPOUND TENSES.

| | | | | | |
|---|---|---|---|---|---|
| Past ind. | J'ai révéré, etc. | *I have revered, etc.* | Cond. past. | J'aurais révéré, etc. | *I should have revered, etc.* |
| Plup. | J'avais révéré, etc. | *I had revered, etc.* | Sub. pres. | Que j'aie révéré, etc. | *that I may have revered, etc.* |
| Past ant. | J'eus révéré, etc. | *I had revered, etc.* | | | |
| Fut. Ant. | J'aurai révéré, etc. | *I shall have revered, etc.* | Sub. imp. | Que j'eusse révéré, etc. | *that I might have revered, etc.* |

* RULE.—The verbs having an *e*, with an acute accent, at the last syllable of the radical, *change the acute accent into a grave one*, before the terminations: *e, es, ent,* but preserve the acute accent in the Future and Conditional Present; *je révérerai, je révérerais, etc.*
Some *Grammarians* write the Future and the Conditional with a grave accent; *je révèrerai, je révèrerais, etc.;* but such is not the spelling of the French Academy, which preserves the acute accent in those two tenses.
N.B.—Formerly verbs ending in *éger*, as (*protéger*, to protect) did not follow the rule and preserved the acute accent over the *e* throughout the verb; but now they follow the above rule of verbs having an acute accent, on the last syllable of the radical (*Dict. of the Acad., last edition*). So we write: *je protège,* and not *je protége.*
(1) *Persons having a grave accent are printed in italic letters.*

## CONJUGATE LIKE *RÉVÉRER.*

| | | | | |
|---|---|---|---|---|
| Abréger | *To shorten.* | Posséder | *To possess.* | Recéler — *To conceal.* |
| Inquiéter | *— disquiet.* | Préférer | *—prefer.* | Régler — *— rule.* |
| Lécher | *— lick.* | Protéger | *—protect.* | Sécher — *— dry.* |

# VERB *ARGUER*, TO ARGUE.*

## INFINITIVE MOOD.

| | | | |
|---|---|---|---|
| PRESENT. | | PAST. | |
| Arguer. | *To argue.* | Avoir argué. | *To have argued.* |
| PARTICIPLE PRESENT. | | COMPOUND OF PARTICIPLE PRESENT. | |
| Arguant. | *Arguing.* | Ayant argué. | *Having argued.* |

PARTICIPLE PAST.

Argué (m.s.), arguée (f.s.), argués (m.pl.), arguées (f.pl.), *argued.*

## INDICATIVE MOOD.

PRESENT.

| | |
|---|---|
| J'*arguë.* | *I argue.* |
| Tu *arguës.* | *thou arguest.* |
| Il *arguë.* | *he argues.* |
| Nous arguons. | *we argue.* |
| Vous arguez. | *you argue.* |
| Ils *arguënt.* | *they argue.* |

IMPERFECT.

| | |
|---|---|
| J'arguais. | *I was arguing.* |
| Tu arguais. | *thou wast arguing.* |
| Il arguait. | *he was arguing.* |
| Nous *arguïons.* | *we were arguing.* |
| Vous *arguïez.* | *you were arguing.* |
| Ils arguaient. | *they were arguing.* |

PAST INDEFINITE.

| | |
|---|---|
| J'arguai. | *I argued.* |
| Tu arguas. | *thou arguedst.* |
| Il argua. | *he argued.* |
| Nous arguâmes. | *we argued.* |
| Vous arguâtes. | *you argued.* |
| Ils arguèrent | *they argued.* |

FUTURE.

| | |
|---|---|
| J'*arguërai.* | *I shall argue.* |
| Tu *arguëras.* | *thou wilt argue.* |
| Il *arguëra.* | *he will argue.* |
| Nous *arguërons.* | *we shall argue.* |
| Vous *arguërez.* | *you will argue.* |
| Ils *arguëront.* | *they will argue.* |

## CONDITIONAL MOOD.

PRESENT.

| | |
|---|---|
| J'*arguërais.* | *I should argue.* |
| Tu *arguërais.* | *thou wouldst argue.* |
| Il *arguërait.* | *he would argue.* |
| Nous *arguërions.* | *we should argue.* |
| Vous *arguëriez.* | *you would argue.* |
| Ils *arguëraient.* | *they would argue.* |

## IMPERATIVE MOOD.

PRESENT OR FUTURE.

| | |
|---|---|
| *Arguë.* | *Argue (thou).* |
| Qu'il *arguë.* | *let him argue.* |
| Arguons. | *let us argue.* |
| Arguez. | *argue (you).* |
| Qu'ils *arguënt.* | *let them argue.* |

## SUBJUNCTIVE MOOD.

| | |
|---|---|
| Que j'*arguë.* | *That I may argue.* |
| Que tu *arguës.* | *that thou mayest argue.* |
| Qu'il *arguë.* | *that he may argue.* |
| Que nous *arguïons.* | *that we may argue.* |
| Que vous *arguïez.* | *that you may argue.* |
| Qu'ils *arguënt.* | *that they may argue.* |

IMPERFECT.

| | | |
|---|---|---|
| Que j'arguasse. | *That I might* | *argue.* |
| Que tu arguasses. | *that thou mightest* | |
| Qu'il arguât. | *that he might* | |
| Que nous arguassions. | *that we might* | |
| Que vous arguassiez. | *that you might* | |
| Qu'ils arguassent. | *that they might* | |

## COMPOUND TENSES.

| | | |
|---|---|---|
| *Past ind.* | J'ai argué, etc. | *I have argued, etc.* |
| *Past ant.* | J'eus argué, etc. | *I had argued, etc.* |
| *Plup.* | J'avais argué, etc. | *I had argued, etc.* |
| *Fut. ant.* | J'aurai argué, etc. | *I shall have argued, etc.* |
| *Cond. past.* | J'aurais argué, etc. | *I should have argued, etc.* |
| *Sub. past.* | Que j'aie argué, etc. | *that I may have argued, etc.* |
| *Sub. imp.* | Que j'eusse argué, etc. | *that I might have argued, etc.* |

* N.B.—As in the verb *arguer*, the *u* should be sounded throughout the verb, *two dots* have been placed over the *e* following *u*, to show that *u* is to be sounded distinctly.

For the same reason, *arguer* takes also *two dots* on the *i*; in the terminations of the *Imperfect of the Indicative* and in the *Present of the Subjunctive*, on the first and second person plural.

# REMARKS ON SOME VERBS.

The following verbs present slight irregularities :

*JOUER*, to play—*TUER*, to kill—*BÉNIR*, to bless—*FLEURIR*, to blossom —*REFLEURIR*, to blossom again—*HAÏR*, to hate—*BATTRE*, to beat— *ROMPRE*, to break.

## *JOUER*, to play ; *TUER*, to kill.

The verbs ending in *ouer* and *uer*, as *Jouer*, *Tuer*, are regular, but some Grammarians think, that in the *Imperfect of the Indicative* and *the Present of the Subjunctive*, two dots ( ·· ) should be put *on the i* of the terminations—*ions*, *iez*, in order to pronounce those persons correctly. *A vowel with dots is pronounced separately in French.*

IMPERFECT (Indicative).—Je jouais, tu jouais, il jouait, *nous jouïons, vous jouïez*, ils jouaient. I was playing, etc.

PRESENT OF SUBJUNCTIVE.—Que je joue, que tu joues, qu'il joue, que *nous jouïons*, que *vous jouïez*, qu'ils jouent. That I may play, etc.

## *BÉNIR*, to bless, to consecrate.

*Bénir*, to bless, is regular, and conjugated like *Finir* (page 23), but the Past Participle has two forms : *Béni and Bénit. Bénit* is used when speaking of things consecrated by a religious ceremony, Ex. :

|   |   |
|---|---|
| *Du pain bénit,* | Consecrated bread. |
| *De l'eau bénite,* | Holy water. |

*Béni* is used in the other senses.

*Le prêtre a béni l'assistance.* The Priest has blessed the congregation.

## *FLEURIR*, to blossom. *REFLEURIR*, to blossom again.

*Fleurir*, to blossom, in its literal sense is regular, and conjugated like *Finir* (page 23).

*Fleurir*, used figuratively signifying—*to be prosperous, to flourish*, etc., is regular also, except in the *Imperfect of the Indicative* and the *Participle Present*, where it has the following forms :

*Imperfect.*—Je florissais, tu florissais, il florissait, nous florissions, vous florissiez, ils florissaient. *I was prosperous*, etc.

*Participle Present*—florissant, *being prosperous.*

In a figurative sense, the *Participle Present :* Florissant is always used. But the forms of the *Imperfect*—Je florissais, etc., have been replaced by some good writers, by the regular forms : Je fleurissais, etc.

Refleurir, *to blossom again*, is conjugated like *Fleurir*, and follows the same rules.

## HAÏR, TO HATE.

A diæresis ( ·· ) is kept over the *i*, in all the tenses of *Haïr*, except in the three persons singular of the :

INDICATIVE, Present—*Je hais, tu hais, il hait.* Nous haïssons, vous haïssez, ils haïssent. *I hate, thou hatest,* etc.

*And the second person singular of the :*

IMPERATIVE—*Hais*, qu'il haïsse, haïssons, haïssez, qu'ils haïssent. *Hate (thou)*, etc.

HAÏR keeps the diæresis in the *past definite, in the first and second person plural.*

Nous *haïmes*, we hated ; vous *haïtes*, you hated ; and in the third person of the *Imperfect of the Subjunctive.*

Qu'il *haït*—that he might hate. Instead of taking, as the other verbs, the circumflex accent on those persons.

———

## BATTRE, TO BEAT.

The only irregularity in verbs ending in *attre* is, that they lose one of the *t*'s of the radical, in the three persons singular of *the Present of the Indicative*, and the second person singular of the Imperative. In the other tenses and persons, they are conjugated like the regular verbs of the fourth conjugation. See *Vendre* (page 27).

| PRESENT OF THE INDICATIVE. | | IMPERATIVE. | |
|---|---|---|---|
| | | | PRESENT. |
| Je *bats.* | *I beat.* | | |
| Tu *bats.* | *thou beatest.* | *Bats.* | *Beat (thou).* |
| Il *bat.* | *he beats.* | Qu'il batte. | *let him beat.* |
| Nous battons. | *we beat.* | Battons. | *let us beat.* |
| Vous battez. | *you beat.* | Battez. | *beat (you.)* |
| Ils battent. | *they beat.* | Qu'ils battent. | *let them beat.* |

CONJUGATE IN THE SAME MANNER :

| Abattre | - | - | - | *To pull down.* | Rabattre - | - | - | - | *To abate.* |
|---|---|---|---|---|---|---|---|---|---|
| Combattre | - | - | - | *— combat, to fight.* | Rebattre - | - | - | - | *— beat again.* |
| Débattre | - | - | - | *— debate, to discuss.* | | | | | |

———

## ROMPRE, TO BREAK.

The only irregularity of the verbs ending in *ompre* is, they take *t*, after the *p* in the *third person singular of the Present of the Indicative.*

Indicative, Present—Je romps, tu romps, *il rompt*, nous rompons, vous rompez, ils rompent. *I break*, etc.

The other tenses and persons are conjugated, like the regular verbs, of the fourth conjugation (see page 27).

CONJUGATE AS *ROMPRE.*

| Corrompre | . | . | - | *To corrupt, to vitiate.* | Interrompre | . | . | . | . | *To interrupt.* |
|---|---|---|---|---|---|---|---|---|---|---|

# CHAPTER 4

# Neuter, Passive, Pronominal, Reciprocal, and Impersonal Verbs

## OF NEUTER OR *INTRANSITIVE* VERBS.

A Neuter verb expresses merely—First: The state of its subject ; as J'existe, *I exist.* Secondly: An action limited to the subject which produces it, as : Je marche, *I walk.*

*Neuter verbs have no separate conjugation of their own ; if not irregular, they are conjugated according to the conjugation to which they belong.*

Most Neuter verbs take the *auxiliary* verb *Avoir*, in their compound tenses, but the following take *être*.

| | | | | | | | | | | |
|---|---|---|---|---|---|---|---|---|---|---|
| Aller | - | - | - | *To go.* | | Naître | - | - | - | *To be born.* |
| Arriver | - | - | - | *— arrive.* | | Parvenir | - | - | - | *— attain.* |
| Décéder | - | - | - | *— die.* | | Provenir | - | - | - | *— come from.* |
| Devenir | - | - | - | *— become.* | | Redevenir | - | - | - | *— become again.* |
| Disconvenir | - | - | - | *— deny.* | | Retourner | - | - | - | *— go back.* |
| Échoir | - | - | - | *— become due.* | | Revenir | - | - | - | *— come back.* |
| Éclore | - | - | - | *— blow, to be hatched.* | | Survenir | - | - | - | *— happen.* |
| Mourir | - | - | - | *— die.* | | Venir | - | - | - | *— come.* |

*In their compound tenses the following Neuter verbs take :*

*Avoir*, if they express an action.

*Être*, if they express the result of that action.

| | | | | | | | | | | |
|---|---|---|---|---|---|---|---|---|---|---|
| Aborder | - | - | - | *To land.* | | Fleurir | - | - | - | *To blossom.* |
| Accourir | - | - | - | *— run to.* | | Grandir | - | - | - | *— grow.* |
| Accroître | - | - | - | *— increase.* | | Monter | - | - | - | *— go up.* |
| Apparaître | - | - | - | *— appear.* | | Partir | - | - | - | *— set out.* |
| Croître | - | - | - | *— grow.* | | Passer | - | - | - | *— pass.* |
| Déborder | - | - | - | *— overflow.* | | Remonter | - | - | - | *— go up (again.)* |
| Déchoir | - | - | - | *— decay.* | | Rentrer | - | - | - | *— come in (again.)* |
| Demeurer | - | - | - | *— stay.* | | Repartir | - | - | - | *— start again.* |
| Descendre | - | - | - | *— go down.* | | Rester | - | - | - | *— remain.* |
| Disparaître | - | - | - | *— disappear.* | | Sortir | - | - | - | *— go out.* |
| Échapper | - | - | - | *— escape.* | | Tomber | - | - | - | *— fall.* |
| Entrer | - | - | - | *— come in.* | | Retomber | - | - | - | *— fall again.* |

*Some Neuter verbs* change their meaning when they change the auxiliary.

Convenir, with *avoir* means :—*To become, to suit,*

Convenir, with *être* means :—*To agree, to settle.*

Ex. : Cette maison m'a convenu.    *That house suited me.*
Nous sommes convenus du prix.    *We agreed upon the price.*

# CONJUGATION OF PASSIVE VERBS.

The *Passive verb* expresses an action received or suffered by its subject or nominative. Ex. : Je suis frappé, *I am struck.*

There is only one way of conjugating passive verbs ; it is to join the *Past Participle* of an active verb, to all the tenses of the verb *être, to be.*

Remark.—Since the Past Participle employed with *être*, agrees in gender and number with the nominative, in conjugating a *passive verb*, the Past Participle ought to have the same gender and number as the nominative.

The Past Participle forms the feminine by adding silent *e* to the masculine form, *aimé*, (m.s.) *aimée*, (f.s.), and the plural by adding *s* to the singular, masculine or feminine form, *aimé*, (m.s), *aimés* (m.pl.) ; *aimée* (f.s.), *aimées* (f.pl.).

## VERB *ÊTRE AIMÉ*, TO BE LOVED.

### INFINITIVE MOOD.

| PRESENT. | | PAST. | |
|---|---|---|---|
| Être aimé. | *To be loved.* | Avoir été aimé. | *To have been loved.* |

| PARTICIPLE PRESENT. | | COMPOUND OF PARTICIPLE PRESENT. | |
|---|---|---|---|
| Étant aimé. | *Being loved.* | Ayant été aimé. | *Having been loved.* |

PARTICIPLE PAST.

Aimé (m.s.), aimée (f.s.), aimés (m.pl.), aimées (f.pl.), *loved.*

### INDICATIVE MOOD.

PRESENT.

*Plural. Singular.*

Je suis aimé. *I am loved.*
Tu es aimé. *thou art loved.*
Il est aimé. *he is loved.*
Nous sommes aimés. *we are loved.*
Vous êtes aimés. *you are loved.*
Ils sont aimés. *they are loved.*

PAST INDEFINITE.

*Plural. Singular.*

J'ai été aimé. *I have been loved.*
Tu as été aimé. *thou hast been loved.*
Il a été aimé. *he has been loved.*
Nous avons été aimés. *we have been loved.*
Vous avez été aimés. *you have been loved.*
Ils ont été aimés. *they have been loved.*

IMPERFECT.

J'étais aimé. *I was loved.*
Tu étais aimé. *thou wast loved.*
Il était aimé. *he was loved.*
Nous étions aimés. *we were loved.*
Vous étiez aimés. *you were loved.*
Ils étaient aimés. *they were loved.*

PLUPERFECT.

J'avais été aimé. *I had been loved.*
Tu avais été aimé. *thou hadst been loved.*
Il avait été aimé. *he had been loved.*
Nous avions été aimés. *we had been loved.*
Vous aviez été aimés. *you had been loved.*
Ils avaient été aimés. *they had been loved.*

PAST DEFINITE.

Je fus aimé. *I was loved.*
Tu fus aimé. *thou wast loved.*
Il fut aimé. *he was loved.*
Nous fûmes aimés. *we were loved.*
Vous fûtes aimés. *you were loved.*
Ils furent aimés. *they were loved.*

PAST ANTERIOR

J'eus été aimé. *I had been loved.*
Tu eus été aimé. *thou hadst been loved.*
Il eut été aimé. *he had been loved.*
Nous eûmes été aimés. *we had been loved.*
Vous eûtes été aimés. *you had been loved.*
Ils eurent été aimés. *they had been loved.*

FUTURE.

Je serai aimé. *I shall be loved.*
Tu seras aimé. *thou wilt be loved.*
Il sera aimé. *he will be loved.*
Nous serons aimés. *we shall be loved.*
Vous serez aimés. *you will be loved.*
Ils seront aimés. *they will be loved.*

FUTURE ANTERIOR.

J'aurai été aimé. *I shall have*
Tu auras été aimé. *thou wilt have*
Il aura été aimé. *he will have*
Nous aurons été aimés. *we shall have*
Vous aurez été aimés. *you will have*
Ils auront été aimés. *they will have*

*been loved.*

## CONDITIONAL MOOD.

| | | | |
|---|---|---|---|
| Je serais aimé. | *I should be loved.* | J'aurais été aimé. | *I should have.* |
| Tu serais aimé. | *thou wouldst be loved.* | Tu aurais été aimé | *thou wouldst have* |
| Il serait aimé. | *he would be loved.* | Il aurait été aimé. | *he would have* |
| Nous serions aimés. | *we should be loved.* | Nous aurions été aimés. | *we should have* |
| Vous seriez aimés. | *you would be loved.* | Vous auriez été aimés. | *you would have* |
| Ils seraient aimés. | *they would be loved.* | Ils auraient été aimés. | *they would have.* |

*been loved.*

## IMPERATIVE MOOD.

### PRESENT.

| | | |
|---|---|---|
| Sois aimé - - - - | - | *Be (thou) loved.* |
| Qu'il soit aimé - - | - | *let him be loved.* |
| Soyons aimés - | - | *let us be loved.* |
| Soyez aimés - - - | - | *be (you) loved.* |
| Qu'ils soient aimés | - - | *let them be loved.* |

## SUBJUNCTIVE MOOD.

### PRESENT.

| | |
|---|---|
| Que je sois aimé. | *That I may be loved.* |
| Que tu sois aimé. | *that thou mayest be loved.* |
| Qu'il soit aimé. | *that he may be loved.* |
| Que nous soyons aimés. | *that we may be loved.* |
| Que vous soyez aimés. | *that you may be loved.* |
| Qu'ils soient aimés. | *that they may be loved.* |

### IMPERFECT.

| | |
|---|---|
| Que je fusse aimé. | *That I might be loved.* |
| Que tu fusses aimé. | *that thou mightest be loved.* |
| Qu'il fût aimé. | *that he might be loved.* |
| Que nous fussions aimés. | *that we might be loved.* |
| Que vous fussiez aimés. | *that you might be loved.* |
| Qu'ils fussent aimés. | *that they might be loved.* |

### PAST.

| | |
|---|---|
| Que j'aie été aimé. | *That I may have been loved.* |
| Que tu aies été aimé. | *that thou mayest have been loved.* |
| Qu'il ait été aimé. | *that he may have been loved.* |
| Que nous ayons été aimés. | *that we may have been loved.* |
| Que vous ayez été aimés. | *that you may have been loved.* |
| Qu'ils aient été aimés. | *that they may have been loved.* |

### PLUPERFECT.

| | |
|---|---|
| Que j'eusse été aimé. | *That I might have been loved.* |
| Que tu eusses été aimé. | *that thou mightest have been loved.* |
| Qu'il eût été aimé. | *that he might have been loved.* |
| Que nous eussions été aimés. | *that we might have been loved.* |
| Que vous eussiez été aimés. | *that you might have been loved.* |
| Qu'ils eussent été aimés. | *that they might have been loved.* |

---

N.B.—The Nominative Pronouns, in the above verb, have been considered in *the masculine gender.*

CONJUGATE PASSIVELY SOME OF THE FOLLOWING ACTIVE VERBS:

| | | | | | | | | |
|---|---|---|---|---|---|---|---|---|
| Visiter | . | . | *To visit.* | Punir | . | *To punish.* | Admirer | . | . | *To admire.* |
| Cacher | . | . | *— hide.* | Recevoir | . | *— receive.* | Choisir | . | *— choose.* |

# PASSIVE VERB CONJUGATED NEGATIVELY.*

## *ÊTRE AIMÉ*, TO BE LOVED.

### INFINITIVE MOOD.

| PRESENT. | | PAST. | |
|---|---|---|---|
| N'être pas aimé. | *Not to be loved.* | N'avoir pas été aimé. | *Not to have been loved.* |
| **PARTICIPLE PRESENT.** | | **COMP. OF PART. PRESENT.** | |
| N'étant pas aimé. | *Not being loved.* | N'ayant pas été aimé. | *Not having been loved.* |

PARTICIPLE PAST.

Aimé (m.s.)—Aimée (f.s.)—Aimés (m.pl.)—Aimées (f.pl.), *loved.*

### INDICATIVE MOOD.

PRESENT.

| | | |
|---|---|---|
| *Plural. Sing.* | Je ne suis pas aimé. | *I am not loved.* |
| | Tu n'es pas aimé. | *thou art not loved.* |
| | Il n'est pas aimé. | *he is not loved.* |
| | Nous ne sommes pas aimés. | *we are not loved.* |
| | Vous n'êtes pas aimés. | *you are not loved.* |
| | Ils ne sont pas aimés. | *they are not loved.* |

| Imperfect. | Je n'étais pas aimé, etc. | *I was not loved, etc.* |
|---|---|---|
| Past definite. | Je ne fus pas aimé, etc. | *I was not loved, etc.* |
| Past indefinite. | Je n'ai pas été aimé, etc. | *I have not been loved, etc.* |
| Pluperfect. | Je n'avais pas été aimé, etc. | *I had not been loved, etc.* |
| Past anterior. | Je n'eus pas été aimé, etc. | *I had not been loved, etc.* |
| Future. | Je ne serai pas aimé, etc. | *I shall not be loved, etc.* |
| Future anterior. | Je n'aurai pas été aimé, etc. | *I shall not have been loved, etc.* |

### CONDITIONAL MOOD.

| Present. | Je ne serais pas aimé, etc. | *I should not be loved, etc.* |
|---|---|---|
| Past. | Je n'aurais pas été aimé, etc. | *I should not have been loved, etc.* |

### IMPERATIVE MOOD.

PRESENT.

| Ne sois pas aimé. | *Be not loved.* |
|---|---|
| Qu'il ne soit pas aimé. | *let him not be loved.* |
| Ne soyons pas aimés. | *let us not be loved.* |
| Ne soyez pas aimés. | *be not loved.* |
| Qu'ils ne soient pas aimés. | *let them not be loved.* |

### SUBJUNCTIVE MOOD.

| Present. | Que je ne sois pas aimé, etc. | *That I may not be loved, etc.* |
|---|---|---|
| Past. | Que je n'aie pas été aimé, etc. | *that I may not have been loved, etc.* |
| Imperfect. | Que je ne fusse pas aimé, etc. | *that I might not be loved, etc.* |
| Pluperfect. | Que je n'eusse pas été aimé, etc. | *that I might not have been loved, etc.* |

* See page 6.

# PASSIVE VERB CONJUGATED INTERROGATIVELY.*

## *ÊTRE AIMÉ*, TO BE LOVED.

### INDICATIVE MOOD.

#### PRESENT.

| | |
|---|---|
| Suis-je aimé? | Am I loved? |
| Es-tu aimé? | art thou loved? |
| Est-il aimé? | is he loved? |
| Sommes-nous aimés? | are we loved? |
| Êtes-vous aimés? | are you loved? |
| Sont-ils aimés? | are they loved? |

| | | |
|---|---|---|
| *Imperfect.* | Étais-je aimé? etc. | Was I loved? etc. |
| *Past definite.* | Fus-je aimé? etc. | was I loved? etc. |
| *Past indefinite.* | Ai-je été aimé? etc. | have I been loved? etc. |
| *Pluperfect.* | Avais-je été aimé? etc. | had I been loved? etc. |
| *Past anterior.* | Eus-je été aimé? etc. | had I been loved? etc. |
| *Future.* | Serai-je aimé? etc. | shall I be loved? etc. |
| *Future anterior.* | Aurai-je été aimé? etc. | shall I have been loved? etc. |

### CONDITIONAL MOOD.

| | | |
|---|---|---|
| *Present.* | Serais-je aimé? etc. | Should I be loved? etc. |
| *Past.* | Aurais-je été aimé? | should I have been loved? etc. |

# PASSIVE VERB CONJUGATED NEGATIVELY AND INTERROGATIVELY.†

## *ÊTRE AIMÉ*, TO BE LOVED.

### INDICATIVE MOOD.

#### PRESENT.

| | |
|---|---|
| Ne suis-je pas aimé? | Am I not loved? |
| N'es-tu pas aimé? | art thou not loved? |
| N'est-il pas aimé? | is he not loved? |
| Ne sommes-nous pas aimés? | are we not loved? |
| N'êtes-vous pas aimés? | are you not loved? |
| Ne sont-ils pas aimés? | are they not loved? |

| | | |
|---|---|---|
| *Imperfect.* | N'étais-je pas aimé? etc. | Was I not loved? etc. |
| *Past definite.* | Ne fus-je pas aimé? etc. | was I not loved? etc. |
| *Past indefinite.* | N'ai-je pas été aimé? etc. | have I not been loved? etc. |
| *Pluperfect.* | N'avais-je pas été aimé? etc. | had I not been loved? etc. |
| *Past anterior.* | N'eus-je pas été aimé? etc. | had I not been loved? etc. |
| *Future.* | Ne serai-je pas aimé? | shall I not be loved? etc. |
| *Future anterior.* | N'aurai je pas été aimé? etc. | shall I not have been loved? etc. |

### CONDITIONAL MOOD.

| | | |
|---|---|---|
| *Present.* | Ne serais-je pas aimé? etc. | Should I not be loved? etc. |
| *Past.* | N'aurais-je pas été aimé? etc. | should I not have been loved? etc. |

# PRONOMINAL VERBS.*

*Pronominal verbs* are those which are conjugated with *two pronouns of the same person ;* those pronouns are:

| Singular. | | | | | Plural. | | | | |
|---|---|---|---|---|---|---|---|---|---|
| Je me | —Pronouns of the 1st Pers. Sing. | | | | Nous nous | —Pronouns of the 1st Pers. Pl. | | | |
| Tu te | — | ,, | ,, 2nd | ,, ,, | Vous vous | — | ,, | ,, 2nd | ,, ,, |
| Il se } | — | ,, | ,, 3rd | ,, ,, | Ils se } | — | ,, | ,, 3rd | ,, ,, |
| Elle se } | | | | | Elles se } | | | | |

*The Compound Tenses* of pronominal verbs, are formed with Être and never with Avoir, as in English :—Ex., *Je me suis flatté*, I have flattered myself, etc. See the compound tenses of *Se Flatter.*

---

## CONJUGATION OF A PRONOMINAL VERB
### MODEL VERB.
### *SE FLATTER*, TO FLATTER ONE'S SELF.
#### INFINITIVE MOOD.

| PRESENT. | | PAST. | |
|---|---|---|---|
| Se flatter. | *To flatter one's self.* | S'être flatté. | *To have flattered one's self.* |

| PARTICIPLE PRESENT. | | COMPOUND OF PARTICIPLE PRESENT. | |
|---|---|---|---|
| Se flattant. | *Flattering one's self.* | S'étant flatté. | *Having flattered one's self.* |

#### PARTICIPLE PAST.
Flatté (m.s.), flattés (m.pl.), flattée (f.s.), flattées (f.pl.), *Flattered.*

## INDICATIVE MOOD.
### SIMPLE TENSES.
#### PRESENT.

| | |
|---|---|
| Je me flatte. | *I flatter myself.* |
| Tu te flattes. | *thou flatterest thyself.* |
| Il se flatte. | *he flatters himself.* |
| Nous nous flattons. | *we flatter ourselves.* |
| Vous vous flattez. | *you flatter yourselves.* |
| Ils se flattent. | *they flatter themselves.* |

#### IMPERFECT.

| | |
|---|---|
| Je me flattais. | *I was flattering myself.* |
| Tu te flattais. | *thou wast flattering thyself.* |
| Il se flattait. | *he was flattering himself.* |
| Nous nous flattions. | *we were flattering ourselves.* |
| Vous vous flattiez. | *you were flattering yourselves.* |
| Ils se flattaient. | *they were flattering themselves.* |

#### PAST DEFINITE.

| | |
|---|---|
| Je me flattai. | *I flattered myself.* |
| Tu te flattas. | *thou flatteredst thyself.* |
| Il se flatta. | *he flattered himself.* |
| Nous nous flattâmes. | *we flattered ourselves.* |
| Vous vous flattâtes. | *you flattered yourselves.* |
| Ils se flattèrent. | *they flattered themselves.* |

#### FUTURE.

| | |
|---|---|
| Je me flatterai. | *I shall flatter myself.* |
| Tu te flatteras. | *thou wilt flatter thyself.* |
| Il se flattera. | *he will flatter himself.* |
| Nous nous flatterons. | *we shall flatter ourselves.* |
| Vous vous flatterez. | *you will flatter yourselves.* |
| Ils se flatteront. | *they will flatter themselves.* |

---

* N.B.—Pronominal Verbs have no separate conjugation of their own ; if not irregular, they are conjugated according to the conjugation to which they belong, each being preceded by the pronouns: *Je me—tu te*, etc.

# INDICATIVE MOOD (*continued.*)

## COMPOUND TENSES.

### PAST INDEFINITE.

| | |
|---|---|
| Je me suis flatté. | *I have flattered myself.* |
| Tu t'es flatté. | *thou hast flattered thyself.* |
| Il s'est flatté. | *he has flattered himself.* |
| Nous nous sommes flattés. | *we have flattered ourselves.* |
| Vous vous êtes flattés. | *you have flattered yourselves.* |
| Ils se sont flattés. | *they have flattered themselves.* |

### PLUPERFECT.

| | |
|---|---|
| Je m'étais flatté. | *I had flattered myself.* |
| Tu t'étais flatté. | *thou hadst flattered thyself.* |
| Il s'était flatté. | *he had flattered himself.* |
| Nous nous étions flattés. | *we had flattered ourselves.* |
| Vous vous étiez flattés. | *you had flattered yourselves.* |
| Ils s'étaient flattés. | *they had flattered themselves.* |

### PAST ANTERIOR.

| | |
|---|---|
| Je me fus flatté. | *I had flattered myself.* |
| Tu te fus flatté. | *thou hadst flattered thyself.* |
| Il se fut flatté. | *he had flattered himself.* |
| Nous nous fûmes flattés. | *we had flattered ourselves.* |
| Vous vous fûtes flattés. | *you had flattered yourselves.* |
| Il se furent flattés. | *they had flattered themselves.* |

### FUTURE ANTERIOR.

| | |
|---|---|
| Je me serai flatté. | *I shall have flattered myself.* |
| Tu te seras flatté. | *thou wilt have flattered thyself.* |
| Il se sera flatté. | *he will have flattered himself.* |
| Nous nous serons flattés. | *we shall have flattered ourselves.* |
| Vous vous serez flattés. | *you will have flattered yourselves.* |
| Ils se seront flattés. | *they will have flattered themselves.* |

# CONDITIONAL MOOD.

## SIMPLE TENSE.

### PRESENT.

| | |
|---|---|
| Je me flatterais. | *I should flatter myself.* |
| Tu te flatterais. | *thou wouldst flatter thyself.* |
| Il se flatterait. | *he would flatter himself.* |
| Nous nous flatterions. | *we should flatter ourselves.* |
| Vous vous flatteriez. | *you would flatter yourselves.* |
| Ils se flatteraient. | *they would flatter themselves.* |

## COMPOUND TENSE.

### PAST.

| | |
|---|---|
| Je me serais flatté. | *I should have flattered myself.* |
| Tu te serais flatté. | *thou wouldst have flattered thyself.* |
| Il se serait flatté. | *he would have flattered himself.* |
| Nous nous serions flattés. | *we should have flattered ourselves.* |
| Vous vous seriez flattés. | *you would have flattered yourselves.* |
| Ils se seraient flattés. | *they would have flattered themselves.* |

# IMPERATIVE MOOD.

### PRESENT OR FUTURE.

| | |
|---|---|
| Flatte-toi. | *Flatter thyself.* |
| Qu'il se flatte. ⎱ | *let him flatter himself.* |
| Qu'elle se flatte. ⎰ | *let her flatter herself.* |
| Flattons-nous. | *let us flatter ourselves.* |
| Flattez-vous. | *flatter yourselves.* |
| Qu'ils *or* qu'elles se flattent. | *let them flatter themselves.* |

---

# SUBJUNCTIVE MOOD.

### SIMPLE TENSES.

#### PRESENT.

| | |
|---|---|
| Que je me flatte. | *That I may flatter myself.* |
| Que tu te flattes. | *that thou mayest flatter thyself.* |
| Qu'il se flatte. | *that he may flatter himself.* |
| Que nous nous flattions. | *that we may flatter ourselves.* |
| Que vous vous flattiez. | *that you may flatter yourselves.* |
| Qu'ils se flattent. | *that they may flatter themselves.* |

#### IMPERFECT.

| | |
|---|---|
| Que je me flattasse, | *That I might flatter myself.* |
| Que tu te flattasses. | *that thou mightest flatter thyself.* |
| Qu'il se flattât. | *that he might flatter himself.* |
| Que nous nous flattassions. | *that we might flatter ourselves.* |
| Que vous vous flattassiez. | *that you might flatter yourselves.* |
| Qu'ils se flattassent. | *that they might flatter themselves.* |

### COMPOUND TENSES

#### PAST.

| | |
|---|---|
| Que je me sois flatté. | *That I may have flattered myself.* |
| Que tu te sois flatté. | *that thou mayest have flattered thyself.* |
| Qu'il se soit flatté. | *that he may have flattered himself.* |
| Que nous nous soyons flattés. | *that we may have flattered ourselves.* |
| Que vous vous soyez flattés. | *that you may have flattered yourselves.* |
| Qu'ils se soient flattés. | *that they may have flattered themselves.* |

#### PLUPERFECT.

| | |
|---|---|
| Que je me fusse flatté. | *That I might have flattered myself.* |
| Que tu te fusses flatté. | *that thou mightest have flattered thyself.* |
| Qu'il se fût flatté. | *that he might have flattered himself.* |
| Que nous nous fussions flattés. | *that we might have flattered ourselves.* |
| Que vous vous fussiez flattés. | *that you might have flattered yourselves.* |
| Qu'ils se fussent flattés. | *that they might have flattered themselves.* |

### CONJUGATE IN THE SAME MANNER:

| | | | |
|---|---|---|---|
| Se baigner | *To bathe.* | S'établir | *To settle.* |
| Se dépêcher | *— make haste.* | S'apercevoir | *— become aware.* |
| S'enrichir | *— grow rich.* | S'attendre à | *— expect.* |

Rule.—*The Past Participle* of a Reflective or Pronominal verb agrees in gender and number with the pronouns: (Me, te, se, nous, vous), *i.e.*, takes the gender and number of those pronouns, when they are the accusatives of the verb.

# PRONOMINAL VERB CONJUGATED NEGATIVELY.*

---

## *NE PAS SE FLATTER,* NOT TO FLATTER ONE'S SELF.

---

### INFINITIVE MOOD.

#### PRESENT.

Ne pas se flatter.                    *Not to flatter one's self.*

#### PAST.

Ne s'être pas flatté. (1)           *Not to have flattered one's self.*

#### PARTICIPLE PRESENT.

Ne se flattant pas.                  *Not flattering one's self.*

#### COMPOUND OF PARTICIPLE PRESENT.

Ne s'étant pas flatté.              *Not having flattered one's self.*

#### PAST PARTICIPLE.

Flatté (m.s.), flattée (f.s.), flattés (m.pl.), flattées (f.pl.), *Flattered.*

### INDICATIVE MOOD.

#### SIMPLE TENSES.—PRESENT.

| | |
|---|---|
| Je ne me flatte pas. | *I do not flatter myself.* |
| Tu ne te flattes pas. | *thou dost not flatter thyself.* |
| Il ne se flatte pas. | *he does not flatter himself.* |
| Nous ne nous flattons pas. | *we do not flatter ourselves.* |
| Vous ne vous flattez pas. | *you do not flatter yourselves.* |
| Ils ne se flattent pas. | *they do not flatter themselves.* |

#### IMPERFECT.

| | |
|---|---|
| Je ne me flattais pas. | *I was not flattering myself.* |
| Tu ne te flattais pas. | *thou wast not flattering thyself.* |
| Il ne se flattait pas. | *he was not flattering himself.* |
| Nous ne nous flattions pas. | *we were not flattering ourselves.* |
| Vous ne vous flattiez pas. | *you were not flattering yourselves.* |
| Ils ne se flattaient pas. | *they were not flattering themselves.* |

---

* N.B.—When the Pronominal Verbs are *conjugated negatively,* ne stands before the verb or the auxiliary, in the *Infinitive Mood,* and *pas* after it, except in the Present (see above). See page 6 No. 3.

In the other tenses *ne* is placed between the two pronouns : Je me, tu te, il se, etc., and *pas* after the verb in simple tenses ; in compound tenses, *pas* is between the Auxiliary and the Past Participle.

In the *Imperative, ne* stands before the verb, and *pas* after it, but in the third persons, *ne* is placed between the two pronouns and *pas* after the verb.

(1) Or : *Ne pas s'être flatté* or *flattée.*

### PAST DEFINITE.

| | |
|---|---|
| Je ne me flattai pas. | *I did not flatter myself.* |
| Tu ne te flattas pas. | *thou didst not flatter thyself.* |
| Il ne se flatta pas. | *he did not flatter himself.* |
| Nous ne nous flattâmes pas. | *we did not flatter ourselves.* |
| Vous ne vous flattâtes pas. | *you did not flatter yourselves.* |
| Ils ne se flattèrent pas. | *they did not flatter themselves.* |

### FUTURE.

| | |
|---|---|
| Je ne me flatterai pas. | *I shall not flatter myself.* |
| Tu ne te flatteras pas. | *thou wilt not flatter thyself.* |
| Il ne se flattera pas. | *he will not flatter himself.* |
| Nous ne nous flatterons pas. | *we shall not flatter ourselves.* |
| Vous ne vous flatterez pas. | *you will not flatter yourselves.* |
| Ils ne se flatteront pas. | *they will not flatter themselves.* |

### COMPOUND TENSES—PAST INDEFINITE.

| | |
|---|---|
| Je ne me suis pas flatté. | *I have not flattered myself.* |
| Tu ne t'es pas flatté. | *thou hast not flattered thyself.* |
| Il ne s'est pas flatté. | *he has not flattered himself.* |
| Nous ne nous sommes pas flattés. | *we have not flattered ourselves.* |
| Vous ne vous êtes pas flattés. | *you have not flattered yourselves.* |
| Ils ne se sont pas flattés. | *they have not flattered themselves.* |

### PLUPERFECT.

| | |
|---|---|
| Je ne m'étais pas flatté. | *I had not flattered myself.* |
| Tu ne t'étais pas flatté. | *thou hadst not flattered thyself.* |
| Il ne s'était pas flatté. | *he had not flattered himself.* |
| Nous ne nous étions pas flattés. | *we had not flattered ourselves.* |
| Vous ne vous étiez pas flattés. | *you had not flattered yourselves.* |
| Ils ne s'étaient pas flattés. | *they had not flattered themselves.* |

### PAST ANTERIOR.

| | |
|---|---|
| Je ne me fus pas flatté. | *I had not flattered myself.* |
| Tu ne te fus pas flatté. | *thou hadst not flattered thyself.* |
| Il ne se fut pas flatté. | *he had not flattered himself.* |
| Nous ne nous fûmes pas flattés. | *we had not flattered ourselves.* |
| Vous ne vous fûtes pas flattés. | *you had not flattered yourselves.* |
| Ils ne se furent pas flattés. | *they had not flattered themselves.* |

### FUTURE ANTERIOR.

| | |
|---|---|
| Je ne me serai pas flatté. | *I shall not have flattered myself.* |
| Tu ne te seras pas flatté. | *thou wilt not have flattered thyself.* |
| Il ne se sera pas flatté. | *he will not have flattered himself.* |
| Nous ne nous serons pas flattés. | *we shall not have flattered ourselves.* |
| Vous ne vous serez pas flattés. | *you will not have flattered yourselves.* |
| Ils ne se seront pas flattés. | *they will not have flattered themselves.* |

## CONDITIONAL MOOD.

### SIMPLE TENSE.—PRESENT.

| | |
|---|---|
| Je ne me flatterais pas. | *I should not flatter myself.* |
| Tu ne te flatterais pas. | *thou wouldst not flatter thyself.* |
| Il ne se flattterait pas. | *he would not flatter himself.* |
| Nous ne nous flatterions pas. | *we should not flatter ourselves.* |
| Vous ne vous flatteriez pas. | *you would not flatter yourselves.* |
| Ils ne se flatteraient pas. | *they would not flatter themselves.* |

### COMPOUND TENSE.—PAST.

| | |
|---|---|
| Je ne me serais pas flatté. | *I should not have flattered myself.* |
| Tu ne te serais pas flatté. | *thou wouldst not have flattered thyself.* |
| Il ne se serait pas flatté. | *he would not have flattered himself.* |
| Nous ne nous serions pas flattés. | *we should not have flattered ourselves.* |
| Vous ne vous seriez pas flattés. | *you would not have flattered yourselves.* |
| Ils ne se seraient pas flattés. | *they would not have flattered themselves.* |

## IMPERATIVE MOOD.

### PRESENT OR FUTURE.

| | |
|---|---|
| Ne te flatte pas. | *Do not flatter thyself.* |
| Qu'il ne se flatte pas. | *let him not flatter himself.* |
| Ne nous flattons pas. | *let us not flatter ourselves.* |
| Ne vous flattez pas. | *do not flatter yourselves.* |
| Qu'ils ne se flattent pas. | *let them not flatter themselves.* |

## SUBJUNCTIVE MOOD.

### SIMPLE TENSES.—PRESENT.

| | |
|---|---|
| Que je ne me flatte pas. | *That I may not flatter myself.* |
| Que tu ne te flattes pas. | *that thou mayest not flatter thyself.* |
| Qu'il ne se flatte pas. | *that he may not flatter himself.* |
| Que nous ne nous flattions pas. | *that we may not flatter ourselves.* |
| Que vous ne vous flattiez pas. | *that you may not flatter yourselves.* |
| Qu'ils ne se flattent pas. | *that they may not flatter themselves.* |

### IMPERFECT.

| | |
|---|---|
| Que je ne me flattasse pas. | *That I might not flatter myself.* |
| Que tu ne te flattasses pas. | *that thou mightest not flatter thyself.* |
| Qu'il ne se flattât pas. | *that he might not flatter himself.* |
| Que nous ne nous flattassions pas. | *that we might not flatter ourselves.* |
| Que vous ne vous flattassiez pas. | *that you might not flatter yourselves.* |
| Qu'ils ne se flattassent pas. | *that they might not flatter themselves.* |

### COMPOUND TENSES.—PAST.

| | |
|---|---|
| Que je ne me sois pas flatté. | *That I may not have flattered myself.* |
| Que tu ne te sois pas flatté. | *that thou mayest not have flattered thyself.* |
| Qu'il ne se soit pas flatté. | *that he may not have flattered himself.* |
| Que nous ne nous soyons pas flattés. | *that we may not have flattered ourselves.* |
| Que vous ne vous soyez pas flattés. | *that you may not have flattered yourselves.* |
| Qu'ils ne se soient pas flattés. | *that they may not have flattered themselves.* |

### PLUPERFECT.

| | |
|---|---|
| Que je ne me fusse pas flatté. | *That I might not have flattered myself.* |
| Que tu ne te fusses pas flatté. | *that thou mightest not have flattered thyself.* |
| Qu'il ne se fût pas flatté. | *that he might not have flattered himself.* |
| Que nous ne nous fussions pas flattés. | *that we might not have flattered ourselves.* |
| Que vous ne vous fussiez pas flattés. | *that you might not have flattered yourselves.* |
| Qu'ils ne se fussent pas flattés. | *that they might not have flattered themselves.* |

CONJUGATE IN THE SAME MANNER:

| | | | | |
|---|---|---|---|---|
| S'arrêter | *To stop, to stay.* | Se figurer | *To fancy, imagine.* |
| Se baisser | *— stoop.* | Se lever | *— get up, rise.* |
| S'enhardir | *— grow bold.* | Se réjouir de | *rejoice.* |

# CONJUGATION OF A PRONOMINAL VERB INTERROGATIVELY.*

*SE FLATTER*, TO FLATTER ONE'S SELF.

## INDICATIVE MOOD.

### SIMPLE TENSES.

#### PRESENT.

| | |
|---|---|
| Me flatté-je ? (1) | *Do I flatter myself?* |
| Te flattes-tu ? | *dost thou flatter thyself?* |
| Se flatte-t-il ? | *does he flatter himself?* |
| Nous flattons-nous ? | *do we flatter ourselves?* |
| Vous flattez-vous ? | *do you flatter yourselves?* |
| Se flattent-ils ? | *do they flatter themselves?* |

#### IMPERFECT.

| | |
|---|---|
| Me flattais-je ? | *Was I flattering myself?* |
| Te flattais-tu ? | *wast thou flattering thyself?* |
| Se flattait-il ? | *was he flattering himself?* |
| Nous flattions-nous ? | *were we flattering ourselves?* |
| Vous flattiez-vous ? | *were you flattering yourselves?* |
| Se flattaient-ils ? | *were they flattering themselves?* |

#### PAST DEFINITE.

| | |
|---|---|
| Me flattai-je ? | *Did I flatter myself?* |
| Te flattas-tu ? | *didst thou flatter thyself?* |
| Se flatta-t-il ? | *did he flatter himself?* |
| Nous flattâmes-nous ? | *did we flatter ourselves?* |
| Vous flattâtes-vous ? | *did you flatter yourselves?* |
| Se flattèrent-ils ? | *did they flatter themselves?* |

#### FUTURE.

| | |
|---|---|
| Me flatterai-je ? | *Shall I flatter myself?* |
| Te flatteras-tu ? | *wilt thou flatter thyself?* |
| Se flattera-t-il ? | *will he flatter himself?* |
| Nous flatterons-nous ? | *shall we flatter ourselves?* |
| Vous flatterez-vous ? | *will you flatter yourselves?* |
| Se flatteront-ils ? | *will they flatter themselves?* |

### COMPOUND TENSES.

#### PAST INDEFINITE.

| | |
|---|---|
| Me suis-je flatté ? | *Have I flattered myself?* |
| T'es-tu flatté ? | *hast thou flattered thyself?* |
| S'est-il flatté ? | *has he flattered himself?* |
| Nous sommes-nous flattés ? | *have we flattered ourselves?* |
| Vous êtes-vous flattés ? | *have you flattered yourselves?* |
| Se sont-ils flattés ? | *have they flattered themselves?* |

* N.B.—To conjugate a Pronominal verb interrogatively the pronouns nominative : *Je, tu, il, elle, nous, vous, ils, elles*, must be placed after the verb in simple tenses; and between the Auxiliary and the Past Participle in compound tenses.  See page 4, No. 2.

The second pronouns : *Me, te, se, nous, vous, se*, stand always before the verb or the auxiliary.

(1) See page 4, No. 4.

## INDICATIVE MOOD *(continued.)*

### COMPOUND TENSES.

#### PLUPERFECT.

| | |
|---|---|
| M'étais-je flatté? | *Had I flattered myself?* |
| T'étais-tu flatté? | *hadst thou flattered thyself?* |
| S'était-il flatté? | *had he flattered himself?* |
| Nous étions-nous flattés? | *had we flattered ourselves?* |
| Vous étiez-vous flattés? | *had you flattered yourselves?* |
| S'étaient-ils flattés? | *had they flattered themselves?* |

#### PAST ANTERIOR.

| | |
|---|---|
| Me fus-je flatté? | *Had I flattered myself?* |
| Te fus-tu flatté? | *hadst thou flattered thyself?* |
| Se fut-il flatté? | *had he flattered himself?* |
| Nous fûmes-nous flattés? | *had we flattered ourselves?* |
| Vous fûtes-vous flattés? | *had you flattered yourselves?* |
| Se furent-ils flattés? | *had they flattered themselves?* |

#### FUTURE ANTERIOR.

| | |
|---|---|
| Me serai-je flatté? | *Shall I have flattered myself?* |
| Te seras-tu flatté? | *wilt thou have flattered thyself?* |
| Se sera-t-il flatté? | *will he have flattered himself?* |
| Nous serons-nous flattés? | *shall we have flattered ourselves?* |
| Vous serez-vous flattés? | *will you have flattered yourselves?* |
| Se seront-ils flattés? | *will they have flattered themselves?* |

## CONDITIONAL MOOD.

### SIMPLE TENSE.—PRESENT.

| | |
|---|---|
| Me flatterais-je? | *Should I flatter myself?* |
| Te flatterais-tu? | *wouldst thou flatter thyself?* |
| Se flatterait-il? | *would he flatter himself?* |
| Nous flatterions-nous? | *should we flatter ourselves?* |
| Vous flatteriez-vous? | *would you flatter yourselves?* |
| Se flatteraient-ils? | *would they flatter themselves?* |

### COMPOUND TENSE.—PAST.

| | |
|---|---|
| Me serais-je flatté? | *Should I have flattered myself?* |
| Te serais-tu flatté? | *wouldst thou have flattered thyself?* |
| Se serait-il flatté? | *would he have flattered himself?* |
| Nous serions-nous flattés? | *should we have flattered ourselves?* |
| Vous seriez-vous flattés? | *would you have flattered yourselves?* |
| Se seraient-ils flattés? | *would they have flattered themselves?* |

CONJUGATE IN THE SAME MANNER:

| | | | |
|---|---|---|---|
| S'abonner à | *To subscribe to.* | S'envoler | *To fly away.* |
| Se douter | *— suspect.* | Se révolter | *— revolt.* |

CARCASSONNE, THE CITY WALLS

CHATEAU DE FONTAINEBLEAU

56

# CONJUGATION OF A PRONOMINAL VERB INTERROGATIVELY AND NEGATIVELY.*

---

## SE FLATTER, TO FLATTER ONE'S SELF.

### INDICATIVE MOOD.

#### SIMPLE TENSES.

##### PRESENT.

| | |
|---|---|
| Ne me flatte-je pas? (1). | *Do I not flatter myself?* |
| Ne te flattes-tu pas ? | *dost thou not flatter thyself?* |
| Ne se flatte-t-il pas ? | *does he not flatter himself?* |
| Ne nous flattons-nous pas ? | *do we not flatter ourselves ?* |
| Ne vous flattez-vous pas ? | *do you not flatter yourselves ?* |
| Ne se flattent-ils pas ? | *do they not flatter themselves?* |

##### IMPERFECT.

| | |
|---|---|
| Ne me flattais-je pas? | *Was I not flattering myself ?* |
| Ne te flattais-tu pas ? | *wast thou not flattering thyself?* |
| Ne se flattait-il pas? | *was he not flattering himslf ?* |
| Ne nous flattions-nous pas? | *were we not flattering ourselves ?* |
| Ne vous flattiez-vous pas ? | *were you not flattering yourselves ?* |
| Ne se flattaient-ils pas? | *were they not flattering themselves?* |

##### PAST DEFINITE.

| | |
|---|---|
| Ne me flattai-je pas ? | *Did I not flatter myself?* |
| Ne te flattas-tu pas ? | *didst thou not flatter thyself?* |
| Ne se flatta-t-il pas ? | *did he not flatter himself ?* |
| Ne nous flattâmes-nous pas ? | *did we not flatter ourselves ?* |
| Ne vous flattâtes-vous pas ? | *did you not flatter yourselves ?* |
| Ne se flattèrent-ils pas? | *did they not flatter themselves!* |

##### FUTURE.

| | |
|---|---|
| Ne me flatterai-je pas? | *Shall I not flatter myself?* |
| Ne te flatteras-tu pas ? | *wilt thou not flatter thyself?* |
| Ne se flattera-t-il pas ? | *will he not flatter himself?* |
| Ne nous flatterons-nous pas? | *shall we not flatter ourselves ?* |
| Ne vous flatterez-vous pas? | *will you not flatter yourselves ?* |
| Ne se flatteront-ils pas? | *will they not flatter themselves ?* |

#### COMPOUND TENSES.

##### PAST INDEFINITE.

| | |
|---|---|
| Ne me suis-je pas flatté ? | *Have I not flattered myself?* |
| Ne t'es-tu pas flatté ? | *hast thou not flattered thyself?* |
| Ne s'est-il pas flatté ? | *has he not flattered himself?* |
| Ne nous sommes-nous pas flattés ? | *have we not flattered ourselves ?* |
| Ne vous êtes-vous pas flattés ? | *have you not flattered yourselves ?* |
| Ne se sont-ils pas flattés ? | *have they not flattered themselves ?* |

---

* N.B.—To conjugate a Pronominal Verb negatively and interrogatively, *ne* must be placed before the pronouns : *Me, te, se—nous, vous, se* (see above); and *pas* after the pronouns nominative : *Je, tu, il, elle, nous, vous, ils, elles,* in simple as well as compound tenses (see page 8).
(1) See page 4, No. 4.

## INDICATIVE MOOD *(continued)*.

---

### COMPOUND TENSES.

#### PLUPERFECT.

| | |
|---|---|
| Ne m'étais-je pas flatté ? | *Had I not flattered myself?* |
| Ne t'étais-tu pas flatté ? | *hadst thou not flattered thyself?* |
| Ne s'était-il pas flatté ? | *had he not flattered himself?* |
| Ne nous étions-nous pas flattés ? | *had we not flattered ourselves?* |
| Ne vous étiez-vous pas flattés ? | *had you not flattered yourselves?* |
| Ne s'étaient-ils pas flattés ? | *had they not flattered themselves?* |

#### PAST ANTERIOR.

| | |
|---|---|
| Ne me fus-je pas flatté ? | *Had I not flattered myself?* |
| Ne te fus-tu pas flatté ? | *hadst thou not flattered thyself?* |
| Ne se fut-il pas flatté ? | *had he not flattered himself?* |
| Ne nous fûmes-nous pas flattés ? | *had we not flattered ourselves?* |
| Ne vous fûtes-vous pas flattés ? | *had you not flattered yourselves?* |
| Ne se furent-ils pas flattés ? | *had they not flattered themselves?* |

#### FUTURE ANTERIOR.

| | |
|---|---|
| Ne me serai-je pas flatté ? | *Shall I not have flattered myself?* |
| Ne te seras-tu pas flatté ? | *wilt thou not have flattered thyself?* |
| Ne se sera-t-il pas flatté ? | *will he not have flattered himself?* |
| Ne nous serons-nous pas flattés ? | *shall we not have flattered ourselves?* |
| Ne vous serez-vous pas flattés ? | *will you not have flattered yourselves?* |
| Ne se seront-ils pas flattés ? | *will they not have flattered themselves?* |

---

## CONDITIONAL MOOD.

#### PRESENT.

| | |
|---|---|
| Ne me flatterais-je pas ? | *Should I not flatter myself?* |
| Ne te flatterais-tu pas ? | *wouldst thou not flatter thyself?* |
| Ne se flatterait-il pas ? | *would he not flatter himself?* |
| Ne nous flatterions-nous pas ? | *should we not flatter ourselves?* |
| Ne vous flatteriez-vous pas ? | *would you not flatter yourselves?* |
| Ne se flatteraient-ils pas ? | *would they not flatter themselves?* |

#### PAST.

| | |
|---|---|
| Ne me serais-je pas flatté ? | *Should I not have flattered myself?* |
| Ne te serais-tu pas flatté ? | *wouldst thou not have flattered thyself?* |
| Ne se serait-il pas flatté ? | *would he not have flattered himself?* |
| Ne nous serions-nous pas flattés ? | *should we not have flattered ourselves?* |
| Ne vous seriez-vous pas flattés ? | *would you not have flattered yourselves?* |
| Ne se seraient-ils pas flattés ? | *would they not have flattered themselves?* |

---

CONJUGATE IN THE SAME MANNER :

Se glisser - - - *To creep (into).* | Se moquer de - - - *To laugh at.*

# CONJUGATION OF RECIPROCAL VERBS.

*Reciprocal Verbs* express a reciprocity of action between two or more subjects, as: Nous nous aimons l'une l'autre. *We love one another.* This sort of verb can only be used in the three persons plural, because there are two or more subjects.

*They are conjugated like the pronominal verbs, both in their simple and compound tenses.* (See N.B. page 48.)

## *SE QUERELLER*, TO QUARREL.

### INDICATIVE MOOD.

#### SIMPLE TENSES.—PRESENT.

| | |
|---|---|
| Nous nous querellons. | *We quarrel.* |
| Vous vous querellez. | *you quarrel.* |
| Ils se querellent. | *they quarrel.* |

#### IMPERFECT.

| | |
|---|---|
| Nous nous querellions. | *We were quarrelling.* |
| Vous vous querelliez. | *you were quarrelling.* |
| Ils se querellaient. | *they were quarrelling.* |

#### PAST DEFINITE.

| | |
|---|---|
| Nous nous querellâmes. | *We quarrelled.* |
| Vous vous querellâtes. | *you quarrelled.* |
| Ils se querellèrent. | *they quarrelled.* |

#### FUTURE.

| | |
|---|---|
| Nous nous querellerons. | *We shall quarrel.* |
| Vous vous querellerez. | *you will quarrel.* |
| Ils se querelleront. | *they will quarrel.* |

#### COMPOUND TENSES.—PAST INDEFINITE.

| | |
|---|---|
| Nous nous sommes querellés. | *We have quarrelled.* |
| Vous vous êtes querellés. | *you have quarrelled.* |
| Ils se sont querellés. | *they have quarrelled.* |

#### PLUPERFECT.

| | |
|---|---|
| Nous nous étions querellés. | *We had quarrelled.* |
| Vous vous étiez querellés. | *you had quarrelled.* |
| Ils s'étaient querellés. | *they had quarrelled.* |

#### PAST ANTERIOR.

| | |
|---|---|
| Nous nous fûmes querellés. | *We had quarrelled.* |
| Vous vous fûtes querellés. | *you had quarrelled.* |
| Ils se furent querellés. | *they had quarrelled.* |

N.B.—To avoid an equivoque, we add to the reciprocal verb the expressions: *L'un l'autre* (m.s.), or *les uns les autres* (m.pl.)—*L'une l'autre* (f.s.), or *les unes les autres* (f.pl.)

*L'un l'autre,* when there are only two subjects, and *Les uns les autres,* if there are more than two. Ex.:

| | |
|---|---|
| Nous nous aimons l'un l'autre. | *We love one another.* |
| Nous nous flattons les uns les autres. | *We flatter one another.* |

But the addition of : *L'un, l'autre,* etc., is not necessary, if the meaning is clearly reciprocal, as in the verb : *Se quereller.*

### FUTURE ANTERIOR.

| | |
|---|---|
| Nous nous serons querellés. | *We shall have quarrelled.* |
| Vous vous serez querellés. | *you will have quarrelled.* |
| Ils se seront querellés. | *they will have quarrelled.* |

## CONDITIONAL MOOD.

### SIMPLE TENSE.—PRESENT.

| | |
|---|---|
| Nous nous querellerions. | *We should quarrel.* |
| Vous vous querelleriez. | *you would quarrel.* |
| Ils se querelleraient. | *they would quarrel.* |

### COMPOUND TENSE.—PAST.

| | |
|---|---|
| Nous nous serions querellés. | *We should have quarrelled.* |
| Vous vous seriez querellés. | *you would have quarrelled.* |
| Ils se seraient querellés. | *they would have quarrelled.* |

## IMPERATIVE MOOD.

### PRESENT OR FUTURE.

| | |
|---|---|
| Querellons-nous | *Let us quarrel.* |
| Querellez-vous | *quarrel (you).* |
| Qu'ils se querellent | *let them quarrel.* |

## SUBJUNCTIVE MOOD.

### SIMPLE TENSES.—PRESENT.

| | |
|---|---|
| Que nous nous querellions. | *That we may quarrel.* |
| Que vous vous querelliez. | *that you may quarrel.* |
| Qu'ils se querellent. | *that they may quarrel.* |

### IMPERFECT.

| | |
|---|---|
| Que nous nous querellassions. | *That we might quarrel.* |
| Que vous vous querellassiez. | *that you might quarrel.* |
| Qu'ils se querellassent. | *that they might quarrel.* |

### COMPOUND TENSES.—PAST.

| | |
|---|---|
| Que nous nous soyons querellés. | *That we may have quarrelled.* |
| Que vous vous soyez querellés. | *that you may have quarrelled.* |
| Qu'ils se soient querellés. | *that they may have quarrelled.* |

### PLUPERFECT.

| | |
|---|---|
| Que nous nous fussions querellés. | *That we might have quarrelled.* |
| Que vous vous fussiez querellés. | *that you might have quarrelled.* |
| Qu'ils se fussent querellés. | *that they might have quarrelled.* |

N.B.—The reciprocal verbs are conjugated: *interrogatively, negatively, and interrogatively and negatively* like the Pronominal Verbs.

CONJUGATE IN THE SAME MANNER:

S'embrasser - *To kiss each other.* | Se détester - *To detest each other.*

# CONJUGATION OF THE IMPERSONAL VERBS.

*The Impersonal Verbs* are those used only, *in the third person singular*, with the pronoun il, *it*, taken in an indefinite sense.

The Impersonal verbs are conjugated, *in the third person singular*, according to the conjugation to which they belong, except if they are irregular.

*Rule*—The Past Participle of Impersonal verbs is invariable.

*The following Impersonal verbs are among those most in use:*

| | | |
|---|---|---|
| S'agir | *The matter is* | See page 62. |
| Advenir *or* Avenir | *To happen, to occur, to come to pass* | See page 65. It takes *être* in its Compound tenses. |
| Y avoir | *There to be* | See page 61. |
| Bruiner | *To drizzle* | See page 66. |
| Conster | *To appear (law term)* | See page 66. It takes *être* in its Compound tenses. |
| Convenir | *To suit, to be expedient, proper, etc.* | Conjugated like *Advenir*, p. 65. |
| Dégeler | *To thaw* | See page 65. |
| Falloir | *Must—to be necessary* | See page 63. |
| S'en falloir | *To be far from* | See page 64. |
| Geler | *To freeze* | See page 65. |
| Grêler | *To hail* | See page 66. |
| Importer | *To be of importance* | See page 66. |
| Neiger | *To snow* | See page 66. |
| Pleuvoir | *To rain* | See page 68. |
| Regeler | *To freeze again* | See page 65. |
| Tonner | *To thunder* | See page 66. |

# CONJUGATION OF *Y AVOIR*, THERE TO BE.*

### INFINITIVE MOOD.

| | | |
|---|---|---|
| *Present.* | Y avoir. | *There to be.* |
| *Part. Pres.* | Y ayant. | *There being.* |
| *Compound.* | Y ayant eu. | *There having been.* |
| *Part. Past.* | Eu, (inv.) | *Been.* |

### INDICATIVE MOOD.

| | | |
|---|---|---|
| *Present.* | Il y a. | *There is* or *there are.* |
| *Imperfect.* | Il y avait. | *There was* or *there were.* |
| *Past Def.* | Il y eut. | *There was* or *there were.* |
| *Past Ind.* | Il y a eu. | *There has been* or *there have been.* |
| *Pluperfect.* | Il y avait eu. | *There had been.* |
| *Past Ant.* | Il y eut eu. | *There had been.* |
| *Future.* | Il y aura. | *There will be.* |
| *Future Ant.* | Il y aura eu. | *There will have been.* |

### CONDITIONAL MOOD.

| | | |
|---|---|---|
| *Present.* | Il y aurait. | *There would be.* |
| *Past.* | Il y aurait eu. | *There would have been.* |

*No Imperative Mood.*

### SUBJUNCTIVE MOOD.

| | | |
|---|---|---|
| *Present.* | Qu'il y ait. | *That there may be.* |
| *Imperfect.* | Qu'il y eût. | *That there might be.* |
| *Past.* | Qu'il y ait eu. | *That there may have been.* |
| *Pluperfect.* | Qu'il y eût eu. | *That there might have been.* |

## Y AVOIR, *CONJUGATED NEGATIVELY.*

### INDICATIVE MOOD.

| | | |
|---|---|---|
| *Present.* | Il n'y a pas. | *There is not* or *There are not.* |
| *Imperfect.* | Il n'y avait pas. | *There was not* or *There were not.* |
| *Past Def.* | Il n'y eut pas. | *There was not* or *There were not.* |
| *Past Indef.* | Il n'y a pas eu. | *There has not been* or *There have not been.* |
| *Pluperfect.* | Il n'y avait pas eu. | *There had not been.* |
| *Past Ant.* | Il n'y eut pas eu. | *There had not been.* |
| *Future.* | Il n'y aura pas. | *There will not be.* |
| *Future Ant.* | Il n'y aura pas eu. | *There will not have been.* |

### CONDITIONAL MOOD.

| | | |
|---|---|---|
| *Present.* | Il n'y aurait pas. | *There would not be.* |
| *Past.* | Il n'y aurait pas eu. | *There would not have been.* |

*No Imperative.*

### SUBJUNCTIVE MOOD.

| | | |
|---|---|---|
| *Present.* | Qu'il n'y ait pas. | *That there may not be.* |
| *Imperfect.* | Qu'il n'y eut pas. | *That there might not be.* |
| *Past.* | Qu'il n'y ait pas eu. | *That there may not have been.* |
| *Pluperfect.* | Qu'il n'y eut pas eu. | *That there might not have been.* |

---

* N.B. 1. In French, *Y avoir*, has only one form *in each tense*, and in English it has two in some.
Ex. : Indicative Present : *Il y a* There is *or* there are.

---

2. *Il y a, il y avait* do not change in French when followed by a noun plural.
Ex.: *Il y a un homme* There is a man.
*Il y a des hommes* There are men.

# Y AVOIR *CONJUGATED.*

## INTERROGATIVELY.

### INDICATIVE MOOD.

| | | |
|---|---|---|
| *Present.* | Y a-t-il? | *Is there? are there?* |
| *Imper.* | Y avait-il? | *Was there? were there?* |
| *Past Def.* | Y eut-il? | *Was there? were there?* |
| *Past Ind.* | Y a-t-il eu? | *Has there been? have there been?* |
| *Plup.* | Y avait-il eu? | *Had there been?* |
| *Past Ant.* | Y eut-il eu? | *Had there been?* |
| *Future.* | Y aura-t-il? | *Will there be?* |
| *Fut. Ant.* | Y aura-t il eu? | *Will there have been?* |

### CONDITIONAL MOOD.

| | | |
|---|---|---|
| *Present.* | Y aurait-il? | *Would there be?* |
| *Past.* | Y aurait-il eu? | *Would there have been?* |

## NEGATIVELY AND INTERROGATIVELY.

### INDICATIVE MOOD.

| | | |
|---|---|---|
| *Present.* | N'y a-t-il pas? | *Is there not? are there not?* |
| *Imperfect.* | N'y avait-il pas? | *Was there not? were there not?* |
| *Past. Def.* | N'y eut-il pas? | *Was there not? were there not?* |
| *Past Ind.* | N'y a-t-il pas eu? | *Has there not been? have there not been?* |
| *Plup.* | N'y avait-il pas eu? | *Had there not been?* |
| *Past Ant.* | N'y eut-il pas eu? | *Had there not been?* |
| *Future.* | N'y aura-t-il pas? | *Will there not be?* |
| *Fut. Ant.* | N'y aura-t-il pas eu? | *Will there not have been?* |

### CONDITIONAL MOOD.

| | | |
|---|---|---|
| *Present.* | N'y aurait-il pas? | *Would there not be?* |
| *Past.* | N'y aurait-il pas eu? | *Would there not have been?* |

---

**VERB *S'AGIR*,** TO BE THE MATTER, TO BE IN QUESTION.

| | SIMPLE TENSES. | | | COMPOUND TENSES. | |
|---|---|---|---|---|---|
| *IND. pres.* | Il s' agit. (1) | *The matter is,* | *Pret. ind.* | Il s'est agi. | *The matter has been.* |
| *Imp.* | Il s'agissait. | *the matter was.* | *Plup.* | Il s'était agi. | *the matter had been.* |
| *Past déf.* | Il s'agit. | *the matter was.* | *Past ant.* | Il se fut agi. | *the matter had been.* |
| *Fut. abs.* | Il s'agira. | *the matter will be.* | *Fut. ant.* | Il se sera agi. | *the matter will have been.* |
| *COND. pres.* | Il s'agirait. | *the matter would be.* | *Cond. past.* | Il se serait agi. | *the matter would have been.* |
| *SUB. pres.* | Qu'il s'agisse. | *that the matter may be.* | *Sub. past.* | Qu'il se soit agi. | *that the matter may have been.* |
| *Imperfect.* | Qu'il s'agît. | *that the matter might be.* | *Plup.* | Qu'il se fût agi. | *that the matter might have been.* |
| *INF. pres.* | S'agir. | *to be the matter.* | | | |

---

### VERB *S'AGIR.*

| INTERROGATIVELY. | NEGATIVELY. | NEGATIVELY & INTERROGATIVELY. |
|---|---|---|
| *Ind. Pres.* S'agit-il? | *Ind. Pres.* Il ne s'agit pas. | *Ind. Pres.* Ne s'agit-il pas? |
| *Pret. Ind.* S'est-il agi? etc. | *Pret. Ind.* Il ne s'est pas agi, etc. | *Pret. Ind.* Ne s'est-il pas agi? etc. |

(1) N.B. The expressions : *Il s'agit, il s'agissait,* etc., take *de.*
Ex. : *Il s'agit de vous* You are concerned. *Il s'agissait de lui* He was concerned.
*Il s'agira de faire* It will be necessary to do.
As *Il s'agit* has several meanings, in English the sense of a sentence will show which expression to take amongst : *The matter is, the question is,* etc.

# VERB *FALLOIR*, TO BE NECESSARY, MUST.

## POSITIVELY.

### INFINITIVE MOOD.

| | | |
|---|---|---|
| *Inf. pres.* | Falloir. | *To be necessary.* |
| *Part. pres.* | (None). | |
| *Part. past.* | Fallu. | *been necessary.* |

### INDICATIVE MOOD.

| | | | |
|---|---|---|---|
| *Present.* | Il faut. | *It is* | \ |
| *Imp.* | Il fallait. | *it was* | |
| *Past def.* | Il fallut. | *it was* | |
| *Past inf.* | Il a fallu. | *it has been* | *necessary.* |
| *Plup.* | Il avait fallu. | *it had been* | |
| *Past ant.* | Il eut fallu. | *it had been* | |
| *Future.* | Il faudra. | *it will be* | |
| *Fut. ant.* | Il aura fallu. | *it will have been* | / |

### CONDITIONAL MOOD.

| | | |
|---|---|---|
| *Pres..* | Il faudrait. | *It would be necessary.* |
| *Past* | Il aurait fallu. | *it would have been necessary.* |

(*No Imperative Mood.*)

### SUBJUNCTIVE MOOD.

| | | | |
|---|---|---|---|
| *Pres.* | Qu'il faille. | *That it may be* | \ |
| *Past* | Qu'il ait fallu. | *that it may have been* | *necessary.* |
| *Imp.* | Qu'il fallût. | *that it might be* | |
| *Plup.* | Qu'il eût fallu. | *that it might have been* | / |

---

## INTERROGATIVELY.

| | | | |
|---|---|---|---|
| *IND. pres.* | Faut-il? | *Is it* | \ |
| *Imp.* | Fallait-il? | *was it* | |
| *Past def.* | Fallut-il? | *was it* | |
| *Past Ind.* | A-t-il fallu? | *has it been* | |
| *Past ant.* | Eut-il fallu? | *had it been* | *necessary?* |
| *Plup.* | Avait-il fallu? | *had it been* | |
| *Future.* | Faudra-t-il? | *will it be* | |
| *Fut. ant.* | Aura-t-il fallu? | *will it have been* | / |
| *COND. pres.* | Faudrait-il? | *would it be* | |
| *Past* | Aurait-il fallu? | *would it have been* | |

## NEGATIVELY.

### INFINITIVE MOOD.

| | | |
|---|---|---|
| *Inf. pres.* | Ne falloir pas. | *Not to be necessary.* |

### INDICATIVE MOOD.

| | | | |
|---|---|---|---|
| *Present* | Il ne faut pas. | *It is not* | \ |
| *Imp.* | Il ne fallait pas. | *it was not* | |
| *Past def.* | Il ne fallut pas. | *it was not* | |
| *Past ind.* | Il n'a pas fallu. | *it has not been* | |
| *Plup.* | Il n'avait pas fallu. | *it had not been* | *necessary.* |
| *Past ant.* | Il n'eut pas fallu. | *it had not been* | |
| *Future* | Il ne faudra pas. | *it will not be* | |
| *Fut. ant.* | Il n'aura pas fallu. | *it will not have been* | / |

### CONDITIONAL MOOD.

| | | |
|---|---|---|
| *Pres.* | Il ne faudrait pas. | *It would not be necessary.* |
| *Past* | Il n'aurait pas fallu. | *it would not have been necessary.* |

(*No Imperative Mood.*)

### SUBJUNCTIVE MOOD.

| | | | |
|---|---|---|---|
| *Pres.* | Qu'il ne faille pas. | *That it may not be* | \ |
| *Past* | Qu'il n'ait pas fallu, | *that it may not have been* | *necessary.* |
| *Imp.* | Qu'il ne fallût pas. | *that it might not be* | |
| *Plup.* | Qu'il n'eût pas fallu. | *that it might not have been* | / |

---

## NEGATIVELY AND INTERROGATIVELY.

| | | | |
|---|---|---|---|
| *IND. pres.* | Ne faut-il pas? | *Is it not* | \ |
| *Imp.* | Ne fallait-il pas? | *was it not* | |
| *Past def.* | Ne fallut-il pas? | *was it not* | |
| *Past ind.* | N'a-t-il pas fallu? | *has it not been* | |
| *Past ant.* | N'eut-il pas fallu? | *had it not been* | *necessary?* |
| *Plup.* | N'avait-il pas fallu? | *had it not been* | |
| *Future* | Ne faudra-t-il pas? | *will it not be* | |
| *Fut. ant.* | N'aura-t-il pas fallu? | *will it not have been* | / |
| *COND. pres.* | Ne faudrait-il pas? | *would it not be* | |
| *Past* | N'aurait-il pas fallu? | *would it not have been* | / |

# REMARKS ON VERB *FALLOIR*, MUST, TO BE NECESSARY,

---

*Falloir* has two distinct meanings : it implies necessity or duty, and want or deficiency.

When *Falloir* expresses duty or necessity, it is translated by *Il faut*, *Il fallait*, etc. (page 63), and requires the Subjunctive after it.  Ex. :

| | |
|---|---|
| *Il faut que je parle.* | I must speak. |
| *Il faut que tu parles, etc.* | Thou must speak, etc. |

The expression, *Il faut que je parle*, *implies personal or individual obligation.*

When *Falloir* suggests general advice, it requires the Infinitive Present after it.  Ex. :

| | |
|---|---|
| *Il faut écrire.* | It is necessary to write. |
| *Il fallait écrire.* | It was necessary to write, etc. |

*Falloir* meaning want, deficiency, is followed by a substantive, and a personal pronoun precedes *Falloir*.  Ex. :

| | |
|---|---|
| I want a hat. | *Il me faut un chapeau.* |

---

## S'EN FALLOIR, TO BE FAR FROM, ETC.

| | | |
|---|---|---|
| *INFIN.* present | S'en falloir. | *To be far from, etc.* |
| —— *past* | S'en être fallu. | *to have been far from. etc.* |
| *Comp. of part. pres.* | S'en étant fallu. | *having been far from. etc.* |
| *Participle past* | Fallu. | *been far from, etc.* |

---

### SIMPLE TENSES.

| | | |
|---|---|---|
| *IND. pres.* | Il s'en faut. | *It is* |
| *Imp.* | Il s'en fallait. | *it was* |
| *Past def.* | Il s'en fallut. | *it was* |
| *Plup.* | Il s'en faudra. | *it will be* |
| *Cond. pres.* | Il s'en faudrait. | *it would be* |
| *SUB. pres.* | Qu'il s'en faille. | *that it may be* |
| —— *imp.* | Qu'il s'en fallût. | *that it might be* |

*far from, etc.*

### COMPOUND TENSES.

| | | |
|---|---|---|
| *Past. indef.* | Il s'en est fallu. | *It has* |
| *Plup.* | Il s'en était fallu. | *it had* |
| *Past ant.* | Il s'en fut fallu. | *it had* |
| *Fut. ant.* | Il s'en sera fallu. | *it will have* |
| *Cond. past* | Il s'en serait fallu. | *it would have* |
| *SUB. past* | Qu'il s'en soit fallu. | *that it may have* |
| —— *imp.* | Qu'il s'en fût fallu. | *that it might have* |

*been far from, etc.*

---

### NEGATIVELY.

| | |
|---|---|
| *IND. pres.* | Il ne s'en faut pas. |
| *Past indef.* | Il ne s'en est pas fallu. |
| | etc. |

### INTERROGATIVELY.

| | |
|---|---|
| *IND. pres.* | S'en faut-il ? |
| *Past ind.* | S'en est-il fallu ? |
| | etc. |

## INTERROGATIVELY AND NEGATIVELY.

| | |
|---|---|
| *Ind pres.* | Ne s'en faut-il pas ? |
| *Past ind.* | Ne s'en est-il pas fallu ? |
| | etc. |

# *ADVENIR* or *AVENIR*, TO COME TO PASS, TO TAKE PLACE, TO HAPPEN.

## INFINITIVE MOOD.

| | | |
|---|---|---|
| *Present.* | Advenir. | *To happen.* |
| *Part. pres.* | Advenant. | *Happening.* |
| *Part. past.* | Advenu. | *Happened.* |

## INDICATIVE MOOD.

| | | |
|---|---|---|
| *Present.* | Il advient. | *It happens.* |
| *Imperfect.* | Il advenait. | *It was happening.* |
| *Past def.* | Il advint. | *It happened.* |
| *Past indef.* | Il est advenu. | *It has happened.* |
| *Pluperfect.* | Il était advenu. | *It had happened.* |
| *Past ant.* | Il fut advenu. | *It had happened.* |
| *Future.* | Il adviendra. | *It will happen.* |
| *Fut. ant.* | Il sera advenu. | *It will have happened.* |

## CONDITIONAL MOOD.

| | | |
|---|---|---|
| *Present.* | Il adviendrait. | *It would happen.* |
| *Past.* | Il serait advenu. | *It would have happened.* |

*No Imperative Mood.*

## SUBJUNCTIVE MOOD.

| | | |
|---|---|---|
| *Present.* | Qu'il advienne. | *That it may happen.* |
| *Imperfect.* | Qu'il advînt. | *That it might happen.* |
| *Past.* | Qu'il soit advenu. | *That it may have happened.* |
| *Pluperfect.* | Qu'il fût advenu. | *That it might have happened.* |

N.B.—I. *Advenir* takes *être* in its compound tenses, and is used preferably to *avenir*.
II. *Convenir*, to suit, etc., is conjugated like *advenir*.

# *GELER*, TO FREEZE.

## INFINITIVE MOOD.

| | | |
|---|---|---|
| *Present.* | Geler. | *To freeze.* |
| *Part. pres.* | Gelant. | *Freezing.* |
| *Part. past.* | Gelé. | *Frozen.* |

## INDICATIVE MOOD.

| | | |
|---|---|---|
| *Present.* | Il gèle. | *It freezes.* |
| *Imperfect.* | Il gelait. | *It was freezing.* |
| *Past def.* | Il gela. | *It froze.* |
| *Past ind.* | Il a gelé. | *It has frozen.* |
| *Pluperfect.* | Il avait gelé. | *It had frozen.* |
| *Past ant.* | Il eut gelé. | *It had frozen.* |
| *Future.* | Il gèlera. | *It will freeze.* |
| *Fut. ant.* | Il aura gelé. | *It will have frozen.* |

## CONDITIONAL MOOD.

| | | |
|---|---|---|
| *Present.* | Il gèlerait. | *It would freeze.* |
| *Past.* | Il aurait gelé. | *It would have frozen.* |

*No Imperative Mood.*

## SUBJUNCTIVE MOOD.

| | | |
|---|---|---|
| *Present.* | Qu'il gèle. | *That it may freeze.* |
| *Imperfect.* | Qu'il gelât. | *That it might freeze.* |
| *Past.* | Qu'il ait gelé. | *That it may have frozen.* |
| *Pluperfect.* | Qu'il eût gelé. | *That it might have frozen.* |

N.B.—See Verbs ending in *eler*, page 32.
Conjugate like Geler; Dégeler, *To thaw*, and Regeler, *To freeze again*

# NEIGER.—TO SNOW.

### INFINITIVE MOOD.

| | | |
|---|---|---|
| *Present.* | Neiger. | *To snow.* |
| *Part. pres.* | Neigeant. | *Snowing.* |
| *Part. past.* | Neigé. | *Snowed.* |

### INDICATIVE MOOD.

| | | |
|---|---|---|
| *Present.* | Il neige. | *It snows.* |
| *Imperfect.* | Il neigeait. | *It was snowing.* |
| *Past def.* | Il neigea. | *It snowed.* |
| *Past ind.* | Il a neigé. | *It has snowed.* |
| *Pluperfect.* | Il avait neigé. | *It had snowed.* |
| *Past ant.* | Il eut neigé. | *It had snowed.* |
| *Future.* | Il neigera. | *It will snow.* |
| *Fut. ant.* | Il aura neigé. | *It will have snowed.* |

### CONDITIONAL MOOD.

| | | |
|---|---|---|
| *Present.* | Il neigerait. | *It would snow.* |
| *Past.* | Il aurait neigé. | *It would have snowed.* |

*No Imperative Mood.*

### SUBJUNCTIVE MOOD.

| | | |
|---|---|---|
| *Present.* | Qu'il neige. | *That it may snow.* |
| *Imperfect.* | Qu'il neigeât. | *That it might snow.* |
| *Past.* | Qu'il ait neigé. | *That it may have snowed.* |
| *Pluperfect.* | Qu'il eût neigé. | *That it might have snowed.* |

**N.B.—See Verbs ending in *ger*, page 31.**

# GRÊLER.—TO HAIL.

### INFINITIVE MOOD.

| | | |
|---|---|---|
| *Present.* | Grêler. | *To hail.* |
| *Part. pres.* | Grêlant. | *Hailing.* |
| *Part. past.* | Grêlé. | *Hailed.* |

### INDICATIVE MOOD.

| | | |
|---|---|---|
| *Present.* | Il grêle. | *It hails.* |
| *Imperfect.* | Il grêlait. | *It was hailing.* |
| *Past def.* | Il grêla. | *It hailed.* |
| *Past ind.* | Il a grêlé. | *It has hailed.* |
| *Pluperfect.* | Il avait grêlé. | *It had hailed.* |
| *Past ant.* | Il eut grêlé. | *It had hailed.* |
| *Future.* | Il grêlera. | *It will hail.* |
| *Fut. ant.* | Il aura grêlé. | *It will have hailed.* |

### CONDITIONAL MOOD.

| | | |
|---|---|---|
| *Present.* | Il grêlerait. | *It would hail.* |
| *Past.* | Il aurait grêlé. | *It would have hailed.* |

*No Imperative Mood.*

### SUBJUNCTIVE MOOD.

| | | |
|---|---|---|
| *Present.* | Qu'il grêle. | *That it may hail.* |
| *Imperfect.* | Qu'il grêlât. | *That it might hail.* |
| *Past.* | Qu'il ait grêlé. | *That it may have hailed.* |
| *Pluperfect.* | Qu'il eût grêlé. | *That it might have hailed.* |

**CONJUGATE IN THE SAME MANNER:**

| | | |
|---|---|---|
| Bruiner | *To drizzle.* | Importer | *To be of importance.* |
| Conster | *— appear (law term.)* | Tonner | *— thunder.* |

# VERB *PLEUVOIR*, TO RAIN.

## POSITIVELY.

### INFINITIVE MOOD.

| | | |
|---|---|---|
| Pres. | Pleuvoir. | To rain. |
| Part. pres. | Pleuvant. | raining. |
| Part. past | Plu (*inv.*) | rained. |

### INDICATIVE MOOD.

| | | |
|---|---|---|
| Pres. | Il pleut. | It rains. |
| Imp. | Il pleuvait. | it was raining. |
| Past def. | Il plut. | it rained. |
| Past ind. | Il a plu. | it has rained. |
| Past ant. | Il eut plu. | it had rained. |
| Plup. | Il avait plu. | it had rained. |
| Future | Il pleuvra. | it will rain. |
| Fut. ant. | Il aura plu. | it will have rained. |

### CONDITIONAL MOOD.

| | | |
|---|---|---|
| Pres. | Il pleuvrait. | It would rain. |
| Past. | Il aurait plu. | It would have rained. |

#### (No Imperative.)

### SUBJUNCTIVE MOOD.

| | | |
|---|---|---|
| Pres. | Qu'il pleuve | That it may rain. |
| Past. | Qu'il ait plu. | that it may have rained. |
| Imp. | Qu'il plût. | that it might rain. |
| Plup. | Qu'il eût plu. | that it might have rained. |

### INTERROGATIVELY.

| | | |
|---|---|---|
| IND. Pres. | Pleut-il ? | Does it rain ? |
| Imp. | Pleuvait-il ? | was it raining ? |
| Past def. | Plut-il ? | did it rain ? |
| Past ind. | A-t-il plu ? | has it rained? |
| Past ant. | Eut-il plu ? | had it rained ? |
| Plup. | Avait-il plu ? | had it rained? |
| Future. | Pleuvra-t-il ? | will it rain ? |
| Fut. ant. | Aura-t-il plu? | will it have rained ? |
| COND. Pres. | Pleuvrait-il ? | would it rain ? |
| Cond past. | Aurait-il plu ? | would it have rained ? |

## NEGATIVELY.

### INFINITIVE MOOD.

| | | |
|---|---|---|
| Pres. | Ne pas pleuvoir. | Not to rain. |
| Part pres. | Ne pleuvant pas. | not raining. |

### INDICATIVE MOOD.

| | | |
|---|---|---|
| Pres. | Il ne pleut pas. | It does not rain |
| Imp. | Il ne pleuvait pas. | it was not raining. |
| Past def. | Il ne plut pas. | it did not rain. |
| Past ind. | Il n'a pas plu. | it has not rained. |
| Past. ant. | Il n'eut pas plu. | it had not rained. |
| Plup. | Il n'avait pas plu. | it had not rained. |
| Future. | Il ne pleuvra pas. | it will not rain |
| Fut. ant. | Il n'aura pas plu. | it will not have rained. |

### CONDITIONAL MOOD.

| | | |
|---|---|---|
| Pres. | Il ne pleuvrait pas. | It would not rain. |
| Past. | Il n'aurait pas plu. | It would not have rained. |

#### (No Imperative.)

### SUBJUNCTIVE MOOD.

| | | |
|---|---|---|
| Pres. | Qu'il ne pleuve pas. | that it may not rain. |
| Past. | Qu'il n'ait pas plu. | that it may not have rained. |
| Imp. | Qu'il ne plût pas. | that it might not rain. |
| Plup. | Qu'il n'eût pas plus. | that it might not have rained. |

## NEGATIVELY AND INTERROGATIVELY.

| | | |
|---|---|---|
| IND. Pres. | Ne pleut-il pas ? | Does it not rain ? |
| Imp. | Ne pleuvait-il pas? | was it not raining ? |
| Past def. | Ne plut-il pas ? | did it not rain ? |
| Past ind. | N'a-t-il pas plu ? | has it not rained ? |
| Past ant. | N'eut-il pas plu ? | had it not rained ? |
| Plup. | N'avait-il pas plu ? | had it not rained ? |
| Future. | Ne pleuvra-t-il pas? | will it not rain ? |
| Fut. ant. | N'aura-t-il pas plu? | will it not have rained ? |
| COND. Pres. | Ne pleuvrait-il pas ? | would it not rain ? |
| Cond past. | N'aurait-il pas plu | would it not have rained ? |

# CHAPTER 5

# Irregular Verbs—First Conjugation

**1.**—*The first person singular of the Present of the Indicative* ends always by *e* or *s*.

When the first person ends by *e*, the second ends by *es* ; and the third by *e*.

If the first person ends by *s*, the second also ends by *s*, and the third by *t* or *d* ; by *d*, if *d* is found in the singular persons.

*The first person plural of the Present of the Indicative* ends always by *ons*, the second by *ez*, the third by *ent*.

The exceptions are :

(1) Verb Aller—Je vais, tu vas, il *va* ; nous allons, vous allez, il *vont*.
  ,,  Dire—Je dis, tu dis, il dit, nous disons, vous *dites*, ils disent.
  ,,  Faire—Je fais. tu fais, il fait, nous faisons, vous *faites*, ils *font*.
  ,,  Convaincre—Je convaincs,  tu convaincs,  il *convainc*, nous convainquons, vous convainquez, ils con-
  ,,  Vaincre—Je vaincs, tu vaincs, il *vainc*, nous vainquons, vous vainquez, ils vainquent.   [vainquent.
  ,,  Pouvoir—Je peux, tu *peux*, il peut, nous pouvons, vous pouvez, ils peuvent.
  ,,  Vouloir—Je *veux*, tu *veux*, il veut, nous voulons, vous voulez, ils veulent.
  ,,  Valoir—Je *vaux*, tu *vaux*, il vaut, nous valons, vous valez, ils valent.

**2.**—*The Imperfect of the Indicative* ends in all verbs in the first person singular by *ais* ; in the second, *ais* ; third, *ait*.  In the person plural in *ions* ; second *iez* ; third, *aient*.

**3.**—*The Past Definite* has four different terminations :

| | | | | | |
|---|---|---|---|---|---|
| 1. | 1st person singular *ai*, 2nd *as*, 3rd *a*. | | 1st person plural *âmes*, 2nd *âtes*, 3rd *èrent*. | | |
| 2. | ,,  ,,  ,, *is* ,, *is* ,, *it*. | | ,,  ,,  *îmes* ,, *îtes* ,, *irent*. | | |
| 3. | ,,  ,,  ,, *us* ,, *us* ,, *ut*. | | ,,  ,,  *ûmes* ,, *ûtes* ,, *urent*. | | |
| 4. | ,,  ,,  ,, *ins* ,, *ins* ,, *int*. | | ,,  .,  *înmes* ,, *întes* ,, *inrent*. | | |

**4.**—*The Future* ends in all verbs in the first person singular by *rai* ;  second, *ras* ;  third *ra*. First person plural in *rons* ; second, *rez* ; third, *ront*.

**5.**—*The Conditional* in all verbs ends in the first person singular in *rais* ; second, *rais* ; third, *rait*.   First person plural in *rions* ; second, *riez* ; third, *raient*.

**6.**—*The Imperative* ends in all  verbs in the second person singular by *e* or *s* ;  in the third by *e* ; in the first person plural by *ons* ; the second by *ez* :  and the third by *ent*.

The exceptions are :
  Dire :  Dis, qu'il dise, disons, *dites*, qu'ils disent.
  Faire :  Fais, qu'il fasse, faisons, *faites*, qu'ils fassent.
  Pouvoir has no Imperative.
  Valoir :  *vaux*, qu'il vaille, valons, valez, qu'il vaillent.

**7.**—*The Present of the Subjunctive* ends in all verbs in the first person singular by *e* ; the second by *es* ; the third by *e*.   In the first person plural by *ions* ; second, *iez* ; third, *ent*.

**8.**—*The Imperfect of the Subjunctive* has four different terminations :

| 1st pers. sing. | 2nd pers. sing. | 3rd pers. sing. | 1st pers. pl. | 2nd pers. pl. | 3rd pers. pl. |
|---|---|---|---|---|---|
| *asse* | *asses* | *ât* | *assions* | *assiez* | *assent*. |
| *isse* | *isses* | *ît* | *issions* | *issiez* | *issent*. |
| *usse* | *usses* | *ût* | *ussions* | *ussiez* | *ussent* |
| *insse* | *insses* | *înt* | *inssions* | *inssiez* | *inssent*. |

**9.**—*The Participle Present* ends in all verbs by *ant*.

**10.**—*The Participle Past* ends by *é, i, u, t* or *s*.

N.B.—The above observations have been summed up in our Paradigm, page 69.
(1) The exceptions are printed in italic letters.

# PARADIGM.

## TO SHOW THE SIMILARITY OF VERBS IN THEIR FINAL SYLLABLES.

| | 1st conj. | 2nd conj. | 3rd conj. | 4th conj. | |
|---|---|---|---|---|---|
| INFINITIVE PRESENT. | er | ir | oir | re | REMARKS I. |
| PARTICIPLE PRESENT. | ant. | ant | ant | ant | The Participle Present ends in *ant* in all verbs. |
| PARTICIPLE PAST. | é, i, u, t, s. | | | | The Participle Past ends in *e, i,* etc. |

| | Singular. | | | Plural. | | | |
|---|---|---|---|---|---|---|---|
| | 1st pers. Je | 2nd pers. Tu | 3rd pers. Il Elle | 1st pers. Nous | 2nd pers. Vous | 3rd pers. Ils Elles | |
| INDICATIVE PRESENT. | { e / s | es / s | e / t *or* d } | ons | ez | ent | **II.** The Present of the Indicative ends in the three persons plural by: *ons, ez, ent.* |
| IMPERFECT. | ais | ais | ait | ions | iez | aient | **III.** The Imperfect of the Indicative ends in *ais, ait,* etc., in all verbs. |
| PAST DEFINITE. | { ai / is / us / ins | as / is / us / ins | a / it / ut / int | âmes / îmes / ûmes / înmes | âtes / îtes / ûtes / întes | èrent / irent / urent / inrent | **IV.** The Past Definite has four different terminations: *ai, as,* etc. *is, is,* etc. *us, us,* etc. *ins, ins,* etc. |
| FUTURE. | rai | ras | ra | rons | rez | ront | **V.** The Future ends in all verbs by: *rai, ras,* etc. |
| CONDITIONAL. | rais | rais | rait | rions | riez | raient | **VI.** The Conditional ends in all verbs in: *rais, rais,* etc. |
| IMPERATIVE. | { | e / s | }e | ons | ez | ent | **VII.** The persons of the Imperative are similar generally to those of the Indicative (present). |
| SUBJUNCTIVE PRESENT. | }e | es | e | ions | iez | ent | **VIII.** The Present of the Subjunctive ends in: *e, es, e,* etc., in all verbs. |
| IMPERFECT OF SUBJUNCTIVE. | { asse / isse / usse / insse | asses / isses / usses / insses | ât / ît / ût / înt | assions / issions / ussions / inssions | assiez / issiez / ussiez / inssiez | assent / issent / ussent / inssent | **IX.** The Imperfect of the Subjunctive has four different terminations: *asse, asses,* etc. *isse, isses,* etc. *usse, usses,* etc. *insse, insses,* etc. |

N.B.—When the first person singular of any tense is known, it is very easy to know the others, by consulting the PARADIGM. Thus: *je mis, je croirais, etc.,* looking for the Past Definite and Conditional, we find: *Je mis, tu mis, il mit, etc. Je croirais, tu croirais, etc.*

# IRREGULAR VERBS.—FIRST CONJUGATION.

## VERB *ALLER*, TO GO.*

### INFINITIVE MOOD.

| PRESENT. | | PAST. | |
|---|---|---|---|
| Aller. | *To go.* | Être allé. | *To have gone.* |
| **PARTICIPLE PRESENT.** | | **COMP. OF PART. PRESENT.** | |
| Allant. | *Going.* | Étant allé. | *Having gone.* |

#### PARTICIPLE PAST.
Allé (m.s.), allés (m.pl.), allée (f.s.), allées (f.pl.), *gone.*

### SIMPLE TENSES.

#### INDICATIVE MOOD.
##### PRESENT.
| | |
|---|---|
| Je *vais.* | *I go* or *I am going.* |
| Tu *vas.* | *thou goest* or *thou art going.* |
| Il *va.* | *he goes* or *he is going.* |
| Nous allons. | *we go* or *we are going.* |
| Vous allez. | *you go* or *or you are going.* |
| Ils *vont.* | *they go* or *they are going.* |

##### IMPERFECT.
| | |
|---|---|
| J'allais. | *I was going.* |
| Tu allais. | *thou wast going.* |
| Il allait. | *he was going.* |
| Nous allions. | *we were going.* |
| Vous alliez. | *you were going.* |
| Ils allaient. | *they were going.* |

##### PAST DEFINITE.
| | |
|---|---|
| J'allai. | *I went.* |
| Tu allas. | *thou wentest.* |
| Il alla. | *he went.* |
| Nous allâmes. | *we went.* |
| Vous allâtes. | *you went.* |
| Ils allèrent. | *they went.* |

##### FUTURE.
| | |
|---|---|
| J'*irai.* | *I shall go.* |
| Tu *iras.* | *thou wilt go.* |
| Il *ira.* | *he will go.* |
| Nous *irons.* | *we shall go.* |
| Vous *irez.* | *you will go.* |
| Ils *iront.* | *they will go.* |

#### CONDITIONAL MOOD.
##### PRESENT.
| | |
|---|---|
| J'*irais.* | *I should go.* |
| Tu *irais.* | *thou wouldst go.* |
| Il *irait.* | *he would go.* |
| Nous *irions.* | *we should go.* |
| Vous *iriez.* | *you would go.* |
| Ils *iraient.* | *they would go.* |

#### IMPERATIVE MOOD.
##### PRESENT.
| | |
|---|---|
| *Va.* | *Go (thou).* |
| Qu'il *aille.* | *let him go.* |
| Allons. | *let us go.* |
| Allez. | *go (you).* |
| Qu'ils *aillent.* | *let them go.* |

#### SUBJUNCTIVE MOOD.
##### PRESENT.
| | |
|---|---|
| Que j'*aille.* | *That I may go.* |
| Que tu *ailles.* | *that thou mayest go.* |
| Qu'il *aille.* | *that he may go.* |
| Que nous allions. | *that we may go.* |
| Que vous alliez. | *that you may go.* |
| Qu'ils *aillent.* | *that they may go.* |

##### IMPERFECT.
| | |
|---|---|
| Que j'allasse. | *That I might go.* |
| Que tu allasses. | *that thou mightest go.* |
| Qu'il allât. | *that he might go.* |
| Que nous allassions. | *that we might go.* |
| Que vous allassiez. | *that you might go.* |
| Qu'ils allassent. | *that they might go.* |

### COMPOUND TENSES.

| | | | |
|---|---|---|---|
| Past Ind. | Je suis allé, etc. | *I have gone, etc.* | |
| Plup. | J'étais allé, etc. | *I had gone, etc.* | |
| Past Ant. | Je fus allé, etc. | *I had gone, etc.* | |
| Fut. Ant. | Je serai allé, etc. | *I shall have gone, etc.* | |
| Cond. Past. | Je serais allé, etc. | *I should have gone, etc.* | |
| Sub. Past. | Que je sois allé, etc. | *that I may have gone, etc.* | |
| Plup. | Que je fusse allé, etc. | *that I might have gone, etc.* | |

NB.—The only irregular verbs of the first conjugation are:
Aller, *to go.*   Envoyer, *to send.*   Renvoyer, *to send back.*

*Remarks on the verb* Aller.—The verb *être* (to be) is used sometimes instead of *aller*, to go; *but only in the compound tenses, never in the simple tenses.*
So we say: *Il a été* and *Il est allé*; but there is a difference between these two expressions: *Il a été à Paris,* means the person has been there and returned, or left the place; and in: *Il est allé à Paris,* the verb *Il est allé* indicates that return has not yet taken place.
II.—In the Imperative: va takes *s* before *y. Vas-y,* go there; and before *en, Vas-en prendre,* go and take some.
III.—*Aller* is conjugated with the auxiliary *être* in all its compound tenses. See above.
* The irregular persons are printed in italic letters.

# VERB *S'EN ALLER*, TO GO AWAY.

## INFINITIVE MOOD.

| PRESENT. | | PAST. | |
|---|---|---|---|
| S'en aller. | *To go away.* | S'en être allé. | *To have gone away.* |

| PARTICIPLE PRESENT. | | COMP. OF PART. PRESENT. | |
|---|---|---|---|
| S'en allant. | *Going away.* | S'en étant allé. | *Having gone away.* |

### PARTICIPLE PAST.

En allé (m.s.), en allée (f.s.), en allés (m.pl.), en allées (f.pl.), *gone away.*

## INDICATIVE MOOD.

### SIMPLE TENSES.

#### PRESENT.

| | |
|---|---|
| Je m'en *vais.* | *I go away* or *I am* |
| Tu t'en *vas.* | *thou goest away* or *thou art* |
| Il s'en *va.* | *he goes away* or *he is* |
| Nous nous en allons. | *we go away* or *we are* |
| Vous vous en allez. | *you go away* or *you are* |
| Ils s'en *vont.* | *they go away* or *they are* |

*going away.*

#### IMPERFECT.

| | |
|---|---|
| Je m'en allais. | *I was going away.* |
| Tu t'en allais. | *thou wast going away.* |
| Ils s'en allait. | *he was going away.* |
| Nous nous en allions. | *we were going away.* |
| Vous vous en alliez. | *you were going away.* |
| Ils s'en allaient. | *they were going away.* |

#### PAST DEFINITE.

| | |
|---|---|
| Je m'en allai. | *I went away.* |
| Tu t'en allas. | *thou wentest away.* |
| Il s'en alla. | *he went away.* |
| Nous nous en allâmes. | *we went away.* |
| Vous vous en allâtes. | *you went away.* |
| Ils s'en allèrent. | *they went away.* |

#### FUTURE.

| | |
|---|---|
| Je m'en *irai.* | *I shall go away.* |
| Tu t'en *iras.* | *thou wilt go away.* |
| Il s'en *ira.* | *he will go away.* |
| Nous nous en *irons.* | *we shall go away.* |
| Vous vous en *irez.* | *you will go away.* |
| Ils s'en *iront.* | *they will go away.* |

### COMPOUND TENSES.

#### PAST INDEFINITE.

| | |
|---|---|
| Je m'en suis allé. | *I have* |
| Tu t'en es allé. | *thou hast* |
| Il s'en est allé. | *he has* |
| Nous nous en sommes allés. | *we have* |
| Vous vous en êtes allés. | *you have* |
| Ils s'en sont allés. | *they have* |

*gone away.*

#### PLUPERFECT.

| | |
|---|---|
| Je m'en étais allé. | *I had gone* |
| Tu t'en étais allé. | *thou hadst gone* |
| Il s'en était allé. | *he had gone* |
| Nous nous en étions allés. | *we had gone* |
| Vous vous en étiez allés. | *you had gone* |
| Ils s'en étaient allés. | *they had gone* |

*away.*

#### PAST ANTERIOR.

| | |
|---|---|
| Je m'en fus allé. | *I had gone* |
| Tu t'en fus allé. | *thou hadst gone* |
| Il s'en fut allé. | *he had gone* |
| Nous nous en fûmes allés. | *we had gone* |
| Vous vous en fûtes allés. | *you had gone* |
| Ils s'en furent allés. | *they had gone* |

*away.*

#### FUTURE ANTERIOR.

| | |
|---|---|
| Je m'en serai allé. | *I shall have* |
| Tu t'en seras allé. | *thou wilt have* |
| Il s'en sera allé. | *he will have* |
| Nous nous en serons allés. | *we shall have* |
| Vous vous en serez allés. | *you will have* |
| Ils s'en seront allés. | *they will have* |

*gone away.*

---

REMARKS ON THE VERB: *S'EN ALLER:*

I.—The particle *en* follows always the second pronoun, in simple and compound tenses, so we say or write: *Je m'en suis allé*, and not *Je me suis en allé*.

II.—It is not correct to write *Va-t'en* with two hyphens (*Va-t-'en*). We use only one and an apostrophe, because the *t* in *va-t'en* is not euphonic, as in *aima-t-il;* but replaces *te*, of which the *e*, is elided, before a vowel.

BAYEUX, CROQUEVIEILLE MILL

CALAIS, TOWN HALL

# CONDITIONAL MOOD.

| SIMPLE TENSES. | | COMPOUND TENSES. | |
|---|---|---|---|

### PRESENT.

| Je m'en *irais*. | *I should go away.* |
| Tu t'en *irais*. | *thou wouldst go away.* |
| Il s'en *irait*. | *he would go away.* |
| Nous nous en *irions*. | *we should go away.* |
| Vous vous en *iriez*. | *you would go away.* |
| Ils s'en *iraient*. | *they would go away.* |

### PAST.

| Je m'en serais allé. | *I should have gone away.* |
| Tu t'en serais allé. | *thou wouldst have gone away.* |
| Il s'en serait allé. | *he would have gone away.* |
| Nous nous en serions allés. | *we should have gone away.* |
| Vous vous en seriez allés. | *you would have gone away.* |
| Ils s'en seraient allés. | *they would have gone away.* |

## IMPERATIVE MOOD.

| *Va*-t'en | - - - | *Go away (thou).* |
| Qu'il s'en *aille* | - - | *let him go away.* |
| Allons-nous-en | - - | *let us go away.* |
| Allez-vous-en | - - | *go away (you).* |
| Qu'ils s'en *aillent* | - | *let them go away.* |

## SUBJUNCTIVE MOOD.

### PRESENT.

| Que je m'en *aille*. | *That I may go away.* |
| Que tu t'en *ailles*. | *that thou mayest go away.* |
| Qu'il s'en *aille*. | *that he may go away.* |
| Que nous nous en allions. | *that we may go away.* |
| Que vous vous en alliez. | *that you may go away.* |
| Qu'ils s'en *aillent*. | *that they may go away.* |

### PAST.

| Que je m'en sois allé. | *That I may have gone away.* |
| Que tu t'en sois allé. | *that thou mayest have gone away.* |
| Qu'il s'en soit allé. | *that he may have gone away.* |
| Que nous nous en soyons allés. | *that we may have gone away.* |
| Que vous vous en soyez allés. | *that you may have gone away.* |
| Qu'ils s'en soient allés. | *that they may have gone away.* |

### IMPERFECT.

| Que je m'en allasse. | *That I might go away.* |
| Que tu t'en allasses. | *that thou mightest go away.* |
| Qu'il s'en allât. | *that he might go away.* |
| Que nous nous en allassions. | *that we might go away.* |
| Que vous vous en allassiez. | *that you might go away.* |
| Qu'ils s'en allassent. | *that they might go away.* |

### PLUPERFECT.

| Que je m'en fusse allé. | *That I might have gone away.* |
| Que tu t'en fusses allé. | *that thou mightest have gone away.* |
| Qu'il s'en fût allé. | *that he might have gone away.* |
| Que nous nous en fussions allés. | *that we might have gone away.* |
| Que vous vous en fussiez allés. | *that you might have gone away.* |
| Qu'ils s'en fussent allés. | *that they might have gone away.* |

N.B.—Many verbs have the particle *en* like the verb: S'en aller. Ex.: S'en retourner, *To go back.* S'en prendre à, *To lay the blame on,* etc. In those verbs the particle *en* has the same place as in: *S'en aller.* Ex.:
*Ind. Pres.* Je m'en retourne, etc. | *Indic. Pres.* Je m'en prends à, etc.
*Imper.* Retourne-t'en, etc. | *Imper.* Prenez-vous-en à, etc.

# VERB *S'EN ALLER*, TO GO AWAY, NEGATIVELY.*

## INFINITIVE MOOD.

**PRESENT.**

Ne pas s'en aller. *Not to go away.*

**PAST.**

Ne s'en être pas allé. *Not to have gone away.*

**PARTICIPLE PRESENT.**

Ne s'en allant pas. *Not going away.*

**COMPOUND OF PARTICIPLE PRESENT.**

Ne s'en étant pas allé. *Not having gone away.*

**PARTICIPLE PAST.**

En allé, *gone.*

### COMPOUND TENSES.

## INDICATIVE MOOD.

**PRESENT.**

| | |
|---|---|
| Je ne m'en vais pas. | *I do not go away.* |
| Tu ne t'en vas pas. | *thou dost not go away.* |
| Il ne s'en va pas. | *he does not go away.* |
| Nous ne nous en allons pas. | *we do not go away.* |
| Vous ne vous en allez pas. | *you do not go away.* |
| Ils ne s'en vont pas. | *they do not go away.* |

**IMPERFECT.**

Je ne m'en allais pas, etc. *I was not going away, etc.*

**PAST DEFINITE.**

Je ne m'en allai pas, etc. *I did not go away, etc.*

**FUTURE.**

Je ne m'en irai pas, etc. *I shall not go away, etc.*

## CONDITIONAL MOOD.

Je ne m'en irais pas, etc. *I should not go away, etc.*

## IMPERATIVE MOOD.

**PRESENT.**

| | |
|---|---|
| Ne t'en va pas. | *Do not go away.* |
| Qu'il ne s'en aille pas. | *let him not go away.* |
| Ne nous en allons pas. | *let us not go away.* |
| Ne vous en allez pas. | *do not go away.* |
| Qu'ils ne s'en aillent pas. | *let them not go away.* |

## SUBJUNCTIVE MOOD.

**PRESENT.**

Que je ne m'en aille pas, etc. *That I may not go away, etc.*

**IMPERFECT.**

Que je ne m'en allasse pas, etc. *That I might not go away, etc.*

### COMPOUND TENSES.

## INDICATIVE MOOD.

**PAST INDEFINITE.**

| | |
|---|---|
| Je ne m'en suis pas allé. | *I have not gone away.* |
| Tu ne t'en es pas allé. | *thou hast not gone away.* |
| Il ne s'en est pas allé. | *he has not gone away.* |
| Nous ne nous en sommes pas allés. | *we have not gone away.* |
| Vous ne vous en êtes pas allés. | *you have not gone away.* |
| Ils ne s'en sont pas allés. | *they have not gone away.* |

**PAST ANTERIOR.**

Je ne m'en fus pas allé, etc. *I had not gone away, etc.*

**PLUPERFECT.**

Je ne m'en étais pas allé, etc. *I had not gone away, etc.*

**FUTURE ANTERIOR.**

Je ne m'en serai pas allé, etc. *I shall not have gone away, etc.*

## CONDITIONAL MOOD.

**PAST.**

Je ne m'en serais pas allé, etc. *I should not have gone away, etc.*

## SUBJUNCTIVE MOOD.

**PAST.**

Que je ne m'en sois pas allé, etc. *That I may not have gone away, etc.*

**PLUPERFECT.**

Que je ne m'en fusse pas allé, etc. *That I might not have gone away, etc.*

*N.B.—See page 51, what has been said to conjugate a Pronominal Verb negatively.

## VERB *S'EN ALLER*, TO GO AWAY.

### INTERROGATIVELY.*

#### SIMPLE TENSES.

##### INDICATIVE.—PRESENT.

| | |
|---|---|
| M'en vais-je ? | Do I go away ? |
| T'en vas-tu ? | dost thou go away ? |
| S'en va-t-il ? | does he go away ? |
| Nous en allons-nous ? | do we go away ? |
| Vous en allez-vous ? | do you go away ? |
| S'en vont-ils ? | do they go away ? |

##### IMPERFECT.

| | |
|---|---|
| M'en allais-je ? etc. | Was I going away ? etc. |

##### PAST DEFINITE.

| | |
|---|---|
| M'en allai-je ? etc. | Did I go away ? etc. |

##### FUTURE.

| | |
|---|---|
| M'en irai-je ? etc. | Shall I go away ? etc. |

##### CONDITIONAL MOOD.

| | |
|---|---|
| M'en irais-je ? etc. | Should I go away ? etc. |

#### COMPOUND TENSES.

##### PAST INDEFINITE.

| | |
|---|---|
| M'en suis-je allé ? | Have I gone away ? |
| T'en es-tu allé ? | hast thou gone away ? |
| S'en est-il allé ? | has he gone away ? |
| Nous en sommes-nous allés ? | have we gone away ? |
| Vous en êtes-vous allés ? | have you gone away ? |
| S'en sont-ils allés ? | have they gone away ? |

##### PLUPERFECT.

| | |
|---|---|
| M'en étais-je allé ? etc. | Had I gone away ? etc. |

##### PAST ANTERIOR.

| | |
|---|---|
| M'en fus-je allé ? etc. | Had I gone away ? etc. |

##### FUTURE.

| | |
|---|---|
| M'en serai-je allé ? etc. | Shall I have gone away ? etc. |

##### CONDITIONAL MOOD.

| | |
|---|---|
| M'en serais-je allé ? | Should I have gone away ? etc. |

### NEGATIVELY AND INTERROGATIVELY.*

#### SIMPLE TENSES.

##### INDICATIVE.—PRESENT.

| | |
|---|---|
| Ne m'en vais-je pas ? | Do I not go away ? |
| Ne t'en vas-tu pas ? | dost thou not go away ? |
| Ne s'en va-t-il pas ? | does he not go away ? |
| Ne nous en allons-nous pas ? | do we not go away ? |
| Ne vous en allez-vous pas ? | do you not go away ? |
| Ne s'en vont-ils pas ? | do they not go away ? |

##### IMPERFECT.

| | |
|---|---|
| Ne m'en allais-je pas ? etc. | Was I not going away ? etc. |

##### PAST DEFINITE.

| | |
|---|---|
| Ne m'en allai-je pas ? etc. | Did I not go away ? etc. |

##### FUTURE.

| | |
|---|---|
| Ne m'en irai-je pas ? etc. | Shall I not go away ? etc. |

##### CONDITIONAL MOOD.

| | |
|---|---|
| Ne m'en irais-je pas ? etc. | Should I not go away ? etc. |

#### COMPOUND TENSES.

##### PAST INDEFINITE.

| | |
|---|---|
| Ne m'en suis-je pas allé ? | Have I not gone away ? |
| Ne t'en es-tu pas allé ? | hast thou not gone away ? |
| Ne s'en est-il pas allé ? | has he not gone away ? |
| Ne nous en sommes-nous pas allés ? | have we not gone away ? |
| Ne vous en êtes-vous pas allés ? | have you not gone away ? |
| Ne s'en sont-ils pas allés ? | have they not gone away ? |

##### PLUPERFECT.

| | |
|---|---|
| Ne m'en étais-je pas allé ? etc. | Had I not gone away ? etc. |

##### PAST ANTERIOR.

| | |
|---|---|
| Ne m'en fus-je pas allé ? etc. | Had I not gone away ? etc. |

##### FUTURE.

| | |
|---|---|
| Ne m'en serai-je pas allé ? etc. | Shall I not have gone away ? etc. |

##### CONDITIONAL MOOD.

| | |
|---|---|
| Ne m'en serais-je pas allé ? etc. | Should I not have gone away ? etc. |

*N.B.—We have given p. 54 the rules to conjugate a Pronominal Verb, *Interrogatively*, and p. 56 to conjugate it Negatively and Interrogatively.

# VERB *ENVOYER*, to send.

## INFINITIVE MOOD.

| PRESENT. | | PAST. | |
|---|---|---|---|
| Envoyer. | *To send.* | Avoir envoyé. | *To have sent.* |

| PARTICIPLE PRESENT. | | COMP. OF PART. PRESENT. | |
|---|---|---|---|
| Envoyant. | *Sending.* | Ayant envoyé. | *Having sent.* |

### PARTICIPLE PAST.

Envoyé (m.s.), envoyée (f.s.), envoyés (m.pl.), envoyées (f.pl.), *sent.*

## SIMPLE TENSES.

### INDICATIVE MOOD.
#### PRESENT.

| | |
|---|---|
| J'envoie. | *I send.* |
| Tu envoies. | *thou sendest.* |
| Il envoie. | *he sends.* |
| Nous envoyons. | *we send.* |
| Vous envoyez. | *you send.* |
| Ils envoient. | *they send.* |

#### IMPERFECT.

| | |
|---|---|
| J'envoyais. | *I was sending.* |
| Tu envoyais. | *thou wast sending.* |
| Il envoyait. | *he was sending.* |
| Nous envoyions. | *we were sending.* |
| Vous envoyiez. | *you were sending.* |
| Ils envoyaient. | *they were sending.* |

#### PAST DEFINITE.

| | |
|---|---|
| J'envoyai. | *I sent.* |
| Tu envoyas. | *thou sentest.* |
| Il envoya. | *he sent.* |
| Nous envoyâmes. | *we sent.* |
| Vous envoyâtes. | *you sent.* |
| Ils envoyèrent. | *they sent.* |

#### FUTURE.

| | |
|---|---|
| J'enverrai. | *I shall send.* |
| Tu enverras. | *thou wilt send.* |
| Il enverra. | *he will send.* |
| Nous enverrons. | *we shall send.* |
| Vous enverrez. | *you will send.* |
| Ils enverront. | *they will send.* |

### CONDITIONAL MOOD.
#### PRESENT.

| | |
|---|---|
| J'enverrais. | *I should send.* |
| Tu enverrais. | *thou wouldst send.* |
| Il enverrait. | *he would send.* |
| Nous enverrions. | *we should send.* |
| Vous enverriez. | *you would send.* |
| Ils enverraient. | *they would send.* |

### IMPERATIVE MOOD.
#### PRESENT.

| | |
|---|---|
| Envoie. - - - | *Send (thou).* |
| Qu'il envoie - - | *let him send.* |
| Envoyons - - | *let us send.* |
| Envoyez - - | *send (you).* |
| Qu'ils envoient - - | *let them send.* |

### SUBJUNCTIVE MOOD.
#### PRESENT.

| | |
|---|---|
| Que j'envoie. | *That I may send.* |
| Que tu envoies. | *that thou mayest send.* |
| Qu'il envoie. | *that he may send.* |
| Que nous envoyions. | *that we may send.* |
| Que vous envoyiez. | *that you may send.* |
| Qu'ils envoient. | *that they may send.* |

#### IMPERFECT.

| | |
|---|---|
| Que j'envoyasse. | *That I might send.* |
| Que tu envoyasses. | *that thou mightest send.* |
| Qu'il envoyât. | *that he might send.* |
| Que nous envoyassions. | *that we might send.* |
| Que vous envoyassiez. | *that you might send.* |
| Qu'ils envoyassent. | *that they might send.* |

## COMPOUND TENSES.

| | | | | | |
|---|---|---|---|---|---|
| *Past def.* | J'ai envoyé, etc. | *I have sent, etc.* | *Cond. past.* | J'aurais envoyé, etc. | *I should have sent, etc.* |
| *Plup.* | J'avais envoyé, etc. | *I had sent, etc.* | | | |
| *Past ant.* | J'eus envoyé, etc. | *I had sent, etc,* | *Sub. past.* | Que j'aie envoyé, etc. | *that I may have sent, etc.* |
| *Fut.* | J'aurai envoyé, etc. | *I shall have sent, etc.* | *Sub. plup.* | Que j'eusse envoyé, etc. | *that I might have sent, etc.* |

N.B.—I. The verb *Envoyer* changes *y* into *i* before an *e mute* (see verbs ending in *yer*, page 34), and takes two *r*'s in the Future and Conditional.

II. Conjugate in the same manner: RENVOYER - - *To send back.*

## VERB *S'ABSTENIR*, TO ABSTAIN.
### INFINITIVE MOOD.

| PRESENT. | | PAST. | |
|---|---|---|---|
| S'abstenir. | *To abstain.* | S'être *abstenu.* | *to have abstained.* |

| PARTICIPLE PRESENT. | | COMPOUND OF PARTICIPLE PRESENT. | |
|---|---|---|---|
| S'*abstenant.* | *abstaining.* | S'étant *abstenu.* | *having abstained.* |

### PARTICIPLE PAST.
*Abstenu (m.s.), abstenue (f.s.), abstenus (m.pl.), abstenues (f.pl.), abstained.*

### SIMPLE TENSES.

#### INDICATIVE MOOD.
##### PRESENT.

| Je m'*abstiens.* | *I abstain.* |
|---|---|
| Tu t'*abstiens.* | *thou abstainest.* |
| Il s'*abstient.* | *he abstains.* |
| Nous nous *abstenons.* | *we abstain.* |
| Vous vous *abstenez.* | *you abstain.* |
| Ils s'*abstiennent.* | *they abstain.* |

##### IMPERFECT.

| Je m'*abstenais.* | *I was abstaining.* |
|---|---|
| Tu t'*abstenais.* | *thou wast abstaining.* |
| Il s'*abstenait.* | *he was abstaining.* |
| Nous nous *abstenions.* | *we were abstaining.* |
| Vous vous *absteniez.* | *you were abstaining.* |
| Ils s'*abstenaient.* | *they were abstaining.* |

##### PAST DEFINITE.

| Je m'*abstins.* | *I abstained.* |
|---|---|
| Tu t'*abstins.* | *thou abstained.* |
| Il s'*abstint.* | *he abstained.* |
| Nous nous *abstinmes.* | *we abstained.* |
| Vous vous *abstintes.* | *you abstained.* |
| Ils s'*abstinrent.* | *they abstained.* |

##### FUTURE.

| Je m *abstiendrai.* | *I shall abstain.* |
|---|---|
| Tu t'*abstiendras.* | *thou wilt abstain.* |
| Il s'*abstiendra.* | *he will abstain.* |
| Nous nous *abstiendrons.* | *we shall abstain.* |
| Vous vous *abstiendrez.* | *you will abstain.* |
| Ils s'*abstiendront.* | *they will abstain.* |

#### CONDITIONAL MOOD.
##### PRESENT.

| Je m'*abstiendrais.* | *I should* | abstain. |
|---|---|---|
| Tu t'*abstiendrais.* | *thou wouldst* | |
| Il s'*abstiendrait.* | *he would* | |
| Nous nous *abstiendrions.* | *we should* | |
| Vous vous *abstiendriez.* | *you would* | |
| Ils s'*abstiendraient.* | *they would* | |

#### IMPERATIVE MOOD.
##### PRESENT OR FUTURE.

| *Abstiens*-toi. | *abstain (thou.)* |
|---|---|
| Qu'il s'*abstienne.* | *let him abstain.* |
| *Abstenons*-nous. | *let us abstain.* |
| *Abstenez*-vous. | *abstain (you.)* |
| Qu'ils s'*abstiennent.* | *let them abstain.* |

#### SUBJUNCTIVE MOOD.
##### PRESENT.

| Que je m'*abstienne.* | *that I may* | abstain. |
|---|---|---|
| Que tu t'*abstiennes.* | *that thou mayest* | |
| Qu'il s'*abstienne.* | *that he may* | |
| Que nous nous *abstenions.* | *that we may* | |
| Que vous vous *absteniez.* | *that you may* | |
| Qu'ils s'*abstiennent.* | *that they may* | |

##### IMPERFECT.

| Que je m'*abstinsse.* | *that I might* | abstain. |
|---|---|---|
| Que tu t'*abstinsses.* | *that thou mightest* | |
| Qu'il s'*abstînt.* | *that he might* | |
| Que nous nous *abstinssions.* | *that we might* | |
| Que vous vous *abstinssiez.* | *that you might* | |
| Qu'ils s'*abstinssent.* | *that they might* | |

### COMPOUND TENSES.

| | | | | | |
|---|---|---|---|---|---|
| *Past Ind.* | Je me suis *ab-stenu,* etc. | *I have abstained,* etc. | *Cond. past.* | Je me serais *abstenu,* etc. | *I should have abstained,* etc. |
| *Plup.* | Je m'étais *ab-stenu,* etc. | *I had abstained,* etc. | *Subj. Past.* | Que je me sois *abstenu,* etc. | *that I may have abstained,* etc. |
| *Past ant.* | Je me fus *ab-stenu,* etc. | *I had abstained,* etc. | *Subj. plup.* | Que je me fusse *abstenu,* etc. | *that I might have abstained,* etc. |
| *Fut. ant.* | Je me serai *ab-stenu,* etc. | *I shall have ab-stained,* etc. | | | |

N.B.—I. The verb *S'abstenir* is conjugated like *Venir*; but being a verb essentially reflective, it must be conjugated with two pronouns. On account of that peculiarity we have fully conjugated it. II.The Irregular persons have been printed in the above verb in italics, *and in all the irregular verbs of the second conjugation.*

# VERB *ACQUÉRIR*, TO ACQUIRE.

## INFINITIVE MOOD.

| PRESENT. | | PAST. | |
|---|---|---|---|
| Acquérir. | *To acquire.* | Avoir *acquis.* | *To have acquired.* |
| PARTICIPLE PRESENT. | | COMPOUND OF PARTICIPLE PRESENT. | |
| Acquérant. | *acquiring.* | Ayant *acquis.* | *Having acquired.* |

PARTICIPLE PAST.

Acquis (m.s.), acquise (f.s.), acquis (m.pl.), acquises (f.pl.), *acquired.*

### SIMPLE TENSES.

#### INDICATIVE MOOD.
PRESENT.

| J'*acquiers.* | *I acquire.* |
|---|---|
| Tu *acquiers.* | *thou acquirest.* |
| Il *acquiert.* | *he acquires.* |
| Nous *acquérons.* | *we acquire.* |
| Vous *acquérez.* | *you acquire.* |
| Ils *acquièrent.* | *they acquire.* |

IMPERFECT.

| J'*acquérais.* | *I was acquiring.* |
|---|---|
| Tu *acquérais.* | *thou wast acquiring.* |
| Il *acquérait.* | *he was acquiring.* |
| Nous *acquérions.* | *we were acquiring.* |
| Vous *acquériez.* | *you were acquiring.* |
| Ils *acquéraient.* | *they were acquiring.* |

PAST DEFINITE.

| J'*acquis.* | *I acquired.* |
|---|---|
| Tu *acquis.* | *thou acquiredst.* |
| Il *acquit.* | *he acquired.* |
| Nous *acquîmes.* | *we acquired.* |
| Vous *acquîtes.* | *you acquired.* |
| Ils *acquirent.* | *they acquired.* |

FUTURE.

| J'*acquerrai.* | *I shall acquire.* |
|---|---|
| Tu *acquerras.* | *thou wilt acquire.* |
| Il *acquerra.* | *he will acquire.* |
| Nous *acquerrons.* | *we shall acquire.* |
| Vous *acquerrez.* | *you will acquire.* |
| Ils *acquerront.* | *they will acquire.* |

#### CONDITIONAL MOOD.
PRESENT.

| J'*acquerrais.* | *I should acquire.* |
|---|---|
| Tu *acquerrais.* | *thou wouldst acquire.* |
| Il *acquerrait.* | *he would acquire.* |
| Nous *acquerrions.* | *we should acquire.* |
| Vous *acquerriez.* | *you would acquire.* |
| Ils *acquerraient.* | *they would acquire.* |

#### IMPERATIVE MOOD.
PRESENT OR FUTURE.

| Acquiers. | *Acquire (thou).* |
|---|---|
| Qu'il *acquière.* | *let him acquire.* |
| Acquérons. | *let us acquire.* |
| Acquérez. | *acquire (you).* |
| Qu'ils *acquièrent.* | *let them acquire.* |

#### SUBJUNCTIVE MOOD.
PRESENT.

| Que j'*acquière.* | *That I may* |
|---|---|
| Que tu *acquières.* | *that thou mayest* |
| Qu'il *acquière.* | *that he may* |
| Que nous *acquérions.* | *that we may* |
| Que vous *acquériez.* | *that you may* |
| Qu'ils *acquièrent.* | *that they may* |

*acquire.*

IMPERFECT.

| Que j'*acquisse.* | *That I might* |
|---|---|
| Que tu *acquisses.* | *that thou mightest* |
| Qu'il *acquît.* | *that he might* |
| Que nous *acquissions.* | *that we might* |
| Que vous *acquissiez.* | *that you might* |
| Qu'ils *acquissent.* | *that they might* |

*acquire.*

### COMPOUND TENSES.

| Past Ind. | J'ai *acquis,* etc. | *I have acquired, etc.* | Cond. past. | J'aurais *acquis,* etc. | *I should have acquired, etc.* |
|---|---|---|---|---|---|
| Plup. | J'avais *acquis,* etc. | *I had acquired, etc.* | Subj. past. | Que j'aie *acquis,* etc. | *that I may have acquired, etc.* |
| Past ant. | J'eus *acquis,* etc. | *I had acquired, etc.* | Subj. plup. | Que j'eusse *acquis,* etc. | *that I might have acquired, etc.* |
| Fut. ant. | J'aurai *acquis,* etc. | *I shall have acquired, etc.* | | | |

CONJUGATE IN THE SAME MANNER:

| Conquérir | *To conquer.* | Reconquérir | *To reconquer.* |
|---|---|---|---|
| Requérir | *To require, to beg.* | S'enquérir | *To inquire.* |

# VERB *ASSAILLIR*—TO ASSAULT.

## INFINITIVE MOOD.

| | PRESENT. | | PAST. |
|---|---|---|---|
| Assaill*ir*. | *To assault.* | Avoir assailli. | *To have assaulted.* |

| | PARTICIPLE PRESENT. | | COMP. OF PART. PRESENT. |
|---|---|---|---|
| *Assaillant.* | *Assaulting.* | Ayant assailli. | *Having assaulted.* |

PARTICIPLE PAST.

Assailli (m.s.), assaillie (f.s.), assaillis (m.pl.), assaillies (f.pl.), *assaulted.*

### SIMPLE TENSES.

## INDICATIVE MOOD.

### PRESENT.

| J'assaille. | *I assault.* |
|---|---|
| Tu assailles. | *thou assaultest.* |
| Il assaille. | *he assaults.* |
| Nous assaillons. | *we assault.* |
| Vous assaillez. | *you assault.* |
| Ils assaillent. | *they assault.* |

### IMPERFECT.

| J'assaillais. | *I was assaulting.* |
|---|---|
| Tu assaillais. | *thou wast assaulting.* |
| Il assaillait. | *he was assaulting.* |
| Nous assaillions. | *we were assaulting.* |
| Vous assailliez. | *you were assaulting.* |
| Ils assaillaient. | *they were assaulting.* |

### PAST DEFINITE.

| J'assaillis. | *I assaulted.* |
|---|---|
| Tu assaillis. | *thou assaultedst.* |
| Il assaillit. | *he assaulted.* |
| Nous assaillîmes. | *we assaulted.* |
| Vous assaillîtes. | *you assaulted.* |
| Ils assaillirent. | *they assaulted.* |

### FUTURE.

| J'assaillirai. | *I shall assault.* |
|---|---|
| Tu assailliras. | *thou wilt assault.* |
| Il assaillira. | *he will assault.* |
| Nous assaillirons. | *we shall assault.* |
| Vous assaillirez. | *you will assault.* |
| Ils assailliront. | *they will assault.* |

## CONDITIONAL MOOD.

### PRESENT.

| J'assaillirais. | *I should assault.* |
|---|---|
| Tu assaillirais. | *thou wouldst assault.* |
| Il assaillirait. | *he would assault.* |
| Nous assaillirions | *we should assault.* |
| Vous assailliriez. | *you would assault.* |
| Ils assailliraient. | *they would assault.* |

## IMPERATIVE MOOD.

### PRESENT OR FUTURE.

| Assaille | - | - | *Assault (thou).* |
|---|---|---|---|
| Qu'il assaille | - | | *let him assault.* |
| Assaillons | - | - | *let us assault.* |
| Assaillez | - | - | *assault (you).* |
| Qu'ils assaillent | - | | *let them assault.* |

## SUBJUNCTIVE MOOD.

### PRESENT.

| Que j'assaille. | *That I may* |
|---|---|
| Que tu assailles. | *that thou mayest* |
| Qu'il assaille. | *that he may* |
| Que nous assaillions. | *that we may* |
| Que vous assailliez. | *that you may* |
| Qu'ils assaillent. | *that they may* |

### IMPERFECT.

| Que j'assaillisse. | *That I might* |
|---|---|
| Que tu assaillisses. | *that thou mightest* |
| Qu'il assaillît. | *that he might* |
| Que nous assaillissions. | *that we might* |
| Que vous assaillissiez. | *that you might* |
| Qu'ils assaillissent. | *that they might* |

### COMPOUND TENSES.

| *Past. ind.* | J'ai assailli, etc. | *I have assaulted, etc.* | *Cond. past.* | J'aurais assailli, etc. | *I should have assaulted, etc.* |
|---|---|---|---|---|---|
| *Plup.* | J'avais assailli, etc. | *I had assaulted, etc.* | *Sub. past.* | Que j'aie assailli, etc. | *that I may have assaulted, etc.* |
| *Past. ant.* | J'eus assailli, etc. | *I had assaulted, etc.* | *Sub. plup.* | Que j'eusse assailli, etc. | *that I might have assaulted, etc.* |
| *Fut. ant.* | J'aurai assailli, etc. | *I shall have assaulted, etc.* | | | |

N.B.—Tressaillir, *to start*, is conjugated like *Assaillir*; the Future and the Conditional are written by some grammarians and authors:

| FUTURE. | CONDITIONAL PRESENT. |
|---|---|
| Je tressaillerai. | Je tressaillerais. |
| Tu tressailleras, etc. | Tu tressaillerais, etc. |

The French Academy writes, in the Future: *Je tressaillirai*, etc., and Conditional: *Je tressaillirais*, etc. See above.

## VERB *BOUILLIR*, TO BOIL.

### INFINITIVE MOOD.

| | PRESENT. | | PAST. |
|---|---|---|---|
| Bouill*ir*. | *To boil.* | Avoir bouilli. | *to have boiled.* |
| | PARTICIPLE PRESENT. | | COMPOUND OF PARTICIPLE PRESENT. |
| *Bouillant.* | *boiling.* | Ayant bouilli. | *having boiled.* |

PARTICIPLE PAST.

Bouilli (m.s.), bouillie (f.s.), bouillis (m.pl.), bouillies (f.pl.), *boiled.*

---

### SIMPLE TENSES.

#### INDICATIVE MOOD.

PRESENT.

| Je *bous*. | *I boil.* |
|---|---|
| Tu *bous*. | *thou boilest.* |
| Il *bout*. | *he boils.* |
| Nous *bouillons*. | *we boil.* |
| Vous *bouillez*. | *you boil.* |
| Ils *bouillent*. | *they boil.* |

IMPERFECT.

| Je *bouillais*. | *I was boiling.* |
|---|---|
| Tu *bouillais*. | *thou wast boiling.* |
| Il *bouillait*. | *he was boiling.* |
| Nous *bouillions*. | *we were boiling.* |
| Vous *bouiliiez*. | *you were boiling.* |
| Ils *bouillaient*. | *they were boiling.* |

PAST DEFINITE.

| Je bouillis. | *I boiled.* |
|---|---|
| Tu bouillis. | *thou boiledst.* |
| Il bouillit. | *he boiled.* |
| Nous bouillîmes. | *we boiled.* |
| Vous bouillîtes. | *you boiled.* |
| Ils bouillirent. | *they boiled.* |

FUTURE.

| Je bouillirai. | *I shall boil.* |
|---|---|
| Tu bouilliras. | *thou wilt boil.* |
| Il bouillira. | *he will boil.* |
| Nous bouillirons. | *we shall boil.* |
| Vous bouillirez. | *you will boil.* |
| Ils bouilliront. | *they will boil.* |

#### CONDITIONAL MOOD.

PRESENT.

| Je bouillirais. | *I should boil.* |
|---|---|
| Tu bouillirais. | *thou wouldst boil.* |
| Il bouillirait. | *he would boil.* |
| Nous bouillirions. | *we should boil.* |
| Vous bouilliriez. | *you would boil.* |
| Ils bouilliraient. | *they would boil.* |

#### IMPERATIVE MOOD.

PRESENT OR FUTURE.

| *Bous*. | *Boil (thou).* |
|---|---|
| Qu'il *bouille*. | *let him boil.* |
| *Bouillons*. | *let us boil.* |
| *Bouillez*. | *boil (you).* |
| Qu'ils *bouillent*. | *let them boil.* |

#### SUBJUNCTIVE MOOD.

PRESENT.

| Que je *bouille*. | *that I may boil.* |
|---|---|
| Que tu *bouilles*. | *that thou mayest boil.* |
| Qu'il *bouille*. | *that he may boil.* |
| Que nous *bouillions*. | *that we may boil.* |
| Que vous *bouilliez*. | *that you may boil.* |
| Qu'ils *bouillent*. | *that they may boil.* |

IMPERFECT.

| Que je bouillisse. | *that I might boil.* |
|---|---|
| Que tu bouillisses. | *that thou mightest boil.* |
| Qu'il bouillît. | *that he might boil.* |
| Que nous bouillissions. | *that we might boil.* |
| Que vous bouillissiez. | *that you might boil.* |
| Qu'ils bouillissent. | *that they might boil.* |

---

### COMPOUND TENSES.

| Past Ind. | J'ai bouilli, etc. | *I have boiled, etc.* | Cond. Past. | J'aurais bouilli, etc. | *I should have boiled, etc.* |
|---|---|---|---|---|---|
| Plup. | J'avais bouilli, etc. | *I had boiled, etc.* | Sub. Past. | Que j'aie bouilli, etc. | *That I may have boiled, etc.* |
| Past Ant. | J'eus bouilli, etc. | *I had boiled, etc.* | Sub. Plup. | Que j'eusse bouilli, etc. | *That I might have boiled, etc.* |
| Fut. Ant. | J'aurai bouilli, etc. | *I shall have boiled, etc.* | | | |

---

\* N.B.—I. *Bouillir*, in a figurative sense, may be used in all its tenses and persons.
Ex.: Je bous de colère.
In its literal meaning it is generally used in the third persons.
L'eau bout. *The water boils.* Le lait a bouilli. *The milk has boiled.*
In the above cases *bouillir* is intransitive or neuter.
II. But when *bouillir* is used transitively, we employ the different tenses of the verb *Faire*, followed by the infinitive *bouillir*: Ex.: Je fais bouillir l'eau. *I am boiling the water.*
Je ferai bouillir la viande. *I shall boil the meat.*
III. Rebouillir, *To boil again*, is conjugated like *Bouillir*.

# VERB *COURIR*, TO RUN.

## INFINITIVE MOOD.

| | |
|---|---|
| **PRESENT.** | **PAST.** |
| Cou*rir.* To run. | Avoir *couru.* To have run. |
| **PARTICIPLE PRESENT.** | **COMPOUND OF PARTICIPLE PRESENT.** |
| *Courant.* Running. | Ayant *couru.* Having run. |

**PARTICIPLE PAST.**

*Couru* (m.s.), *courue* (f.s.), *courus* (m.pl.), *courues* (f.pl.), *run.*

## SIMPLE TENSES.

### INDICATIVE MOOD.

**PRESENT.**

| | |
|---|---|
| Je *cours.* | I run. |
| Tu *cours.* | thou runnest. |
| Il *court.* | he runs. |
| Nous *courons.* | we run. |
| Vous *courez.* | you run. |
| Ils *courent.* | they run. |

**IMPERFECT.**

| | |
|---|---|
| Je *courais.* | I was running. |
| Tu *courais.* | thou wast running. |
| Il *courait.* | he was running. |
| Nous *courions.* | we were running. |
| Vous *couriez.* | you were running. |
| Ils *couraient.* | they were running. |

**PAST DEFINITE.**

| | |
|---|---|
| Je *courus.* | I ran. |
| Tu *courus.* | thou rannest. |
| Il *courut.* | he ran. |
| Nous *courûmes.* | we ran. |
| Vous *courûtes.* | you ran. |
| Ils *coururent.* | they ran. |

**FUTURE.**

| | |
|---|---|
| Je courrai. | I shall run. |
| Tu courras. | thou wilt run. |
| Il courra. | he will run. |
| Nous courrons. | we shall run. |
| Vous courrez. | you will run. |
| Ils courront. | they will run. |

### CONDITIONAL MOOD.

**PRESENT.**

| | |
|---|---|
| Je courrais. | I should run. |
| Tu courrais. | thou wouldst run. |
| Il courrait. | he would run. |
| Nous courrions. | we should run. |
| Vous courriez. | you would run. |
| Ils courraient. | they would run. |

### IMPERATIVE MOOD.

**PRESENT OR FUTURE.**

| | |
|---|---|
| Cours. | Run (thou). |
| Qu'il coure. | let him run. |
| Courons. | let us run. |
| Courez. | run (you). |
| Qu'ils *courent.* | let them run. |

### SUBJUNCTIVE MOOD.

**PRESENT.**

| | |
|---|---|
| Que je coure. | That I may run. |
| Que tu coures. | that thou mayest run. |
| Qu'il coure. | that he may run. |
| Que nous courions. | that we may run. |
| Que vous couriez. | that you may run. |
| Qu'ils courent. | that they may run. |

**IMPERFECT.**

| | |
|---|---|
| Que je courusse. | That I might run. |
| Que tu courusses. | that thou mightest run. |
| Qu'il courût. | that he might run. |
| Que nous courussions. | that we might run. |
| Que vous courussiez. | that you might run. |
| Qu'ils courussent. | that they might run. |

## COMPOUND TENSES.

| | | |
|---|---|---|
| Past ind. | J'ai *couru,* etc. | I have run, etc. |
| Plup. | J'avais *couru,* etc. | I had run, etc. |
| Past ant. | J'eus *couru,* etc. | I had run, etc. |
| Fut. ant. | J'aurai *couru,* etc. | I shall have run, etc. |

| | | |
|---|---|---|
| Cond. past. | J'aurais *couru,* | I should have run, etc. |
| Sub. past. | Que j'aie *couru,* etc. | that I may have run, etc. |
| Sub. plup. | Que j'eusse *couru,* etc. | that I might have run, etc. |

### CONJUGATE IN THE SAME MANNER:

| | | | |
|---|---|---|---|
| Accourir | To run (or flock) together. | Parcourir | To run over. |
| Accourir à | — run to. | Recourir | — run again. |
| Concourir | — concur. | Recourir à | — apply to. |
| Discourir | — discourse. | Secourir | — relieve. |
| Encourir | — incur. | | |

Observe that the above verbs have two *r*'s in the Future and Conditional.

N.B.—*Accourir* is conjugated with *to have* (avoir) and *to be* (être). We use *avoir* when we intend to express the action: *to run to,* and *être* to express the result of that action, i.e., *the state.*

## VERB *CUEILLIR*, TO GATHER.

### INFINITIVE MOOD.

| | PRESENT. | | PAST. |
|---|---|---|---|
| Cueillir. | To gather. | Avoir cueilli. | To have gathered. |
| | PARTICIPLE PRESENT. | | COMPOUND OF PARTICIPLE PRESENT. |
| Cueillant. | Gathering. | Ayant cueilli. | Having gathered. |

PARTICIPLE PAST.

Cueilli (m.s.), cueillie (f.s.), cueillis (m.pl.), cueillies (f.pl.), *gathered.*

SIMPLE TENSES.

### INDICATIVE MOOD.
#### PRESENT.

| | |
|---|---|
| Je *cueille.* | I gather |
| Tu *cueilles.* | thou gatherest. |
| Il *cueille.* | he gathers. |
| Nous *cueillons.* | we gather. |
| Vous *cueillez.* | you gather. |
| Ils *cueillent.* | they gather. |

#### IMPERFECT.

| | |
|---|---|
| Je *cueillais.* | I was gathering. |
| Tu *cueillais.* | thou wast gathering. |
| Il *cueillait.* | he was gathering. |
| Nous *cueillions.* | we were gathering. |
| Vous *cueilliez.* | you were gathering. |
| Ils *cueillaient.* | they were gathering. |

#### PAST DEFINITE.

| | |
|---|---|
| Je cueillis. | I gathered. |
| Tu cueillis. | thou gatheredst. |
| Il cueillit. | he gathered. |
| Nous cueillîmes. | we gathered. |
| Vous cueillîtes. | you gathered. |
| Ils cueillirent. | they gathered. |

#### FUTURE.

| | |
|---|---|
| Je *cueillerai.* | I shall gather. |
| Tu *cueilleras.* | thou wilt gather. |
| Il *cueillera.* | he will gather. |
| Nous *cueillerons.* | we shall gather. |
| Vous *cueillerez.* | you will gather. |
| Ils *cueilleront.* | they will gather. |

### CONDITIONAL MOOD.
#### PRESENT.

| | |
|---|---|
| Je *cueillerais.* | I should gather. |
| Tu *cueillerais.* | thou wouldst gather. |
| Il *cueillerait.* | he would gather. |
| Nous *cueillerions.* | we should gather. |
| Vous *cueilleriez.* | you would gather. |
| Ils *cueilleraient.* | they would gather. |

### IMPERATIVE MOOD.
#### PRESENT OR FUTURE.

| | |
|---|---|
| Cueille. | Gather (thou). |
| Qu'il *cueille.* | let him gather. |
| Cueillons. | let us gather. |
| Cueillez. | gather (you). |
| Qu'ils *cueillent.* | let them gather. |

### SUBJUNCTIVE MOOD.
#### PRESENT.

| | |
|---|---|
| Que je *cueille.* | That I may gather. |
| Que tu *cueilles.* | that thou mayest gather. |
| Qu'il *cueille.* | that he may gather. |
| Que nous *cueillions.* | that we may gather. |
| Que vous *cueilliez.* | that you may gather. |
| Qu'ils *cueillent.* | that they may gather. |

#### IMPERFECT.

| | |
|---|---|
| Que je cueillisse. | That I might gather. |
| Que tu cueillisses. | That thou mightest gather. |
| Qu'il cueillît. | that he might gather. |
| Que nous cueillissions. | that we might gather. |
| Que vous cueillissiez. | that you might gather. |
| Qu'ils cueillissent. | that they might gather. |

COMPOUND TENSES.

| | | |
|---|---|---|
| *Past ind.* | J'ai cueilli, etc. | I have gathered, etc. |
| *Plup.* | J'avais cueilli, etc. | I had gathered, etc. |
| | etc. | |
| *Past ant.* | J'eus cueilli, etc. | I had gathered, etc. |
| *Fut. ant.* | J'aurai cueilli, | I shall have gathered, etc. |
| | etc. | |

| | | |
|---|---|---|
| *Cond. past.* | J'aurais cueilli, | I should have gathered, etc. |
| | etc. | |
| *Sub. past.* | Que j'aie cueilli, | that I may have gathered, etc. |
| | etc. | |
| *Sub. plup.* | Que j'eusse cueilli, etc. | that I might have gathered, etc. |

CONJUGATE IN THE SAME MANNER:

| | | |
|---|---|---|
| Accueillir | - - To receive, to welcome. | Recueillir - - - To collect, to reap. |
| Se recueillir - - - | { To collect one's thoughts. { — meditate. | |

# VERB *DORMIR*, TO SLEEP.

## INFINITIVE MOOD.

| | PRESENT. | | PAST. |
|---|---|---|---|
| **Dormir.** | *To sleep.* | Avoir dormi. | *To have slept.* |
| | PARTICIPLE PRESENT. | | COMPOUND OF PARTICIPLE PRESENT. |
| *Dormant.* | *Sleeping.* | Ayant dormi. | *Having slept.* |

### PARTICIPLE PRESENT.

Dormi, (invariable) *slept.*

## SIMPLE TENSES.

### INDICATIVE MOOD.
#### PRESENT.

| Je *dors.* | *I sleep.* |
|---|---|
| Tu *dors.* | *thou sleepest.* |
| Il *dort.* | *he sleeps.* |
| Nous *dormons.* | *we sleep.* |
| Vous *dormez.* | *you sleep.* |
| Ils *dorment.* | *they sleep.* |

#### IMPERFECT.

| Je *dormais.* | *I was sleeping.* |
|---|---|
| Tu *dormais.* | *thou wast sleeping.* |
| Il *dormait.* | *he was sleeping.* |
| Nous *dormions.* | *we were sleeping.* |
| Vous *dormiez.* | *you were sleeping.* |
| Ils *dormaient.* | *they were sleeping.* |

#### PAST DEFINITE.

| Je dormis. | *I slept.* |
|---|---|
| Tu dormis. | *thou sleptest.* |
| Il dormit. | *he slept.* |
| Nous dormîmes. | *we slept.* |
| Vous dormîtes. | *you slept.* |
| Ils dormirent. | *they slept.* |

#### FUTURE.

| Je dormirai. | *I shall sleep.* |
|---|---|
| Tu dormiras. | *thou wilt sleep.* |
| Il dormira. | *he will sleep.* |
| Nous dormirons. | *we shall sleep.* |
| Vous dormirez. | *you will sleep.* |
| Ils dormiront. | *they will sleep.* |

### CONDITIONAL MOOD.
#### PRESENT.

| Je dormirais. | *I should sleep.* |
|---|---|
| Tu dormirais. | *thou wouldst sleep.* |
| Il dormirait. | *he would sleep.* |
| Nous dormirions. | *we should sleep.* |
| Vous dormiriez. | *you would sleep.* |
| Ils dormiraient. | *they would sleep.* |

### IMPERATIVE MOOD.
#### PRESENT OR FUTURE.

| Dors. | *Sleep (thou).* |
|---|---|
| Qu'il *dorme.* | *let him sleep.* |
| Dormons. | *let us sleep.* |
| Dormez. | *sleep (you).* |
| Qu'ils *dorment.* | *let them sleep.* |

### SUBJUNCTIVE MOOD.
#### PRESENT.

| Que je *dorme.* | *That I may sleep.* |
|---|---|
| Que tu *dormes.* | *that thou mayest sleep.* |
| Qu'il *dorme.* | *that he may sleep.* |
| Que nous *dormions.* | *that we may sleep.* |
| Que vous *dormiez.* | *that you may sleep.* |
| Qu'ils *dorment.* | *that they may sleep.* |

#### IMPERFECT.

| Que je dormisse. | *That I might sleep.* |
|---|---|
| Que tu dormisses. | *that thou mightest sleep.* |
| Qu'il dormît. | *that he might sleep.* |
| Que nous dormissions. | *that we might sleep.* |
| Que vous dormissiez. | *that you might sleep.* |
| Qu'il dormissent. | *that they might sleep.* |

## COMPOUND TENSES.

| Past ind. | J'ai dormi, etc. | *I have slept, etc.* | Cond. past. | J'aurais dormi, etc. | *I should have slept, etc.* |
|---|---|---|---|---|---|
| Plup. | J'avais dormi, etc. | *I had slept, etc.* | Sub. past. | Que j'aie dormi, etc. | *that I may have slept, etc.* |
| Past ant. | J'eus dormi, etc. | *I had slept, etc.* | Sub. plup. | Que j'eusse dormi, etc. | *that I might have slept, etc.* |
| Fut. ant. | J'aurai dormi, etc. | *I shall have slept, etc.* | | | |

### CONJUGATE IN THE SAME MANNER:

| Endormir | *To lull to sleep.* | Redormir | *To sleep again.* |
|---|---|---|---|
| S'endormir | *— fall asleep.* | Rendormir | *— lull to sleep again, to lay asleep again.* |
| | | Se rendormir | *— fall asleep again.* |

## VERB *FUIR*, TO FLY, TO RUN AWAY.

### INFINITIVE MOOD.

| PRESENT. | | PAST. | |
|---|---|---|---|
| Fu*ir*. | *To fly.* | Avoir fui. | *To have flown.* |
| PARTICIPLE PRESENT. | | COMPOUND OF PARTICIPLE PRESENT. | |
| *Fuyant.* | *Flying.* | Ayant fui. | *Having flown.* |

PARTICIPLE PAST.

Fui (m.s.), fuie (f.s.), fuis (m.pl.), fuies (f.pl.), *flown.*

---

### SIMPLE TENSES.

#### INDICATIVE MOOD.

##### PRESENT.

| | |
|---|---|
| Je fuis. | *I fly.* |
| Tu fuis. | *thou fliest.* |
| Il fuit. | *he flies.* |
| Nous *fuyons.* | *we fly.* |
| Vous *fuyez.* | *you fly.* |
| Ils *fuient.* | *they fly.* |

##### IMPERFECT.

| | |
|---|---|
| Je *fuyais.* | *I was flying.* |
| Tu *fuyais.* | *thou wast flying.* |
| Il *fuyait.* | *he was flying.* |
| Nous *fuyions.* | *we were flying.* |
| Vous *fuyiez.* | *you were flying.* |
| Ils *fuyaient.* | *they were flying.* |

##### PAST DEFINITE.

| | |
|---|---|
| Je fuis. | *I flew.* |
| Tu fuis. | *thou flewest.* |
| Il fuit. | *he flew.* |
| Nous fuîmes. | *we flew.* |
| Vous fuîtes. | *you flew.* |
| Ils fuirent. | *they flew.* |

##### FUTURE.

| | |
|---|---|
| Je fuirai. | *I shall fly.* |
| Tu fuiras. | *thou wilt fly.* |
| Il fuira. | *he will fly.* |
| Nous fuirons. | *we shall fly.* |
| Vous fuirez. | *you will fly.* |
| Ils fuiront. | *they will fly.* |

#### CONDITIONAL MOOD.

##### PRESENT.

| | |
|---|---|
| Je fuirais. | *I should fly.* |
| Tu fuirais. | *thou wouldst fly.* |
| Il fuirait. | *he would fly.* |
| Nous fuirions. | *we should fly.* |
| Vous fuiriez. | *you would fly.* |
| Ils fuiraient. | *they would fly.* |

#### IMPERATIVE MOOD.

##### PRESENT.

| | |
|---|---|
| Fuis - - - | *Fly (thou).* |
| Qu'il *fuie* - - | *let him fly.* |
| *Fuyons* | *let us fly.* |
| *Fuyez* - - | *fly (you).* |
| Qu'ils *fuient* - | *let them fly.* |

#### SUBJUNCTIVE MOOD.

##### PRESENT.

| | |
|---|---|
| Que je *fuie.* | *That I may fly.* |
| Que tu *fuies.* | *that thou mayest fly.* |
| Qu'il *fuie.* | *that he may fly.* |
| Que nous *fuyions.* | *that we may fly.* |
| Que vous *fuyiez.* | *that you may fly.* |
| Qu'ils *fuient.* | *that they may fly.* |

##### IMPERFECT.

| | |
|---|---|
| Que je fuisse. | *That I might fly.* |
| Que tu fuisses. | *that thou mightest fly.* |
| Qu'il fuît. | *that he might fly.* |
| Que nous fuissions. | *that we might fly.* |
| Que vous fuissiez. | *that you might fly.* |
| Qu'ils fuissent. | *that they might fly.* |

### COMPOUND TENSES.

| | | | | | |
|---|---|---|---|---|---|
| *Past. ind.* | J'ai fui, etc. | *I have flown, etc.* | *Cond. past.* | J'aurais fui, etc. | *I should have flown, ete.* |
| *Plup.* | J'avais fui, etc. | *I had flown, etc.* | | | |
| *Past ant.* | J'eus fui, etc. | *I had flown, etc.* | *Sub. past.* | Que j'aie fui etc. | *That I may have flown, etc.* |
| *Fut. ant.* | J'aurai fui, etc. | *I shall have flown, etc.* | *Sub. plup.* | Que j'eusse fui, etc. | *That I might have flown, etc.* |

---

CONJUGATE IN THE SAME MANNER:

S'enfuir - - - - - - *To run away.*

*S'enfuir* is conjugated with two pronouns, being a pronominal verb.

INDICATIVE PRESENT.

Je m'enfuis.

Tu t'enfuis, etc.

See the pronominal verb. **page 48.**

PAST INDEFINITE.

Je me suis enfui.

Tu t'es enfui, etc.

# VERB *MOURIR* TO DIE.

## INFINITIVE MOOD.

| PRESENT. | | PAST. | |
|---|---|---|---|
| Mour*ir*. | *To die.* | Être *mort*. | *To have died.* |

| PARTICIPLE PRESENT. | | COMPOUND OF PARTICIPLE PRESENT. | |
|---|---|---|---|
| *Mourant.* | *Dying.* | Étant *mort*. | *Having died.* |

### PARTICIPLE PAST.

*Mort* (m.s.), *morte* (f.s.), *morts* (m.pl.), *mortes* (f.pl.), *died.*

## INDICATIVE MOOD.

### PRESENT.

| Je *meurs*. | *I die.* |
|---|---|
| Tu *meurs*. | *thou diest.* |
| Il *meurt*. | *he dies.* |
| Nous *mourons*. | *we die.* |
| Vous *mourez*. | *you die.* |
| Ils *meurent*. | *they die.* |

### IMPERFECT.

| Je *mourais*. | *I was dying.* |
|---|---|
| Tu *mourais*. | *thou wast dying.* |
| Il *mourait*. | *he was dying.* |
| Nous *mourions*. | *we were dying.* |
| Vous *mouriez*. | *you were dying.* |
| Ils *mouraient*. | *they were dying.* |

### PAST DEFINITE.

| Je *mourus*. | *I died.* |
|---|---|
| Tu *mourus*. | *thou diedst.* |
| Il *mourut*. | *he died.* |
| Nous *mourûmes*. | *we died.* |
| Vous *mourûtes*. | *you died.* |
| Ils *moururent* | *they died.* |

### FUTURE.

| Je *mourrai*. | *I shall die.* |
|---|---|
| Tu *mourras*. | *thou wilt die.* |
| Il *mourra*. | *he will die.* |
| Nous *mourrons*. | *we shall die.* |
| Vous *mourrez*. | *you will die.* |
| Ils *mourront*. | *they will die.* |

## CONDITIONAL MOOD.

### PRESENT.

| Je *mourrais*. | *I should die.* |
|---|---|
| Tu *mourrais*. | *thou wouldst die.* |
| Il *mourrait*. | *he would die.* |
| Nous *mourrions*. | *we should die.* |
| Vous *mourriez*. | *you would die.* |
| Ils *mourraient*. | *they would die.* |

## IMPERATIVE MOOD.

### PRESENT OR FUTURE.

| *Meurs* | - | - | - | *Die* (thou). |
|---|---|---|---|---|
| Qu'il *meure* | | | - | *let him die.* |
| *Mourons* | - | | - | *let us die.* |
| *Mourez* | | - | - | *die ( you.)* |
| Qu'ils *meurent* | - | | - | *let them die.* |

## SUBJUNCTIVE MOOD.

### PRESENT.

| Que je *meure*. | *That I may die.* |
|---|---|
| Que tu *meures*. | *that thou mayest die.* |
| Qu'il *meure*. | *that he may die.* |
| Que nous *mourions*. | *that we may die.* |
| Que vous *mouriez*. | *that you may die.* |
| Qu'ils *meurent*. | *that they may die.* |

### IMPERFECT.

| Que je *mourusse*. | *That I might die.* |
|---|---|
| Que tu *mourusses*. | *that thou mightest die.* |
| Qu'il *mourût*. | *that he might die.* |
| Que nous *mourussions*. | *that we might die.* |
| Que vous *mourussiez*. | *that you might die.* |
| Qu'ils *mourussent*. | *that they might die.* |

## COMPOUND TENSES.

| | | | | | |
|---|---|---|---|---|---|
| *Past ind.* | Je suis mort, etc. | *I have died, etc.* | *Cond. past.* | Je serais mort, etc. | *I should have died, etc.* |
| *Plup.* | J'étais mort, etc. | *I had died, etc.* | *Sub. past.* | Que je sois mort, etc. | *That I may have died, etc.* |
| *Past ant.* | Je fus mort, etc. | *I had died, etc.* | | | |
| *Fut. ant.* | Je serai mort, etc. | *I shall have died, etc.* | *Sub. plup.* | Que je fusse mort, etc. | *That I might have died, etc.* |

N.B.—*Mourir* is conjugated with the auxiliary *(être)* in its compound tenses.
Se mourir, *to be at the point of death.* See the Defective Verbs, page 139.

# VERB *OUVRIR*, TO OPEN.

## INFINITIVE MOOD.

| PRESENT. | | PAST. | |
|---|---|---|---|
| Ouvri*r*. | *To open.* | Avoir *ouvert*. | *To have opened.* |
| **PARTICIPLE PRESENT.** | | **COMP. OF PART. PRESENT.** | |
| *Ouvrant*. | *Opening.* | Ayant *ouvert*. | *Having opened.* |

**PARTICIPLE PAST.**

*Ouvert* (m.s.), *ouverte* (f.s.), *ouverts* (m.pl.), *ouvertes* (f.pl.), *opened.*

---

## INDICATIVE MOOD.

### PRESENT.

| | |
|---|---|
| J'*ouvre*. | *I open.* |
| Tu *ouvres*. | *thou openest.* |
| Il *ouvre*. | *he opens.* |
| Nous *ouvrons*. | *we open.* |
| Vous *ouvrez*. | *you open.* |
| Ils *ouvrent*. | *they open.* |

### IMPERFECT.

| | |
|---|---|
| J'*ouvrais*. | *I was opening.* |
| Tu *ouvrais*. | *thou wast opening.* |
| Il *ouvrait*. | *he was opening.* |
| Nous *ouvrions*. | *we were opening.* |
| Vous *ouvriez*. | *you were opening.* |
| Ils *ouvraient*. | *they were opening.* |

### PAST DEFINITE.

| | |
|---|---|
| J'ouvris. | *I opened.* |
| Tu ouvris. | *thou openedst.* |
| Il ouvrit. | *he opened.* |
| Nous ouvrîmes. | *we opened.* |
| Vous ouvrîtes. | *you opened.* |
| Ils ouvrirent. | *they opened.* |

### FUTURE.

| | |
|---|---|
| J'ouvrirai. | *I shall open.* |
| Tu ouvriras. | *thou wilt open.* |
| Il ouvrira. | *he will open.* |
| Nous ouvrirons. | *we shall open.* |
| Vous ouvrirez. | *you will open.* |
| Ils ouvriront. | *they will open.* |

## CONDITIONAL MOOD.

### PRESENT.

| | |
|---|---|
| J'ouvrirais. | *I should open.* |
| Tu ouvrirais. | *thou wouldst open.* |
| Il ouvrirait. | *he would open.* |
| Nous ouvririons. | *we should open.* |
| Vous ouvririez. | *you would open.* |
| Ils ouvriraient. | *they would open.* |

## IMPERATIVE MOOD.

### PRESENT OR FUTURE.

| | | |
|---|---|---|
| Ouvr*e* . - - | *Open (thou).* |
| Qu'il *ouvre* - - | *let him open.* |
| Ouvrons - - | *let us open.* |
| Ouvrez - - | *open (you).* |
| Qu'ils *ouvrent* - | *let them open.* |

## SUBJUNCTIVE MOOD.

### PRESENT.

| | |
|---|---|
| Que j'*ouvre*. | *That I may open.* |
| Que tu *ouvres*. | *that thou mayest open.* |
| Qu'il *ouvre*. | *that he may open.* |
| Que nous *ouvrions*. | *that we may open.* |
| Que vous *ouvriez*. | *that you may open.* |
| Qu'ils *ouvrent*. | *that they may open.* |

### IMPERFECT.

| | |
|---|---|
| Que j'ouvrisse. | *that I might open.* |
| Que tu ouvrisses. | *that thou mightest open.* |
| Qu'il ouvrît. | *that he might open.* |
| Que nous ouvrissions. | *that we might open.* |
| Que vous ouvrissiez. | *that you might open.* |
| Qu'ils ouvrissent. | *that they might open.* |

---

## COMPOUND TENSES.

| | | | |
|---|---|---|---|
| *Past ind.* J'ai ouvert, etc. | *I have opened, etc.* | *Cond. past.* J'aurais ouvert, etc. | *I should have opened, etc.* |
| *Plup.* J'avais ouvert, etc. | *I had opened, etc.* | *Sub. past.* Que j'aie ouvert, etc. | *That I may have opened, etc.* |
| *Past ant.* J'eus ouvert, etc. | *I had opened, etc.* | | |
| *Fut. ant.* J'aurai ouvert, etc. | *I shall have opened, etc.* | *Sub. plup.* Que j'eusse ouvert, etc. | *That I might have opened, etc.* |

## CONJUGATE LIKE *OUVRIR*:

| | | |
|---|---|---|
| Couvrir - | - | *To cover.* |
| Découvrir - | — | *discover, to uncover.* |
| Entr'ouvrir - | — | *open a little, to open half-way.* |
| Offrir . - | — | *offer.* |
| Mésoffrir - | - | *To underbid.* |
| Recouvrir - | - | *— cover again.* |
| Rouvrir - | - | *— open again.* |
| Souffrir - - | - | *— suffer.* |

## VERB *PARTIR*, TO SET OUT, TO GO AWAY.

### INFINITIVE MOOD.

| PRESENT. | | PAST. | |
|---|---|---|---|
| Part*ir*. | To set out. | Être parti. | To have set out. |

| PARTICIPLE PRESENT. | | COMP. OF PARTICIPLE PRESENT. | |
|---|---|---|---|
| *Partant.* | Setting out. | Étant parti. | Having set out. |

#### PARTICIPLE PAST.
Parti (m.s.), partie (f.s.), partis (m.pl.), parties (f.pl.), *set out.*

---

### SIMPLE TENSES.

#### INDICATIVE MOOD.

**PRESENT.**

| Je *pars*. | I set out. |
|---|---|
| Tu *pars*. | thou settest out. |
| Il *part*. | he sets out. |
| Nous *partons*. | we set out. |
| Vous *partez*. | you set out. |
| Ils *partent*. | they set out. |

**IMPERFECT.**

| Je *partais*. | I was setting out. |
|---|---|
| Tu *partais*. | thou wast setting out. |
| Il *partait*. | he was setting out. |
| Nous *partions*. | we were setting out. |
| Vous *partiez*. | you were setting out. |
| Ils *partaient*. | they were setting out. |

**PAST DEFINITE.**

| Je partis. | I set out. |
|---|---|
| Tu partis. | thou settest out. |
| Il partit. | he set out. |
| Nous partîmes. | we set out. |
| Vous partîtes. | you set out. |
| Ils partirent. | they set out. |

**FUTURE.**

| Je partirai. | I shall set out. |
|---|---|
| Tu partiras. | thou wilt set out. |
| Il partira. | he will set out. |
| Nous partirons. | we shall set out. |
| Vous partirez. | you will set out. |
| Ils partiront. | they will set out. |

#### CONDITIONAL MOOD.

**PRESENT.**

| Je partirais. | I should set out. |
|---|---|
| Tu partirais. | thou wouldst set out. |
| Il partirait. | he would set out. |
| Nous partirions. | we should set out. |
| Vous partiriez. | you would set out. |
| Ils partiraient. | they would set out. |

#### IMPERATIVE MOOD.

**PRESENT.**

| Pars | - | - | Set out (thou). |
|---|---|---|---|
| Qu'il *parte* | - | | let him set out. |
| Partons | - | | let us set out. |
| Partez | - | - | set out (you). |
| Qu'ils *partent* | - | | let them set out. |

#### SUBJUNCTIVE MOOD.

**PRESENT.**

| Que je *parte*. | That I may set out. |
|---|---|
| Que tu *partes*. | that thou mayest set out. |
| Qu'il *parte*. | that he may set out. |
| Que nous *partions*. | that we may set out. |
| Que vous *partiez*. | that you may set out. |
| Qu'ils *partent*. | that they may set out. |

**IMPERFECT.**

| Que je partisse. | That I might |
|---|---|
| Que tu partisses. | that thou mightest |
| Qu'il partît. | that he might |
| Que nous partissions. | that we might |
| Que vous partissiez. | that you might |
| Qu'ils partissent. | that they might |

---

### COMPOUND TENSES.

| Past ind. | Je suis parti, etc. I have set out, etc. | Cond. past. | Je serais parti, etc. | I should have set out, etc. |
|---|---|---|---|---|
| Plup. | J'étais parti, etc. I had set out, etc. | | | |
| Past ant. | Je fus parti, etc. I had set out, etc. | Sub. past. | Que je sois parti, etc. | That I may have set out, etc. |
| Fut. ant. | Je serai parti, etc. I shall have set out, etc. | Sub. plup. | Que je fusse parti, etc. | That I might have set out, etc. |

N.B.—I. *Partir,* to set out, to go away, is conjugated with *être.*
II. Repartir, *to set out again,* is conjugated like *partir;* but Repartir, *to reply,* although conjugated like *partir,* takes only *avoir,* in its compound tenses.
III. Répartir (with an accent over the é) *to divide, to distribute,* is regular and conjugated like *finir.* Page 23.
IV. Départir, *to dispense, to distribute,* and Se départir, *to desist, to deviate,* are also conjugated like the verb *partir.*

# VERB *SENTIR*, TO FEEL.

## INFINITIVE MOOD.

| PRESENT. | | PAST. | |
|---|---|---|---|
| Sent*ir*. | *To feel.* | Avoir senti. | *To have felt.* |

| PARTICIPLE PRESENT | | COMP. OF PART. PRESENT. | |
|---|---|---|---|
| *Sentant.* | *Feeling.* | Ayant senti. | *Having felt.* |

### PARTICIPLE PAST.

Senti (m.s.), sentie (f.s.), sentis (m.pl.), senties (f.pl.), *felt.*

---

### SIMPLE TENSES.

#### INDICATIVE MOOD.

**PRESENT.**

| Je *sens.* | *I feel.* |
|---|---|
| Tu *sens.* | *thou feelest.* |
| Il *sent.* | *he feels.* |
| Nous *sentons.* | *we feel.* |
| Vous *sentez.* | *you feel.* |
| Ils *sentent.* | *they feel.* |

**IMPERFECT.**

| Je *sentais.* | *I was feeling.* |
|---|---|
| Tu *sentais.* | *thou wast feeling.* |
| Il *sentait.* | *he was feeling.* |
| Nous *sentions.* | *we were feeling.* |
| Vous *sentiez.* | *you were feeling.* |
| Ils *sentaient.* | *they were feeling.* |

**PAST DEFINITE.**

| Je *sentis.* | *I felt.* |
|---|---|
| Tu *sentis.* | *thou feltest.* |
| Il *sentit.* | *he felt.* |
| Nous *sentîmes.* | *we felt.* |
| Vous *sentîtes.* | *you felt.* |
| Ils *sentirent.* | *they felt.* |

**FUTURE.**

| Je *sentirai.* | *I shall feel.* |
|---|---|
| Tu *sentiras.* | *thou wilt feel.* |
| Il *sentira.* | *he will feel.* |
| Nous *sentirons.* | *we shall feel.* |
| Vous *sentirez.* | *you will feel.* |
| Ils *sentiront.* | *they will feel.* |

#### CONDITIONAL MOOD.

**PRESENT.**

| Je sentirais. | *I should feel.* |
|---|---|
| Tu sentirais. | *thou wouldst feel.* |
| Il sentirait. | *he would feel.* |
| Nous sentirions. | *we should feel.* |
| Vous sentiriez. | *you would feel.* |
| Ils sentiraient. | *they would feel.* |

#### IMPERATIVE MOOD.

**PRESENT.**

| Sens. | *Feel (thou).* |
|---|---|
| Qu'il *sente.* | *let him feel.* |
| Sentons. | *let us feel.* |
| Sentez. | *feel (you).* |
| Qu'ils *sentent.* | *let them feel.* |

#### SUBJUNCTIVE MOOD.

**PRESENT.**

| Que je *sente.* | *That I may feel.* |
|---|---|
| Que tu *sentes.* | *that thou mayest feel.* |
| Qu'il *sente.* | *that he may feel.* |
| Que nous *sentions.* | *that we may feel.* |
| Que vous *sentiez.* | *that you may feel.* |
| Qu'ils *sentent.* | *that they may feel.* |

**IMPERFECT.**

| Que je sentisse. | *That I might feel.* |
|---|---|
| Que tu sentisses. | *that thou mightest feel.* |
| Qu'il sentît. | *that he might feel.* |
| Que nous sentissions. | *that we might feel.* |
| Que vous sentissiez. | *that you might feel.* |
| Qu'ils sentissent. | *that they might feel.* |

---

### COMPOUND TENSES.

| *Past ind.* | J'ai senti, etc. | *I have felt, etc.* | *Cond. past.* | J'aurais senti, etc. | *I should have felt, etc.* |
|---|---|---|---|---|---|
| *Plup.* | J'avais senti, etc. | *I had felt, etc.* | *Sub. past.* | Que j'aie senti, etc. | *That I may have felt, etc.* |
| *Past ant.* | J'eus senti, etc. | *I had felt, etc.* | *Sub. plup.* | Que j'eusse senti, etc. | *That I might have felt, etc.* |
| *Fut. ant.* | J'aurai senti, etc. | *I shall have felt, etc.* | | | |

---

### CONJUGATE IN THE SAME MANNER:

| Consentir | - | - | - | To consent. | Pressentir | - | - | To foresee, to foreknow. |
|---|---|---|---|---|---|---|---|---|
| Démentir | - | - | - | — contradict. | Ressentir | - | - | — resent. |
| Mentir | - | - | - | — to lie. | Se repentir | - | - | — repent. |

N.B.—1. *Se repentir*, being a verb essentially pronominal, is conjugated with two pronouns of the same person. Ex.: *Je me repens, tu te repens, il se repent*, etc. See page 48.

# VERB *SERVIR*, TO SERVE, TO HELP TO.

## INFINITIVE MOOD.

| | PRESENT. | | | PAST. |
|---|---|---|---|---|
| Servir. | *To serve.* | | Avoir servi. | *To have served.* |
| | PRESENT PARTICIPLE. | | | COMP. OF PART. PRESENT. |
| Servant. | *Serving.* | | Ayant servi. | *Having served.* |

### PARTICIPLE PAST.
Servi (m.s.), servie (f.s.), servis (m.pl.), servies (f.pl.), *served.*

---

## INDICATIVE MOOD.

### PRESENT.

| | |
|---|---|
| Je *sers.* | *I serve.* |
| Tu *sers.* | *thou servest.* |
| Il *sert.* | *he serves.* |
| Nous *servons.* | *we serve.* |
| Vous *servez.* | *you serve.* |
| Ils *servent.* | *they serve.* |

### IMPERFECT.

| | |
|---|---|
| Je *servais.* | *I was serving.* |
| Tu *servais.* | *thou wast serving.* |
| Il *servait.* | *he was serving.* |
| Nous *servions.* | *we were serving.* |
| Vous *serviez.* | *you were serving.* |
| Ils *servaient.* | *they were serving.* |

### PAST DEFINITE.

| | |
|---|---|
| Je servis. | *I served.* |
| Tu servis. | *thou servedst.* |
| Il servit. | *he served.* |
| Nous servîmes. | *we served.* |
| Vous servîtes. | *you served.* |
| Ils servirent. | *they served.* |

### FUTURE.

| | |
|---|---|
| Je servirai. | *I shall serve.* |
| Tu serviras. | *thou wilt serve.* |
| Il servira. | *he will serve.* |
| Nous servirons. | *we shall serve.* |
| Vous servirez. | *you will serve.* |
| Ils serviront. | *they will serve.* |

## CONDITIONAL MOOD.

### PRESENT.

| | |
|---|---|
| Je servirais. | *I should serve.* |
| Tu servirais. | *thou wouldst serve.* |
| Il servirait. | *he would serve.* |
| Nous servirions. | *we should serve.* |
| Vous serviriez. | *you would serve.* |
| Ils serviraient. | *they would serve.* |

## IMPERATIVE MOOD.

### PRESENT.

| | |
|---|---|
| Sers. | *Serve (thou).* |
| Qu'il *serve.* | *let him serve.* |
| Servons. | *let us serve.* |
| Servez. | *serve (you).* |
| Qu'ils *servent.* | *let them serve.* |

## SUBJUNCTIVE MOOD.

### PRESENT.

| | |
|---|---|
| Que je *serve.* | *That I may serve.* |
| Que tu *serves.* | *that thou mayest serve.* |
| Qu'il *serve.* | *that he may serve.* |
| Que nous *servions.* | *that we may serve.* |
| Que vous *serviez.* | *that you may serve.* |
| Qu'ils *servent.* | *that they may serve.* |

### IMPERFECT.

| | |
|---|---|
| Que je servisse. | *That I might serve.* |
| Que tu servisses. | *that thou mightest serve.* |
| Qu'il servît. | *that he might serve.* |
| Que nous servissions. | *that we might serve.* |
| Que vous servissiez. | *that you might serve.* |
| Qu'ils servissent. | *that they might serve.* |

---

## COMPOUND TENSES.

| | | | | | |
|---|---|---|---|---|---|
| *Past ind.* | J'ai servi, etc. | *I have served, etc.* | *Cond. past.* | J'aurais servi, etc. | *I should have served, etc.* |
| *Plup.* | J'avais servi, etc. | *I had served, etc.* | *Sub. past.* | Que j'aie servi, etc. | *that I may have served, etc.* |
| *Past ant.* | J'eus servi, etc. | *I had served, etc.* | *Sub. plup.* | Que j'eusse servi, etc. | *that I might have served, etc.* |
| *Fut. ant.* | J'aurai servi, etc. | *I shall have served, etc.* | | | |

---

CONJUGATE IN THE SAME MANNER:

Desservir - - - - - *To clear the table.*

N.B.—Asservir, *to enslave, to subject,* although ending by *servir,* is regular, and conjugated like *finir.* Page 23.

# VERB *SORTIR*, TO GO OUT.

## INFINITIVE MOOD.

| PRESENT. | | PAST. | |
|---|---|---|---|
| Sortir. | To go out. | Être sorti. | To have gone out. |
| **PARTICIPLE PRESENT.** | | **COMPOUND OF PARTICIPLE PRESENT** | |
| Sortant. | Going out. | Étant sorti. | Having gone out. |

### PARTICIPLE PAST.

Sorti (m.s.), sortie (f.s.) sortis (m.pl.), sorties, (f.pl.), *gone out.*

## INDICATIVE MOOD.

### PRESENT.

| Je sors. | I go out. |
|---|---|
| Tu sors. | thou goest out. |
| Il sort. | he goes out. |
| Nous sortons. | we go out. |
| Vous sortez. | you go out. |
| Ils sortent. | they go out. |

### IMPERFECT.

| Je sortais. | I was going out. |
|---|---|
| Tu sortais. | thou wast going out. |
| Il sortait. | he was going out. |
| Nous sortions. | we were going out. |
| Vous sortiez. | you were going out. |
| Ils sortaient. | they were going out. |

### PAST DEFINITE.

| Je sortis. | I went out. |
|---|---|
| Tu sortis. | thou wentest out. |
| Il sortit. | he went out. |
| Nous sortîmes. | we went out. |
| Vous sortîtes. | you went out. |
| Ils sortirent. | they went out. |

### FUTURE.

| Je sortirai. | I shall go out. |
|---|---|
| Tu sortiras. | thou wilt go out. |
| Il sortira. | he will go out. |
| Nous sortirons. | we shall go out. |
| Vous sortirez. | you will go out. |
| Ils sortiront. | they will go out. |

## CONDITIONAL MOOD.

### PRESENT.

| Je sortirais. | I should go out. |
|---|---|
| Tu sortirais. | thou wouldst go out. |
| Il sortirait. | he would go out. |
| Nous sortirions. | we should go out. |
| Vous sortiriez. | you would go out. |
| Ils sortiraient. | they would go out. |

## IMPERATIVE MOOD.

### PRESENT.

| Sors. | Go out (thou). |
|---|---|
| Qu'il sorte. | let him go out. |
| Sortons. | let us go out. |
| Sortez. | go out (you). |
| Qu'ils sortent. | let them go out. |

## SUBJUNCTIVE MOOD.

### PRESENT.

| Que je sorte. | That I may go out. |
|---|---|
| Que tu sortes. | that thou mayest go out. |
| Qu'il sorte. | that he may go out. |
| Que nous sortions. | that we may go out. |
| Que vous sortiez. | that you may go out. |
| Qu'ils sortent. | that they may go out. |

### IMPERFECT.

| Que je sortisse. | That I might go out. |
|---|---|
| Que tu sortisses. | that thou mightest go out. |
| Qu'il sortît. | that he might go out. |
| Que nous sortissions. | that we might go out. |
| Que vous sortissiez. | that you might go out. |
| Qu'ils sortissent. | that they might go out. |

## COMPOUND TENSES.

| Past. Ind. | Je suis sorti, I have gone out, etc. | Cond. past. | Je serais sorti, etc. I should have gone out, etc. |
|---|---|---|---|
| Plup. | J'étais sorti, I had gone out, etc. | Sub. Past. | Que je sois sorti, etc. that I may have gone out, etc. |
| Past. ant. | Je fus sorti, I had gone out, etc. | Sub. plup. | Que je fusse sorti, etc. that I might have gone out, etc. |
| Fut. ant. | Je serai sorti, I shall have gone out, etc. | | |

### CONJUGATE IN THE SAME MANNER:

Sortir, *to go out,* and *Ressortir*, to go out again, are conjugated with *être.*
*Sortir* and *ressortir*, used actively, are of course conjugated with *avoir.*
Ressortir, *to be under the jurisdiction of*, is regular. See *Finir*, page 23.

# VERB *TENIR*, TO HOLD, TO KEEP.

## INFINITIVE MOOD.

| PRESENT. | | PAST. | |
|---|---|---|---|
| Tenir | To hold. | Avoir tenu. | To have held. |
| PARTICIPLE PRESENT. | | COMPOUND OF PARTICIPLE PRESENT. | |
| Tenant | Holding. | Ayant tenu. | Having held. |

PARTICIPLE PAST.

*Tenu* (m.s.), *tenue* (f.s.), *tenus* (m.pl.), *tenues* (f.pl.), *held.*

## INDICATIVE MOOD.

### PRESENT.
| | |
|---|---|
| Je tiens. | I hold. |
| Tu tiens. | thou holdest. |
| Il tient. | he holds |
| Nous tenons. | we hold. |
| Vous tenez. | you hold. |
| Ils tiennent. | they hold. |

### IMPERFECT.
| | |
|---|---|
| Je tenais. | I was holding. |
| Tu tenais. | thou wast holding. |
| Il tenait. | he was holding. |
| Nous tenions. | we were holding. |
| Vous teniez. | you were holding. |
| Ils tenaient. | they were holding. |

### PAST DEFINITE.
| | |
|---|---|
| Je tins. | I held. |
| Tu tins. | thou heldest. |
| Il tint. | he held. |
| Nous tînmes. | we held. |
| Vous tîntes. | you held. |
| Ils tinrent. | they held. |

### FUTURE.
| | |
|---|---|
| Je tiendrai. | I shall hold. |
| Tu tiendras. | thou wilt hold. |
| Il tiendra. | he will hold. |
| Nous tiendrons. | we shall hold. |
| Vous tiendrez. | you will hold. |
| Ils tiendront. | they will hold. |

## CONDITIONAL MOOD.

### PAST.
| | |
|---|---|
| Je tiendrais. | I should hold. |
| Tu tiendrais. | thou wouldst hold. |
| Il tiendrait. | he would hold. |
| Nous tiendrions. | we should hold. |
| Vous tiendriez. | you would hold. |
| Ils tiendraient. | they would hold. |

### PRESENT.
| | |
|---|---|
| Tiens. | Hold (thou). |
| Qu'il tienne. | let him hold. |
| Tenons. | let us hold. |
| Tenez. | hold (you) |
| Qu'ils tiennent. | let them hold. |

## SUBJUNCTIVE MOOD.

### PRESENT.
| | |
|---|---|
| Que je tienne. | That I may hold. |
| Que tu tiennes. | that thou mayest hold. |
| Qu'il tienne. | that he may hold. |
| Que nous tenions. | that we may hold. |
| Que vous teniez. | that you may hold. |
| Qu'ils tiennent. | that they may hold. |

### IMPERFECT.
| | |
|---|---|
| Que je tinsse. | That I might hold. |
| Que tu tinsses. | that thou mightest hold. |
| Qu'il tînt. | that he might hold. |
| Que nous tinssions. | that we might hold. |
| Que vous tinssiez. | that you might hold. |
| Qu'ils tinssent. | that they might hold. |

## COMPOUND TENSES.

| | | | |
|---|---|---|---|
| Past ind. | J'ai tenu, etc. I have held, etc. | Cond. past. | J'aurais tenu, I should have etc. held, etc. |
| Plup. | J'avais tenu, I had held, etc. etc. | Sub. past. | Que j'aie tenu. that I may have etc. held. etc. |
| Past ant. | J'eus tenu, etc. I had held, etc. | | |
| Fut. ant. | J'aurai tenu, I shall have held, etc. etc. | Sub. plup. | Que j'eusse that I might have tenu, etc. held, etc. |

### CONJUGATE LIKE *TENIR*:

| | | | |
|---|---|---|---|
| S'abstenir | To abstain. See p. 76. | Maintenir | To maintain. |
| Appartenir | — belong. | Obtenir | — obtain. |
| Contenir | — contain. | Retenir | — retain. |
| Détenir | — detain, to keep. | Soutenir | — sustain. |
| Entretenir | — maintain, to converse. | | |

N.B.—I. In the above verbs, the *n* is doubled, in the following tenses:—Indicative Present, third person plural; Imperative, third persons; Subjunctive Present, first, second, third person singular, and third person plural; *i.e.*, when the *n* is followed by *e* mute.

II. The verbs conjugated like *Tenir* take *avoir* in their compound tenses.

# VERB *VENIR*, TO COME.

## INFINITIVE MOOD.

| | PRESENT. | | PAST. |
|---|---|---|---|
| Ven*ir*. | *To come.* | Être *venu.* | *To have come.* |
| | PARTICIPLE PRESENT. | | COMP. OF PART. PRESENT |
| *Venant* | *Coming.* | Étant *venu.* | *Having come.* |

PARTICIPLE PAST.
*Venu* (m.s.), *venue* (f.s.), *venus* (m.pl.), *venues* (f.pl.), come.

SIMPLE TENSES.

### INDICATIVE MOOD.
PRESENT.

| Je *viens.* | *I come.* |
|---|---|
| Tu *viens.* | *thou comest.* |
| Il *vient.* | *he comes.* |
| Nous *venons.* | *we come.* |
| Vous *venez.* | *you come.* |
| Ils *viennent.* | *they come.* |

IMPERFECT.

| Je *venais.* | *I was coming.* |
|---|---|
| Tu *venais.* | *thou wast coming.* |
| Il *venait.* | *he was coming.* |
| Nous *venions.* | *we were coming.* |
| Vous *veniez.* | *you were coming.* |
| Ils *venaient.* | *they were coming.* |

PAST DEFINITE.

| Je *vins.* | *I came.* |
|---|---|
| Tu *vins.* | *thou camest.* |
| Il *vint.* | *he came.* |
| Nous *vînmes.* | *we came.* |
| Vous *vîntes.* | *you came.* |
| Ils *vinrent.* | *they came.* |

FUTURE.

| Je *viendrai.* | *I shall come.* |
|---|---|
| Tu *viendras.* | *thou wilt come.* |
| Il *viendra.* | *he will come.* |
| Nous *viendrons.* | *we shall come.* |
| Vous *viendrez.* | *you will come.* |
| Ils *viendront.* | *they will come.* |

### CONDITIONAL MOOD.
PRESENT.

| Je *viendrais.* | *I should come.* |
|---|---|
| Tu *viendrais.* | *thou wouldst come.* |
| Il *viendrait.* | *he would come.* |
| Nous *viendrions.* | *we should come.* |
| Vous *viendriez.* | *you would come.* |
| Ils *viendraient.* | *they would come.* |

### IMPERATIVE MOOD.
PRESENT.

| *Viens.* | *Come (thou).* |
|---|---|
| Qu'il *vienne.* | *let him come.* |
| *Venons.* | *let us come.* |
| *Venez.* | *come (you).* |
| Qu'ils *viennent.* | *let them come.* |

### SUBJUNCTIVE MOOD.
PRESENT.

| Que je *vienne.* | *That I may come.* |
|---|---|
| Que tu *viennes.* | *that thou mayest come.* |
| Qu'il *vienne.* | *that he may come.* |
| Que nous *venions.* | *that we may come.* |
| Que vous *veniez.* | *that you may come.* |
| Qu'ils *viennent.* | *that they may come.* |

IMPERFECT.

| Que je *vinsse.* | *That I might come.* |
|---|---|
| Que tu *vinsses.* | *that thou mightest come.* |
| Qu'il *vînt.* | *that he might come.* |
| Que nous *vinssions.* | *that we might come.* |
| Que vous *vinssiez.* | *that you might come.* |
| Qu'ils *vinssent.* | *that they might come.* |

## COMPOUND TENSES.

| *Past ind.* | Je suis *venu,* etc. | *I have come, etc.* | *Cond. past.* | Je serais *venu,* etc. | *I should have come, etc.* |
|---|---|---|---|---|---|
| *Plup.* | J'étais *venu,* etc. | *I had come, etc.* | | | |
| *Past ant.* | Je fus *venu,* etc. | *I had come, etc.* | *Sub. past.* | Que je sois *venu,* etc. | *That I may have come, etc.* |
| *Fut. ant.* | Je serai *venu,* etc. | *I shall have come, etc.* | *Sub. plup.* | Que je fusse *venu,* etc. | *That I might have come, etc.* |

## CONJUGATE LIKE *VENIR:*

| | | |
|---|---|---|
| Circonvenir | - - - | *To circumvent.* |
| Contrevenir | - - - | *— contravene, transgress.* |
| Convenir à (with *avoir*) | - | *— to please, to suit.* |
| Se Convenir (with *être*) | } | *— please or suit each other, or one another.* |
| Convenir (with *être*) | } | *— agree to do something, to engage oneself, to bind oneself.* |
| Convenir (impersonal) | - | *— be proper, to be seemly.* |
| Devenir | - - - | *— become.* |
| Disconvenir | - - | *— deny, to disown.* |
| Intervenir | - - - | *To intervene, to interfere.* |
| Prévenir | - - - | *— inform, prevent.* |
| Parvenir | - - - | *— reach, to attain.* |
| Provenir de - | - | *— proceed from, arise from.* |
| Redevenir | - - | *— become again.* |
| Se souvenir de | - | *— remember, to recollect.* |
| Revenir | - - - | *— come back.* |
| Se ressouvenir | - | *— remember, to recollect.* |
| Subvenir à - | - | *— relieve.* |
| Survenir | - - } | *— survene, to come or arrive unexpectedly.* |

N.B.—I. *Circonvenir, contrevenir, prévenir,* and *subvenir,* are conjugated with the auxiliary verb *avoir.*
II. *Venir* is conjugated like *tenir;* only *venir* takes *être* in its compound tenses, and *tenir* takes *avoir.*
III. *Venir* and the verbs conjugated like *venir* double the *n* in the same persons as *tenir.*(Page 90, N.B.I.)

AIGUEZE, GARD

NICE, HOTEL NEGRESCO

# VERB *VÊTIR*, TO CLOTHE.

## INFINITIVE MOOD.

| | | | |
|---|---|---|---|
| | PRESENT. | | PAST. |
| Vêt*ir*. | *To clothe.* | Avoir *vêtu*. | *To have clothed.* |
| | PARTICIPLE PRESENT. | | COMP. OF PART. PRESENT. |
| *V êtant*. | *Clothing.* | Ayant *vêtu*. | *Having clothed.* |

PARTICIPLE PAST.

*Vêtu* (m.s.), *vêtue* (f,s.), *vêtus* (m.pl.), *vêtues* (f.pl.), *clothed.*

## SIMPLE TENSES.

### INDICATIVE MOOD.

#### PRESENT.

| | |
|---|---|
| Je *vêts*. | *I clothe.* |
| Tu *vêts*. | *thou clothest.* |
| Il *vêt*. | *he clothes.* |
| Nous *vêtons*. | *we clothe.* |
| Vous *vêtez*. | *you clothe.* |
| Ils *vêtent*. | *they clothe.* |

#### IMPERFECT.

| | |
|---|---|
| Je *vêtais*. | *I was clothing.* |
| Tu *vêtais*. | *thou wast clothing.* |
| Il *vêtait*. | *he was clothing.* |
| Nous *vêtions*. | *we were clothing.* |
| Vous *vêtiez*. | *you were clothing.* |
| Ils *vêtaient*. | *they were clothing.* |

#### PAST DEFINITE.

| | |
|---|---|
| Je vêtis. | *I clothed.* |
| Tu vêtis. | *thou clothedst.* |
| Il vêtit. | *he clothed.* |
| Nous vêtîmes. | *we clothed.* |
| Vous vêtîtes. | *you clothed.* |
| Ils vêtirent. | *they clothed.* |

#### FUTURE.

| | |
|---|---|
| Je vêtirai. | *I shall clothe.* |
| Tu vêtiras. | *thou wilt clothe.* |
| Il vêtira. | *he will clothe.* |
| Nous vêtirons. | *we shall clothe.* |
| Vous vêtirez. | *you will clothe.* |
| Ils vêtiront. | *they will clothe.* |

### CONDITIONAL MOOD.

#### PRESENT.

| | |
|---|---|
| Je vêtirais. | *I should clothe.* |
| Tu vêtirais. | *thou wouldst clothe.* |
| Il vêtirait. | *he would clothe,* |
| Nous vêtirions. | *we should clothe.* |
| Vous vêtiriez. | *you would clothe.* |
| Ils vêtiraient. | *they would clothe.* |

### IMPERATIVE MOOD.

#### PRESENT.

| | |
|---|---|
| *Vêts*. | *Clothe ( thou ).* |
| Qu'il *vête*. | *let him clothe.* |
| *Vêtons*. | *let us clothe.* |
| *Vêtez*. | *clothe (you).* |
| Qu'ils *vêtent*. | *let them clothe.* |

### SUBJUNCTIVE MOOD.

#### PRESENT.

| | |
|---|---|
| Que je *vête*. | *That I may clothe.* |
| Que tu *vêtes*. | *that thou mayest clothe.* |
| Qu'il *vête*. | *that he may clothe.* |
| Que nous *vêtions*. | *that we may clothe.* |
| Que vous *vêtiez*. | *that you may clothe.* |
| Qu'ils *vêtent*. | *that they may clothe.* |

#### IMPERFECT.

| | |
|---|---|
| Que je vêtisse. | *That I might clothe.* |
| Que tu vêtisses. | *that thou mightest clothe.* |
| Qu'il vêtît. | *that he might clothe.* |
| Que nous vêtissions. | *that we might clothe.* |
| Que vous vêtissiez. | *that you might clothe.* |
| Qu'ils vêtissent. | *that they might clothe.* |

## COMPOUND TENSES.

| | | | | | |
|---|---|---|---|---|---|
| Past. ind. | J'ai vêtu, etc. | *I have clothed, etc.* | Cond. past. | J'aurais vêtu, etc. | *I should have clothed, etc.* |
| Plup. | J'avais vêtu, etc. | *I had clothed, etc.* | | | |
| Past ant. | J'eus vêtu, etc. | *I had clothed, etc.* | Sub. past. | Que j'aie vêtu, etc. | *That I may have clothed, etc.* |
| Fut. ant. | J'aurai vêtu, etc. | *I shall have clothed, etc.* | Sub. plup. | Que j'eusse vêtu, etc. | *That I might have clothed, etc.* |

CONJUGATE IN THE SAME MANNER:

| | | |
|---|---|---|
| Dévêtir - - - | *To divest, to strip.* | |
| Se dévêtir . . . | { *— divest one's self,*<br>{ *— undress one's self,* | |
| Revêtir - - - | *To clothe, to invest.* | |
| Se revêtir . - - | *— to dress one's self.* | |

# CHAPTER 7

# Irregular Verbs—Third Conjugation

### VERB *ASSEOIR*, to seat.
### INFINITIVE MOOD.

#### PRESENT.

| First Form. | Second Form. | |
|---|---|---|
| Asseoir. | *Asseoir.* | To seat. |

#### PARTICIPLE PRESENT.

| Asseyant. | *Assoyant.* | Seating. |
|---|---|---|

#### INFINITIVE PAST.

| Avoir assis. | *Avoir assis.* | To have seated. |
|---|---|---|

#### COMP. OF PART. PRESENT.

| Ayant assis. | *Ayant assis.* | Having seated. |
|---|---|---|

#### PARTICIPLE PAST.

Assis (m.s.), assise (f.s.), assis (m.pl.), assises (f.pl.), *seated.*

### INDICATIVE MOOD.
#### PRESENT.

| J'assieds. | *J'assois.* | I seat. |
|---|---|---|
| Tu assieds. | *tu assois.* | thou seatest. |
| Il assied. | *il assoit.* | he seats. |
| Nous asseyons. | *nous assoyons.* | we seat. |
| Vous asseyez. | *vous assoyez.* | you seat. |
| Ils asseyent. | *ils assoient.* | they seat. |

#### IMPERFECT.

| J'asseyais. | *J'assoyais.* | I was seating. |
|---|---|---|
| Tu asseyais. | *tu assoyais.* | thou wast seating. |
| Il asseyait. | *il assoyait.* | he was seating. |
| Nous asseyions. | *nous assoyions.* | we were seating. |
| Vous asseyiez. | *vous assoyiez.* | you were seating. |
| Ils asseyaient. | *ils assoyaient.* | they were seating. |

#### PAST DEFINITE.

| J'assis. | *J'assis.* | I seated. |
|---|---|---|
| Tu assis. | *tu assis.* | thou seatedst. |
| Il assit. | *il assit.* | he seated. |
| Nous assîmes. | *nous assîmes.* | we seated. |
| Vous assîtes. | *vous assîtes.* | you seated. |
| Ils assirent. | *ils assirent.* | they seated. |

#### FUTURE.

| J'assiérai. | *J'assoirai.* | I shall seat. |
|---|---|---|
| Tu assiéras. | *tu assoiras.* | thou wilt seat. |
| Il assiéra. | *il assoira.* | he will seat. |
| Nous assiérons. | *nous assoirons.* | we shall seat. |
| Vous assiérez. | *vous assoirez.* | you will seat. |
| Ils assiéront. | *ils assoiront.* | they will seat. |

N.B.—The Past Definite, the Imperfect of the Subjunctive, and the Past Participle, are similar in both forms.

## VERB *ASSEOIR*, TO SEAT. (*Continued.*)

---

### CONDITIONAL MOOD.

#### PRESENT.

| First Form. | Second Form. | |
|---|---|---|
| J'assiérais. | *J'assoirais.* | I should seat. |
| Tu assiérais. | *tu assoirais.* | thou wouldst seat. |
| Il assiérait. | *il assoirait.* | he would seat. |
| Nous assiérions. | *nous assoirions.* | we should seat. |
| Vous assiériez. | *vous assoiriez.* | you would seat. |
| Ils assiéraient. | *ils assoiraient.* | they would seat. |

### IMPERATIVE MOOD.

#### PRESENT.

| | | |
|---|---|---|
| Assieds. | *Assois.* | Seat (thou). |
| Qu'il asseye. | *qu'il assoie.* | let him seat. |
| Asseyons. | *assoyons.* | let us seat. |
| Asseyez. | *assoyez.* | seat (you). |
| Qu'ils asseyent. | *qu'ils assoient.* | let them seat. |

### SUBJUNCTIVE MOOD.

#### PRESENT.

| | | |
|---|---|---|
| Que j'asseye. | *Que j'assoie.* | That I may seat. |
| Que tu asseyes. | *que tu assoies.* | that thou mayest seat. |
| Qu'il asseye. | *qu'il assoie.* | that he may seat. |
| Que nous asseyions. | *que nous assoyions.* | that we may seat. |
| Que vous asseyiez. | *que vous assoyiez.* | that you may seat. |
| Qu'ils asseyent. | *qu'ils assoient.* | that they may seat. |

#### IMPERFECT.

| | | |
|---|---|---|
| Que j'assisse. | *Que j'assisse.* | That I might seat. |
| Que tu assisses. | *que tu assisses.* | that thou mightest seat. |
| Qu'il assît. | *qu'il assît.* | that he might seat. |
| Que nous assissions. | *que nous assissions.* | that we might seat. |
| Que vous assissiez. | *que vous assissiez.* | that you might seat. |
| Qu'ils assissent. | *qu'ils assissent.* | that they might seat. |

### COMPOUND TENSES.

| | | |
|---|---|---|
| *Past ind.* | J'ai assis, etc. | *I have seated, etc.* |
| *Plup.* | J'avais assis, etc. | *I had seated, etc.* |
| *Past ant.* | J'eus assis, etc. | *I had seated, etc.* |
| *Fut. ant.* | J'aurai assis, etc. | *I shall have seated, etc.* |
| *Cond. past.* | J'aurais assis, etc. | *I should have seated, etc.* |
| *Sub. past.* | Que j'aie assis, etc. | *that I may have seated, etc.* |
| *Sub. plup.* | Que j'eusse assis, etc. | *that I might have seated, etc.* |

---

N.B.—I. The verb *Asseoir* has two forms for its conjugation ; the first form is generally used.
II. The *Future* and the *Conditional* have another form:
Future : J'asseyerai, tu asseyeras, il asseyera, nous asseyerons, vous asseyerez, ils asseyeront, *I shall seat, etc.*
Conditional : J'asseyerais, tu asseyerais, il asseyerait, nous asseyerions, vous asseyeriez, ils asseyeraient, *I should seat, etc.*

### CONJUGATE IN THE SAME MANNER:

Rasseoir . . . . { *To reseat, to place again.* / *— calm, to settle.*

# VERB *S'ASSEOIR*, TO SIT DOWN.

## INFINITIVE MOOD.

*First Form.*     *Second Form.*

### PRESENT.

| S'asseoir. | *S'assesoir.* | To sit down. |

### PARTICIPLE PRESENT.

| S'asseyant. | *S'assoyant.* | Sitting down. |

### INFINITIVE PAST.

| S'être assis. | *S'être assis.* | To have sat down. |

### COMPOUND OF PARTICIPLE PRESENT.

| S'étant assis. | *S'étant assis.* | Having sat down. |

### PARTICIPLE PAST.

Assis (m.s.), assise (f.s.), assis (m.pl.), assises (f.pl.), *sat down.*

---

## SIMPLE TENSES.

---

## INDICATIVE MOOD.

### PRESENT.

| | | |
|---|---|---|
| Je m'assieds. | *Je m'assois.* | I sit down. |
| Tu t'assieds. | *tu t'assois.* | thou sittest down. |
| Il s'assied. | *il s'assoit.* | he sits down. |
| Nous nous asseyons. | *nous nous assoyons.* | we sit down. |
| Vous vous asseyez. | *vous vous assoyez.* | you sit down. |
| Ils s'asseyent. | *ils s'assoient.* | they sit down. |

### IMPERFECT.

| | | |
|---|---|---|
| Je m'asseyais. | *Je m'assoyais.* | I was sitting down. |
| Tu t'asseyais. | *tu t'assoyais.* | thou wast sitting down. |
| Il s'asseyait. | *il s'assoyait.* | he was sitting down. |
| Nous nous asseyions. | *nous nous assoyions.* | we were sitting down. |
| Vous vous asseyiez. | *vous vous assoyiez.* | you were sitting down. |
| Ils s'asseyaient. | *ils s'assoyaient.* | they were sitting down. |

### PAST DEFINITE.*

| | | |
|---|---|---|
| Je m'assis. | *Je m'assis.* | I sat down. |
| Tu t'assis. | *tu t'assis.* | thou sattest down. |
| Il s'assit. | *il s'assit.* | he sat down. |
| Nous nous assîmes. | *nous nous assîmes.* | we sat down. |
| Vous vous assîtes. | *vous vous assîtes.* | you sat down. |
| Ils s'assirent. | *ils s'assirent.* | they sat down. |

### FUTURE.

| | | |
|---|---|---|
| Je m'assiérai. | *Je m'assoirai.* | I shall sit down. |
| Tu t'assiéras. | *tu t'assoiras.* | thou wilt sit down. |
| Il s'assiéra. | *il s'assoira.* | he will sit down. |
| Nous nous assiérons. | *nous nous assoirons.* | we shall sit down. |
| Vous vous assiérez. | *vous vous assoirez.* | you will sit down. |
| Ils s'assiéront. | *ils s'assoiront.* | they will sit down. |

*See N.B., page 93.

## VERB *S'ASSEOIR*, to sit down (*Continued*).

### CONDITIONAL MOOD.

#### PRESENT.

| | | |
|---|---|---|
| Je m'assiérais. | *Je m'assoirais.* | I should sit down. |
| Tu t'assiérais. | *tu t'assoirais.* | thou wouldst sit down. |
| Il s'assiérait. | *il s'assoirait.* | he would sit down. |
| Nous nous assiérions. | *nous nous assoirions.* | we should sit down. |
| Vous vous assiériez. | *vous vous assoiriez.* | you would sit down. |
| Ils s'assiéraient. | *ils s'assoiraient.* | they would sit down. |

### IMPERATIVE MOOD.

#### PRESENT.

| | | |
|---|---|---|
| Assieds-toi. | *Assois-toi.* | Sit down (thou). |
| Qu'il s'asseye. | *qu'il s'assoie.* | let him sit down. |
| Asseyons-nous. | *assoyons-nous.* | let us sit down. |
| Asseyez-vous. | *assoyez-vous.* | sit down (you). |
| Qu'ils s'asseyent. | *qu'ils s'assoient.* | let them sit down. |

### SUBJUNCTIVE MOOD.

#### PRESENT.

| | | |
|---|---|---|
| Que je m'asseye. | *Que je m'assoie.* | That I may sit down. |
| Que tu t'asseyes. | *que tu t'assoies.* | that thou mayest sit down. |
| Qu'il s'asseye. | *qu'il s'assoie.* | that he may sit down. |
| Que nous nous asseyions. | *que nous nous assoyons.* | that we may sit down. |
| Que vous vous asseyiez. | *que vous vous assoyez.* | that you may sit down. |
| Qu'ils s'asseyent. | *qu'ils s'assoient.* | that they may sit down. |

#### IMPERFECT.

| | | |
|---|---|---|
| Que je m'assisse. | *Que je m'assisse.* | That I might sit down. |
| Que tu t'assisses. | *que tu t'assisses.* | that thou mightest sit down. |
| Qu'il s'assît. | *qu'il s'assît.* | that he might sit down. |
| Que nous nous assissions. | *que nous nous assissions.* | that we might sit down. |
| Que vous vous assissiez. | *que vous vous assissiez.* | that you might sit down. |
| Qu'il s'assissent. | *qu'ils s'assissent.* | that they might sit down. |

---

### COMPOUND TENSES.

| | | |
|---|---|---|
| *Past ind.* | Je me suis assis, etc. | *I have sat down, etc.* |
| *Past ant.* | Je me fus assis, etc. | *I had sat down, etc.* |
| *Pluperfect.* | Je m'étais assis, etc. | *I had sat down, etc.* |
| *Future.* | Je me serai assis, etc. | *I shall have sat down, etc.* |
| *Cond past.* | Je me serais assis, etc. | *I should have sat down, etc.* |
| *Sub. pres.* | Que je me sois assis, etc. | *That I may have sat down, etc.* |
| *— plup.* | Que je me fusse assis, etc. | *That I might have sat down, etc.* |

---

N.B.—I. The Verb *Asseoir* is principally used as a Pronominal verb; pronominally employed it has also two forms, the first form is generally used.

II. The *Future* and *Conditional* have another form:

*Future*: Je m'asseyerai, tu t'asseyeras, il s'asseyera, nous nous asseyerons, vous vous asseyerez, ils s'asseyeront, *I shall sit down, etc.*

*Conditional*: Je m'asseyerais, tu t'asseyerais, il s'asseyerait, nous nous asseyerions, vous vous asseyeriez, ils s'asseyeraient, *I should sit down, etc.*

### CONJUGATE IN THE SAME MANNER:

Se Rasseoir · · · { *To sit down again.* / *— calm.* }

# VERB *MOUVOIR*, TO MOVE.

## INFINITIVE MOOD.

| | PRESENT. | | PAST. |
|---|---|---|---|
| Mouv*oir*. | *To move.* | Avoir *mû*. | *To have moved.* |
| | PARTICIPLE PRESENT. | | COMP. OF PARTICIPLE PRESENT. |
| Mouvant. | *Moving.* | Ayant *mû*. | *Having moved.* |

PARTICIPLE PAST.

*Mû* (m.s.), *mue* (f.s.), *mus* (m.pl.), *mues* (f.pl.), *moved.*

## SIMPLE TENSES.

### INDICATIVE MOOD.
#### PRESENT.
| | |
|---|---|
| Je *meus*. | *I move.* |
| Tu *meus*. | *thou movest.* |
| Il *meut*. | *he moves.* |
| Nous mouvons. | *we move.* |
| Vous mouvez. | *you move.* |
| Ils meuvent. | *they move.* |

#### IMPERFECT.
| | |
|---|---|
| Je mouvais. | *I was moving.* |
| Tu mouvais. | *thou wast moving.* |
| Il mouvait. | *he was moving.* |
| Nous mouvions. | *we were moving.* |
| Vous mouviez. | *you were moving.* |
| Ils mouvaient. | *they were moving.* |

#### PAST DEFINITE.
| | |
|---|---|
| Je *mus*. | *I moved.* |
| Tu *mus*. | *thou movedst.* |
| Il *mut*. | *he moved.* |
| Nous *mûmes*. | *we moved.* |
| Vous *mûtes*. | *you moved.* |
| Ils *murent*. | *they moved.* |

#### FUTURE.
| | |
|---|---|
| Je mouvrai. | *I shall move.* |
| Tu mouvras. | *thou wilt move.* |
| Il mouvra. | *he will move.* |
| Nous mouvrons. | *we shall move.* |
| Vous mouvrez. | *you will move.* |
| Ils mouvront. | *they will move.* |

### CONDITIONAL MOOD.
#### PRESENT.
| | |
|---|---|
| Je mouvrais. | *I should move.* |
| Tu mouvrais. | *thou wouldst move.* |
| Il mouvrait. | *he would move.* |
| Nous mouvrions. | *we should move.* |
| Vous mouvriez. | *you would move.* |
| Ils mouvraient. | *they would move.* |

### IMPERATIVE MOOD.
#### PRESENT.
| | |
|---|---|
| *Meus*. | *Move (thou).* |
| Qu'il *meuve*. | *let him move.* |
| Mouvons. | *let us move.* |
| Mouvez. | *move (you).* |
| Qu'ils *meuvent*. | *let them move.* |

### SUBJUNCTIVE MOOD.
#### PRESENT.
| | |
|---|---|
| Que je *meuve*. | *That I may move.* |
| Que tu *meuves*. | *that thou mayest move.* |
| Qu'il *meuve*. | *that he may move.* |
| Que nous mouvions. | *that we may move.* |
| Que vous mouviez. | *that you may move.* |
| Qu'ils *meuvent*. | *that they may move.* |

#### IMPERFECT.
| | |
|---|---|
| Que je *musse*. | *That I might move.* |
| Que tu *musses*. | *that thou mightest move.* |
| Qu'il *mût*. | *that he might move.* |
| Que nous *mussions*. | *that we might move.* |
| Que vous *mussiez*. | *that you might move.* |
| Qu'ils *mussent*. | *that they might move.* |

## COMPOUND TENSES.

| | | | | | |
|---|---|---|---|---|---|
| *Past def.* | J'ai *mû*, etc. | *I have moved, etc.* | *Cond. past.* | J'aurais *mû*, etc. | *I should have moved, etc.* |
| *Plup.* | J'avais *mû*, etc. | *I had moved, etc.* | | | |
| *Past ant.* | J'eus *mû*, etc. | *I had moved, etc.* | *Sub. past.* | Que j'aie *mû*, etc. | *That I may have moved, etc.* |
| *Fut. ant.* | J'aurai *mû*, etc. | *I shall have moved, etc.* | *Sub. plup.* | Que j'eusse *mû*, etc. | *That I might have moved, etc.* |

---

CONJUGATE LIKE *MOUVOIR*:

Émouvoir - - - *To stir up, to move.* | Promouvoir - *To promote* (see the Defective Verbs).
N.B.—The Past Participle of *Mouvoir* takes a circumflex accent only in the m.s., *mû*.

# VERB *POURVOIR*, TO PROVIDE.

## INFINITIVE MOOD.

| | | | |
|---|---|---|---|
| **PRESENT.** | | **PAST.** | |
| Pourv*oir*. | *To provide.* | Avoir pourvu. | *To have provided.* |
| **PARTICIPLE PRESENT.** | | **COMP. OF PART. PRESENT.** | |
| *Pourvoyant*. | *Providing.* | Ayant pourvu. | *Having provided.* |

**PARTICIPLE PAST.**

*Pourvu* (m.s.), *pourvue* (f.s.), *pourvus* (m.pl.), *pourvues* (f.pl.), *provided.*

**SIMPLE TENSES.**

### INDICATIVE MOOD.
**PRESENT.**

| | |
|---|---|
| Je pourvois. | *I provide.* |
| Tu pourvois. | *thou providest.* |
| Il pourvoit. | *he provides.* |
| Nous *pourvoyons*. | *we provide.* |
| Vous *pourvoyez*. | *you provide.* |
| Ils pourvoient. | *they provide.* |

**IMPERFECT.**

| | |
|---|---|
| Je *pourvoyais*. | *I was providing.* |
| Tu *pourvoyais*. | *thou wast providing.* |
| Il *pourvoyait*. | *he was providing.* |
| Nous *pourvoyions*. | *we were providing.* |
| Vous *pourvoyiez*. | *you were providing.* |
| Ils *pourvoyaient*. | *they were providing.* |

**PAST DEFINITE.**

| | |
|---|---|
| Je pourvus. | *I provided.* |
| Tu pourvus. | *thou providedst.* |
| Il pourvut. | *he provided.* |
| Nous pourvûmes. | *we provided.* |
| Vous pourvûtes. | *you provided.* |
| Ils pourvurent. | *they provided.* |

**FUTURE.**

| | |
|---|---|
| Je pourvoirai. | *I shall provide.* |
| Tu pourvoiras. | *thou wilt provide.* |
| Il pourvoira. | *he will provide.* |
| Nous pourvoirons. | *we shall provide.* |
| Vous pourvoirez. | *you will provide.* |
| Ils pourvoiront. | *they will provide.* |

### CONDITIONAL MOOD.
**PRESENT.**

| | |
|---|---|
| Je pourvoirais. | *I should provide.* |
| Tu pourvoirais. | *thou wouldst provide.* |
| Il pourvoirait. | *he would provide.* |
| Nous pourvoirions. | *we should provide.* |
| Vous pourvoiriez. | *you would provide.* |
| Ils pourvoiraient. | *they would provide.* |

### IMPERATIVE MOOD.
**PRESENT.**

| | |
|---|---|
| Pourvois. | *Provide (thou).* |
| Qu'il *pourvoie*. | *let him provide.* |
| Pourvoyons. | *let us provide.* |
| Pourvoyez. | *provide (you).* |
| Qu'ils *pourvoient*. | *let them provide.* |

### SUBJUNCTIVE MOOD.
**PRESENT.**

| | |
|---|---|
| Que je *pourvoie*. | *That I may* |
| Que tu *pourvoies*. | *that thou mayest* |
| Qu'il *pourvoie*. | *that he may* |
| Que nous *pourvoyions*. | *that we may* |
| Que vous *pourvoyiez*. | *that you may* |
| Qu'ils *pourvoient*. | *that they may* |

*provide.*

**IMPERFECT.**

| | |
|---|---|
| Que je pourvusse. | *That I might* |
| Que tu pourvusses. | *that thou mightest* |
| Qu'il pourvût. | *that he might* |
| Que nous pourvussions. | *that we might* |
| Que vous pourvussiez. | *that you might* |
| Qu'ils pourvussent. | *that they might* |

*provide.*

---

**COMPOUND TENSES.**

| | | | |
|---|---|---|---|
| *Past ind.* | J'ai pourvu, etc. | *I have provided, etc.* | |
| *Plup.* | J'avais pourvu, etc. | *I had provided, etc.* | |
| *Past ant.* | J'eus pourvu, etc. | *I had provided, etc.* | |
| *Fut. ant.* | J'aurai pourvu, etc. | *I shall have provided, etc.* | |
| *Cond. past.* | J'aurais pourvu, etc. | *I should have provided, etc.* | |
| *Sub. past.* | Que j'aie pourvu, etc. | *That I may have provided, etc.* | |
| *Sub. plup.* | Que j'eusse pourvu, etc. | *That I might have provided, etc.* | |

---

CONJUGATE AS *POURVOIR*:

Dépourvoir - - - - - *To divest, to strip.*

**N.B.—I.** The French Academy says—*Dépourvoir* is mostly used in the Past Definite, and the Infinitive.
**II.** In Littré's Dict. *Dépourvoir* is conjugated like *Pourvoir*.

# VERB *POUVOIR*, CAN, TO BE ABLE.

## INFINITIVE MOOD.

| | | | | |
|---|---|---|---|---|
| **PRESENT.** | | | **PAST.** | |
| Pou*voir*. | *To be able.* | | Avoir *pu*. | *To have been able.* |
| **PARTICIPLE PRESENT.** | | | **COMP. OF PART. PRESENT.** | |
| Pouvant. | *Being able.* | | Ayant *pu*. | *Having been able.* |

**PARTICIPLE PAST.**
*Pu* (invariable), *been able.*

## SIMPLE TENSES.

### INDICATIVE MOOD.

#### PRESENT.

| | |
|---|---|
| Je *puis* or je *peux*. | *I am able.* |
| Tu *peux*. | *thou art able.* |
| Il *peut*. | *he is able.* |
| Nous pouvons. | *we are able.* |
| Vous pouvez. | *you are able.* |
| Ils peuvent. | *they are able.* |

#### IMPERFECT.

| | |
|---|---|
| Je pouvais. | *I was able.* |
| Tu pouvais. | *thou wast able.* |
| Il pouvait. | *he was able.* |
| Nous pouvions. | *we were able.* |
| Vous pouviez. | *you were able.* |
| Ils pouvaient. | *they were able.* |

#### PAST DEFINITE.

| | |
|---|---|
| Je *pus*. | *I was able.* |
| Tu *pus*. | *thou wast able.* |
| Il *put*. | *he was able.* |
| Nous *pûmes*. | *we were able.* |
| Vous *pûtes*. | *you were able.* |
| Ils *purent*. | *they were able.* |

#### FUTURE.

| | |
|---|---|
| Je *pourrai*. | *I shall be able.* |
| Tu *pourras*. | *thou wilt be able.* |
| Il *pourra*. | *he will be able.* |
| Nous *pourrons*. | *we shall be able.* |
| Vous *pourrez*. | *you will be able.* |
| Ils *pourront*. | *they will be able.* |

### CONDITIONAL MOOD.

#### PRESENT.

| | |
|---|---|
| Je *pourrais*. | *I should be able.* |
| Tu *pourrais*. | *thou wouldst be able.* |
| Il *pourrait*. | *he would be able.* |
| Nous *pourrions*. | *we should be able.* |
| Vous *pourriez*. | *you would be able.* |
| Ils *pourraient*. | *they would be able.* |

*(No Imperative.)*

### SUBJUNCTIVE MOOD.

#### PRESENT.

| | |
|---|---|
| Que je *puisse*. | *That I may be able.* |
| Que tu *puisses*. | *that thou mayest be able.* |
| Qu'il *puisse*. | *that he may be able.* |
| Que nous *puissions*. | *that we may be able.* |
| Que vous *puissiez*. | *that you may be able.* |
| Qu'ils *puissent*. | *that they may be able.* |

#### IMPERFECT.

| | |
|---|---|
| Que je *pusse*. | *That I might be able.* |
| Que tu *pusses*. | *that thou mightest be able.* |
| Qu'il *pût*. | *that he might be able.* |
| Que nous *pussions*. | *that we might be able.* |
| Que vous *pussiez*. | *that you might be able.* |
| Qu'ils *pussent*. | *that they might be able.* |

## COMPOUND TENSES.

| | | | | |
|---|---|---|---|---|
| Past ind. | J'ai *pu*, etc. | *I have been able, etc.* | Cond. past. | J'aurais *pu*, etc. | *I should have been able, etc.* |
| Plup. | J'avais *pu*, etc. | *I had been able, etc.* | | | |
| Past ant. | J'eus *pu*, etc. | *I had been able, etc.* | Sub. past. | Que j'aie *pu*, etc. | *That I may have been able, etc.* |
| Fut. ant. | J'aurai *pu*, etc. | *I shall have been able, etc.* | Sub. plup. | Que j'eusse *pu*, etc. | *That I might have been able, etc.* |

N.B.—I. The first person of the Present of the Indicative has two forms : *je puis* and *je peux*. *Je puis* is much more used than *je peux*, and ought to be preferred. Interrogatively we say : *Puis-je*, and not *Peux-je*.

II. With the Verb *Pouvoir* we may suppress the negations *pas* and *point*. I cannot, *je ne puis*. We cannot go out, *Nous ne pouvons sortir*. However, there is a difference between : *Je ne puis* and *Je ne puis pas* or *point*.

*Je ne puis* implies difficulties.

*Je ne puis pas* or *point* expresses impossibility.

III. In the *Future* and the *Conditional* only one *r* is sounded.

# VERB *SAVOIR*, TO KNOW.

## INFINITIVE MOOD.

| PRESENT. | | PAST. | |
|---|---|---|---|
| Savoir. | To know. | Avoir su. | To have known. |

| PARTICIPLE PRESENT. | | COMP. OF PART. PRESENT. | |
|---|---|---|---|
| Sachant. | Knowing. | Ayant su. | Having known. |

PARTICIPLE PAST.

*Su* (m.s.), *sue* (f.s.), *sus* (m.pl.), *sues*, (f.pl.), **known.**

### SIMPLE TENSES.

## INDICATIVE MOOD.

### PRESENT.

| Je sais. | I know. |
|---|---|
| Tu sais. | thou knowest. |
| Il sait. | he knows. |
| Nous savons. | we know. |
| Vous savez. | you know. |
| Ils savent. | they know. |

### IMPERFECT.

| Je savais. | I was knowing. |
|---|---|
| Tu savais. | thou wast knowing. |
| Il savait. | he was knowing. |
| Nous savions. | we were knowing. |
| Vous saviez. | you were knowing. |
| Ils savaient. | they were knowing. |

### PAST DEFINITE.

| Je sus. | I knew. |
|---|---|
| Tu sus. | thou knewest. |
| Il sut. | he knew. |
| Nous sûmes. | we knew. |
| Vous sûtes. | you knew. |
| Ils surent. | they knew. |

### FUTURE.

| Je saurai. | I shall know. |
|---|---|
| Tu sauras. | thou wilt know. |
| Il saura. | he will know. |
| Nous saurons. | we shall know. |
| Vous saurez. | you will know. |
| Ils sauront. | they will know. |

## CONDITIONAL MOOD.

### PRESENT.

| Je saurais. | I should know. |
|---|---|
| Tu saurais. | thou wouldst know. |
| Il saurait. | he would know. |
| Nous saurions. | we should know. |
| Vous sauriez. | you would know. |
| Ils sauraient. | they would know. |

## IMPERATIVE MOOD.

### PRESENT.

| Sache. | Know (thou). |
|---|---|
| Qu'il sache. | let him know. |
| Sachons. | let us know. |
| Sachez. | know (you). |
| Qu'ils sachent. | let them know. |

## SUBJUNCTIVE MOOD.

### PRESENT.

| Que je sache. | That I may know. |
|---|---|
| Que tu saches. | that thou mayest know. |
| Qu'il sache. | that he may know. |
| Que nous sachions. | that we may know. |
| Que vous sachiez. | that you may know. |
| Qu'ils sachent. | that they may know. |

### IMPERFECT.

| Que je susse. | That I might know. |
|---|---|
| Que tu susses. | that thou mightest know. |
| Qu'il sût. | that he might know. |
| Que nous sussions. | that we might know. |
| Que vous sussiez. | that you might know. |
| Qu'ils sussent. | that they might know. |

### COMPOUND TENSES.

| Past ind. | J'ai su, etc. | I have known, etc. | Cond. past. | J'aurais su, etc. | I should have known, etc. |
|---|---|---|---|---|---|
| Past ant. | J'eus su, etc. | I had known, etc. | Sub. past. | Que j'aie su, etc. | that I may have known, etc. |
| Plup. | J'avais su, etc. | I had known, etc. | Sub. plup. | Que j'eusse su, etc. | that I might have known, etc. |
| Fut. ant. | J'aurai su, etc. | I shall have known, etc. | | | |

## DIFFERENCE BETWEEN SAVOIR AND CONNAÎTRE.

*Savoir*, to know, means mental knowledge, information, science.

Ex : He knows French, *Il sait le français.* I know that she will write, *Je sais qu'elle écrira.* Do you know your lesson? *Savez-vous votre leçon?*

*Connaître*, to know, means to be acquainted with, to know by sight.

Ex. : I know your father, *Je connais votre père.* Do you know his house? *Connaissez-vous sa maison?*

# VERB *SURSEOIR*, to delay, to suspend (Law term.)

## INFINITIVE MOOD.

| PRESENT. | | PAST. | |
|---|---|---|---|
| Surs*eoir*. | *To delay.* | Avoir *sursis*. | *To have delayed.* |
| PARTICIPLE PRESENT. | | COMP. OF PART. PRESENT. | |
| Sursoyant. | *Delaying.* | Ayant *sursis*. | *Having delayed.* |

PARTICIPLE PAST.

*Sursis* (m.s.), *sursise* (f.s.), *sursis* (m.pl.), *sursises* (f.pl.), *delayed.*

### SIMPLE TENSES.

## INDICATIVE MOOD.

### PRESENT.

| | |
|---|---|
| Je sursois. | *I delay.* |
| Tu sursois. | *thou delayest.* |
| Il sursoit. | *he delays.* |
| Nous *sursoyons*. | *we delay.* |
| Vous *sursoyez*. | *you delay.* |
| Ils sursoient. | *they delay.* |

### IMPERFECT.

| | |
|---|---|
| Je *sursoyais*. | *I was delaying.* |
| Tu *sursoyais*. | *thou wast delaying.* |
| Il *sursoyait*. | *he was delaying.* |
| Nous *sursoyions*. | *we were delaying.* |
| Vous *sursoyiez*. | *you were delaying.* |
| Ils *sursoyaient*. | *they were delaying.* |

### PAST DEFINITE.

| | |
|---|---|
| Je *sursis*. | *I delayed.* |
| Tu *sursis*. | *thou delayedst.* |
| Il *sursit*. | *he delayed.* |
| Nous *sursîmes*. | *we delayed.* |
| Vous *sursîtes*. | *you delayed.* |
| Ils *sursirent*. | *they delayed.* |

### FUTURE.

| | |
|---|---|
| Je surseoirai. | *I shall delay.* |
| Tu surseoiras. | *thou wilt delay.* |
| Il surseoira. | *he will delay.* |
| Nous surseoirons. | *we shall delay.* |
| Vous surseoirez. | *you will delay.* |
| Ils surseoiront. | *they will delay.* |

## CONDITIONAL MOOD.

### PRESENT.

| | |
|---|---|
| Je surseoirais. | *I should delay.* |
| Tu surseoirais. | *thou wouldst delay.* |
| Il surseoirait. | *he would delay.* |
| Nous surseoirions. | *we should delay.* |
| Vous surseoiriez. | *you would delay.* |
| Ils surseoiraient. | *they would delay.* |

## IMPERATIVE MOOD.
### PRESENT.

| | |
|---|---|
| Sursois. | *Delay (thou).* |
| Qu'il *sursoie*. | *let him delay.* |
| Sursoyons. | *let us delay.* |
| Sursoyez. | *delay (you).* |
| Qu'ils *sursoient*. | *let them delay.* |

## SUBJUNCTIVE MOOD.
### PRESENT.

| | |
|---|---|
| Que je *sursoie*. | *That I may delay.* |
| Que tu *sursoies*. | *that thou mayest delay.* |
| Qu'il *sursoie*. | *that he may delay.* |
| Que nous *sursoyions*. | *that we may delay.* |
| Que vous *sursoyiez*. | *that you may delay.* |
| Qu'ils *sursoient*. | *that they may delay.* |

### IMPERFECT.

| | |
|---|---|
| Que je *sursisse*. | *That I might delay.* |
| Que tu *sursisses*. | *that thou mightest delay.* |
| Qu'il *sursît*. | *that he might delay.* |
| Que nous *sursissions*. | *that we might delay.* |
| Que vous *sursissiez*. | *that you might delay.* |
| Qu'ils *sursissent*. | *that they might delay.* |

### COMPOUND TENSES.

| | | | | | |
|---|---|---|---|---|---|
| *Past ind.* | J'ai *sursis*, etc. | *I have delayed, etc.* | *Cond. past.* | J'aurais *sursis*, etc. | *I should have delayed, etc.* |
| *Past ant.* | J'eus *sursis*, etc. | *I had delayed, etc.* | | | |
| *Plup.* | J'avais *sursis*, etc. | *I had delayed, etc.* | *Sub. past.* | Que j'aie *sursis*, etc. | *that I may have delayed, etc.* |
| *Fut. ant.* | J'aurai *sursis*, etc. | *I shall have delayed, etc.* | *Sub. plup.* | Que j'eusse *sursis*, etc. | *that I might have delayed, etc.* |

N.B.—Laveaux, Littré in their Dict., conjugate *Surseoir* as above, but the Academy gives neither the Imperative nor the Present of the Subjunctive of that verb.

# VERB *VALOIR*, TO BE WORTH.

## INFINITIVE MOOD.

| | PRESENT. | | PAST. |
|---|---|---|---|
| Val*oir*. | *To be worth.* | Avoir valu. | *To have been worth.* |
| | PARTICIPLE PRESENT. | | COMPOUND OF PARTICIPLE PRESENT. |
| Valant. | *Being worth.* | Ayant valu. | *Having been worth.* |

PARTICIPLE PAST.

Valu (m.s.), value (f.s.), valus (m.pl.), values (f.pl.), *been worth.*

### SIMPLE TENSES.

## INDICATIVE MOOD.

### PRESENT.

| | |
|---|---|
| Je *vaux.* | *I am worth.* |
| Tu *vaux.* | *thou art worth.* |
| Il *vaut.* | *he is worth.* |
| Nous valons. | *we are worth.* |
| Vous valez. | *you are worth.* |
| Ils valent. | *they are worth.* |

### IMPERFECT.

| | |
|---|---|
| Je valais. | *I was worth.* |
| Tu valais. | *thou wast worth.* |
| Il valait. | *he was worth.* |
| Nous valions. | *we were worth.* |
| Vous valiez. | *you were worth.* |
| Ils valaient. | *they were worth.* |

### PAST DEFINITE.

| | |
|---|---|
| Je valus. | *I was worth.* |
| Tu valus. | *thou wast worth.* |
| Il valut. | *he was worth.* |
| Nous valûmes. | *we were worth.* |
| Vous valûtes. | *you were worth.* |
| Ils valurent. | *they were worth.* |

### FUTURE.

| | |
|---|---|
| Je *vaudrai.* | *I shall be worth.* |
| Tu *vaudras.* | *thou wilt be worth.* |
| Il *vaudra.* | *he will be worth.* |
| Nous *vaudrons.* | *we shall be worth.* |
| Vous *vaudrez.* | *you will be worth.* |
| Ils *vaudront.* | *they will be worth.* |

## CONDITIONAL MOOD.

### PRESENT.

| | |
|---|---|
| Je *vaudrais.* | *I should be worth.* |
| Tu *vaudrais.* | *thou wouldst be worth.* |
| Il *vaudrait.* | *he would be worth.* |
| Nous *vaudrions.* | *we should be worth.* |
| Vous *vaudriez.* | *you would be worth.* |
| Ils *vaudraient.* | *they would be worth.* |

## IMPERATIVE MOOD.

### PRESENT.

| | |
|---|---|
| *Vaux.* | *Be worth (thou).* |
| Qu'il *vaille.* | *let him be worth.* |
| Valons. | *let us be worth.* |
| Valez. | *be worth (you).* |
| Qu'ils *vaillent.* | *let them be worth.* |

## SUBJUNCTIVE MOOD.

### PRESENT.

| | | |
|---|---|---|
| Que je *vaille.* | *That I may be* | |
| Que tu *vailles.* | *that thou mayest be* | |
| Qu'il *vaille.* | *that he may be* | *worth.* |
| Que nous *valions.* | *that we may be* | |
| Que vous *valiez.* | *that you may be* | |
| Qu'ils *vaillent.* | *that they may be* | |

### IMPERFECT.

| | | |
|---|---|---|
| Que je valusse. | *That I might* | |
| Que tu valusses. | *that thou mightest* | |
| Qu'il valût. | *that he might* | *be worth.* |
| Que nous valussions. | *that we might* | |
| Que vous valussiez. | *that you might* | |
| Qu'ils valussent. | *that they might* | |

### COMPOUND TENSES.

| | | |
|---|---|---|
| *Past Ind.* | J'ai valu, etc. | *I have been worth, etc.* |
| *Plup.* | J'avais valu, etc. | *I had been worth, etc.* |
| *Past Ant.* | J'eus valu, etc. | *I had been worth, etc.* |
| *Fut. Ant.* | J'aurai valu, etc. | *I shall have been worth, etc.* |
| *Cond. Past.* | J'aurais valu, etc. | *I should have been worth, etc.* |
| *Sub. Past.* | Que j'aie valu, etc. | *That I may have been worth, etc.* |
| *Sub. Plup.* | Que j'eusse valu, etc. | *That I might have been worth, etc.* |

CONJUGATE LIKE *VALOIR*:

Revaloir - - *To return (like for like).* | Équivaloir - - - *To be equivalent.*

N.B.—Prévaloir, *to prevail,* is conjugated like *valoir,* except in the Subjunctive Present, it makes, *Que je prévale, que tu prévales, qu'il prévale, que nous prévalions, que vous prévaliez, qu'ils prévalent.*

# VERB *VOIR*, TO SEE.

## INFINITIVE MOOD.

| PRESENT. | | PAST. | |
|---|---|---|---|
| Voir. | To see. | Avoir vu. | To have seen. |
| PARTICIPLE PRESENT. | | COMP. OF PART. PRESENT. | |
| Voyant. | Seeing. | Ayant vu. | Having seen. |

PARTICIPLE PAST.

*Vu* (m.s.), *vue* (f.s.), *vus*, (m.pl.). *vues* (f.pl.) *seen*.

---

SIMPLE TENSES.

### INDICATIVE MOOD.

**PRESENT.**

| Je vois. | I see. |
|---|---|
| Tu vois. | thou seest. |
| Il voit. | he sees. |
| Nous voyons. | we see. |
| Vous voyez. | you see. |
| Ils voient. | they see. |

**IMPERFECT.**

| Je voyais. | I was seeing. |
|---|---|
| Tu voyais. | thou wast seeing. |
| Il voyait. | he was seeing. |
| Nous voyions. | we were seeing. |
| Vous voyiez. | you were seeing. |
| Ils voyaient. | they were seeing. |

**PAST DEFINITE.**

| Je vis. | I saw. |
|---|---|
| Tu vis. | thou sawest. |
| Il vit. | he saw. |
| Nous vîmes. | we saw. |
| Vous vîtes. | you saw. |
| Ils virent. | they saw. |

**FUTURE.**

| Je verrai. | I shall see. |
|---|---|
| Tu verras. | thou wilt see. |
| Il verra. | he will see. |
| Nous verrons. | we shall see. |
| Vous verrez. | you will see. |
| Ils verront. | they will see. |

### CONDITIONAL MOOD.

**PAST.**

| Je verrais. | I should see. |
|---|---|
| Tu verrais. | thou wouldst see. |
| Il verrait. | he would see. |
| Nous verrions. | we should see. |
| Vous verriez. | you would see. |
| Ils verraient. | they would see. |

### IMPERATIVE MOOD.

**PRESENT.**

| Vois - | - See (thou). |
|---|---|
| Qu'il voie | - let him see. |
| Voyons - | - let us see. |
| Voyez - | - see (you). |
| Qu'ils voient - | let them see. |

### SUBJUNCTIVE MOOD.

**PRESENT.**

| Que je voie. | That I may see. |
|---|---|
| Que tu voies. | that thou mayest see. |
| Qu'il voie. | that he may see. |
| Que nous voyions. | that we may see. |
| Que vous voyiez. | that you may see. |
| Qu'ils voient. | that they may see. |

**IMPERFECT.**

| Que je visse. | That I might see. |
|---|---|
| Que tu visses. | that thou mightest see. |
| Qu'il vît. | that he might see. |
| Que nous vissions. | that we might see. |
| Que vous vissiez. | that you might see. |
| Qu'ils vissent. | that they might see. |

---

COMPOUND TENSES.

| Past. ind. | J'ai vu, etc. | I have seen, etc. | Cond. past | J'aurais vu, etc. | I should have seen, etc. |
|---|---|---|---|---|---|
| Plup. | J'avais vu, etc. | I had seen, etc. | Sub. past | Que j'aie vu, etc. | that I may have seen, etc. |
| Past ant. | J'eus vu, etc. | I had seen, etc. | Sub. plup. | Que j'eusse vu, etc. | that I might have seen, etc. |
| Fut. ant. | J'aurai vu, etc. | I shall have seen, etc. | | | |

---

CONJUGATE IN THE SAME MANNER:

Entrevoir - - - *To have a glimpse of.* | Revoir - - - - *To see again.*

N.B.—Prévoir, *to foresee*, is conjugated like *Voir*, except in the Future and the Conditional:—
*Future :* Je prévoirai, tu prévoiras, il prévoira, nous prévoirons, vous prévoirez, ils prévoiront.
*Conditional :* Je prévoirais, tu prévoirais, il prévoirait, nous prévoirions, vous prévoiriez, ils prévoiraient.

# VERB *VOULOIR*, TO WILL, TO BE WILLING, TO WISH.

## INFINITIVE MOOD.

| | PRESENT. | | PAST. |
|---|---|---|---|
| Vouloir. | *To wish.* | Avoir voulu. | *To have wished.* |
| | PARTICIPLE PRESENT. | | COMPOUND OF PARTICIPLE PRESENT. |
| Voulant. | *Wishing.* | Ayant voulu. | *Having wished.* |

PARTICIPLE PAST.

Voulu (m.s.), voulue (f.s.), voulus (m.pl.), voulues (f.pl.), *wished.*

## SIMPLE TENSES.

### INDICATIVE MOOD.

PRESENT.

| | |
|---|---|
| Je *veux.* | *I wish.* |
| Tu *veux.* | *thou wishest.* |
| Il *veut.* | *he wishes.* |
| Nous voulons. | *we wish.* |
| Vous voulez. | *you wish.* |
| Ils veulent. | *they wish.* |

IMPERFECT.

| | |
|---|---|
| Je voulais. | *I was wishing.* |
| Tu voulais. | *thou wast wishing.* |
| Il voulait. | *he was wishing.* |
| Nous voulions. | *we were wishing.* |
| Vous vouliez. | *you were wishing.* |
| Ils voulaient. | *they were wishing.* |

PAST DEFINITE.

| | |
|---|---|
| Je voulus. | *I wished.* |
| Tu voulus. | *thou wishedst.* |
| Il voulut. | *he wished.* |
| Nous voulûmes. | *we wished.* |
| Vous voulûtes. | *you wished.* |
| Ils voulurent. | *they wished.* |

FUTURE.

| | |
|---|---|
| Je voudrai. | *I shall wish.* |
| Tu voudras. | *thou wilt wish.* |
| Il voudra. | *he will wish.* |
| Nous voudrons. | *we shall wish.* |
| Vous voudrez. | *you will wish.* |
| Ils voudront. | *they will wish.* |

### CONDITIONAL MOOD.

PRESENT.

| | |
|---|---|
| Je *voudrais.* | *I should wish.* |
| Tu *voudrais.* | *thou wouldst wish.* |
| Il *voudrait.* | *he would wish.* |
| Nous *voudrions.* | *we should wish.* |
| Vous *voudries.* | *you would wish.* |
| Ils *voudraient.* | *they would wish.* |

### IMPERATIVE MOOD.

PRESENT.

| | | |
|---|---|---|
| *Veuille* veux - - - | *Wish (thou).* |
| *Veuillons* voulons - - | *let us wish.* |
| *Veuillez* voulez - - | *wish (you).* |

### SUBJUNCTIVE MOOD.

PRESENT.

| | |
|---|---|
| Que je *veuille.* | *That I may wish.* |
| Que tu *veuilles.* | *that thou mayest wish.* |
| Qu'il *veuille.* | *that he may wish.* |
| Que nous voulions. | *that we may wish.* |
| Que vous vouliez. | *that you may wish.* |
| Qu'ils *veuillent.* | *that they may wish.* |

IMPERFECT.

| | |
|---|---|
| Que je voulusse. | *That I might wish.* |
| Que tu voulusses. | *that thou mightest wish.* |
| Qu'il voulût. | *that he might wish.* |
| Que nous voulussions. | *that we might wish.* |
| Que vous voulussiez. | *that you might wish.* |
| Qu'ils voulussent. | *that they might wish.* |

## COMPOUND TENSES.

| | | | | | |
|---|---|---|---|---|---|
| *Past Ind.* | J'ai voulu, etc. | *I have wished, etc.* | *Cond. past.* | J'aurais voulu, etc. | *I should have wished, etc,* |
| *Plup.* | J'avais voulu, etc. | *I had wished, etc.* | | | |
| *Past ant.* | J'eus voulu, etc. | *I had wished, etc.* | *Subj. Past.* | Que j'aie voulu, etc. | *That I may have wished, etc.* |
| *Fut. ant.* | J'aurai voulu, etc. | *I shall have wished, etc.* | *Subj. Plup.* | Que j'eusse voulu, etc. | *That I might have wished, etc.* |

N.B.—I. The Imperative *Veux, voulons, voulez,* is very seldom used, and only to excite in a person a strong determined will (Academy). Ex.: *Veux et tu réussiras. Voulez et l'on vous obéira. Voulons et il cédera.*

II. The Imperative is *veuille, veuillons, veuillez.* (Littré's Dict.) The second person plural *Veuillez* is the one generally used, and means : *Be so good as, be so kind as.*

Ex. : *Veuillez me prêter votre livre.* Be so good as to lend me your book.

III. According to "Littré's Dict." it would be more correct to write in the Present of the Subjunctive : *Que nous veuillions, que vous veuilliez,* than : Que nous *voulions,* que vous *vouliez.*

IV. REVOULOIR, *To wish anew, to will again,* is conjugated like *Vouloir.*

# CHAPTER 8

# Irregular Verbs—Fourth Conjugation

## VERB *ABSOUDRE*, TO ABSOLVE.

### INFINITIVE MOOD.

| PRESENT. | | PAST. | |
|---|---|---|---|
| Absoud*re*. | *To absolve.* | Avoir *absous*. | *To have absolved.* |
| **PARTICIPLE PRESENT.** | | **COMPOUND OF PARTICIPLE PRESENT.** | |
| *Absolvant.* | *Absolving.* | Ayant *absous*. | *Having absolved.* |

#### PARTICIPLE PAST.

*Absous* (m.s.), *absoute* (f.s.), *absous* (m.pl.), *absoutes* (f.pl.), *absolved.*

### SIMPLE TENSES.

#### INDICATIVE MOOD.

##### PRESENT.

| | |
|---|---|
| J'*absous.* | *I absolve.* |
| Tu *absous.* | *thou absolvest.* |
| Il *absout.* | *he absolves.* |
| Nous *absolvons.* | *we absolve.* |
| Vous *absolvez.* | *you absolve.* |
| Ils *absolvent.* | *they absolve.* |

##### IMPERFECT.

| | |
|---|---|
| J'*absolvais.* | *I was absolving.* |
| Tu *absolvais.* | *thou wast absolving.* |
| Il *absolvait.* | *he was absolving.* |
| Nous *absolvions.* | *we were absolving.* |
| Vous *absolviez.* | *you were absolving.* |
| Ils *absolvaient.* | *they were absolving.* |

*(No Past Definite.)*

##### FUTURE.

| | |
|---|---|
| J'*absoudrai.* | *I shall absolve.* |
| Tu *absoudras.* | *thou wilt absolve.* |
| Il *absoudra.* | *he will absolve.* |
| Nous *absoudrons.* | *we shall absolve.* |
| Vous *absoudrez.* | *you will absolve.* |
| Ils *absoudront.* | *they will absolve.* |

#### CONDITIONAL MOOD.

##### PRESENT.

| | |
|---|---|
| J'*absoudrais.* | *I should absolve.* |
| Tu *absoudrais.* | *thou wouldst absolve.* |
| Il *absoudrait.* | *he would absolve.* |
| Nous *absoudrions.* | *we should absolve.* |
| Vous *absoudriez.* | *you would absolve.* |
| Ils *absoudraient.* | *they would absolve.* |

#### IMPERATIVE MOOD.

##### PRESENT.

| | | |
|---|---|---|
| *Absous* | - - | *Absolve (thou).* |
| Qu'il *absolve* | | *let him absolve.* |
| *Absolvons* - | - | *let us absolve.* |
| *Absolvez* | - - | *absolve (you).* |
| Qu'ils *absolvent* - | | *let them absolve.* |

#### SUBJUNCTIVE MOOD.

##### PRESENT.

| | |
|---|---|
| Que j'*absolve.* | *That I may absolve.* |
| Que tu *absolves.* | *that thou mayest absolve.* |
| Qu'il *absolve.* | *that he may absolve.* |
| Que nous *absolvions.* | *that we may absolve.* |
| Que vous *absolviez.* | *that you may absolve.* |
| Qu'ils *absolvent.* | *that they may absolve.* |

*(No Imperfect of the Subjunctive)*

### COMPOUND TENSES.

| | | | | |
|---|---|---|---|---|
| *Past ind.* | J'ai *absous*, etc. *I have absolved, etc.* | | *Cond. past.* | J'aurais *absous*, *I should have ab-*  etc. *solved, etc.* |
| *Plup.* | J'avais *absous*, *I had absolved, etc.*  etc. | | *Sub. past.* | Que j'aie *absous*, etc. *That I may have absolved, etc.* |
| *Past ant.* | J'eus *absous*, *I had absolved, etc.*  etc. | | *Sub. plup.* | Que j'eusse *absous*, etc. *That I might have absolved, etc.* |
| *Fut. ant.* | J'aurai *absous*. *I shall have absolved, etc.*  etc. | | | |

---

CONJUGATE IN THE SAME MANNER:

Dissoudre - - - - - - *To dissolve.*

N.B.—I. *Dissoudre*, like *absoudre*, has neither Past definite nor Imperfect of the Subjunctive.

II. The irregular persons have been printed in italics in all the verbs of the fourth conjugation.

# VERB *BOIRE*, TO DRINK.

## INFINITIVE MOOD.

| | PRESENT. | | PAST. |
|---|---|---|---|
| Boire. | *To drink.* | Avoir *bu.* | *To have drunk.* |
| | PARTICIPLE PRESENT. | | COMPOUND OF PARTICIPLE PRESENT. |
| *Buvant.* | *Drinking.* | Ayant *bu.* | *Having drunk.* |

PARTICIPLE PAST.

*Bu* (m.s.), *bue* (f.s.), *bus* (m.pl.), *bues* (f.pl.), *drunk.*

## SIMPLE TENSES.

### INDICATIVE MOOD.

#### PRESENT.

| Je bois. | *I drink.* |
|---|---|
| Tu bois. | *thou drinkest.* |
| Il boit. | *he drinks.* |
| Nous *buvons.* | *we drink.* |
| Vous *buvez.* | *you drink.* |
| Ils *boivent.* | *they drink.* |

#### IMPERFECT.

| Je *buvais.* | *I was drinking.* |
|---|---|
| Tu *buvais.* | *thou wast drinking.* |
| Il *buvait.* | *he was drinking.* |
| Nous *buvions.* | *we were drinking.* |
| Vous *buviez.* | *you were drinking.* |
| Ils *buvaient.* | *they were drinking.* |

#### PAST DEFINITE.

| Je *bus.* | *I drank.* |
|---|---|
| Tu *bus.* | *thou drankest.* |
| Il *but.* | *he drank.* |
| Nous *bûmes.* | *we drank.* |
| Vous *bûtes.* | *you drank.* |
| Ils *burent.* | *they drank.* |

#### FUTURE.

| Je boirai. | *I shall drink.* |
|---|---|
| Tu boiras. | *thou wilt drink.* |
| Il boira. | *he will drink.* |
| Nous boirons. | *we shall drink.* |
| Vous boirez. | *you will drink.* |
| Ils boiront. | *they will drink.* |

### CONDITIONAL MOOD.

#### PRESENT.

| Je boirais. | *I should drink.* |
|---|---|
| Tu boirais. | *thou wouldst drink.* |
| Il boirait. | *he would drink.* |
| Nous boirions. | *we should drink.* |
| Vous boiriez. | *you would drink.* |
| Ils boiraient. | *they would drink.* |

### IMPERATIVE MOOD.

#### PRESENT.

| Bois - - - | *Drink (thou).* |
|---|---|
| Qu'il *boive* - - | *let him drink.* |
| *Buvons* - - | *let us drink.* |
| *Buvez* - - | *drink (you).* |
| Qu'ils *boivent* - | *let them drink.* |

### SUBJUNCTIVE MOOD.

#### PRESENT.

| Que je *boive.* | *That I may drink.* |
|---|---|
| Que tu *boives.* | *that thou mayest drink.* |
| Qu'il *boive.* | *that he may drink.* |
| Que nous *buvions.* | *that we may drink.* |
| Que vous *buviez.* | *that you may drink.* |
| Qu'ils *boivent.* | *that they may drink.* |

#### IMPERFECT.

| Que je *busse.* | *That I might drink.* |
|---|---|
| Que tu *busses.* | *that thou mightest drink.* |
| Qu'il *bût.* | *that he may drink.* |
| Que nous *bussions.* | *that we might drink.* |
| Que vous *bussiez.* | *that you might drink.* |
| Qu'ils *bussent.* | *that they might drink.* |

## COMPOUND TENSES.

| | | | | | |
|---|---|---|---|---|---|
| Past ind. | J'ai *bu,* etc. | *I have drunk, etc.* | Cond. past. | J'aurais *bu,* etc. | *I should have drunk, etc.* |
| Plup. | J'avais *bu,* etc. | *I had drunk, etc.* | | | |
| Past ant. | J'eus *bu,* etc. | *I had drunk, etc.* | Sub. past. | Que j'aie *bu,* etc. | *That I may have drunk, etc.* |
| Fut. ant. | J'aurai *bu,* etc. | *I shall have drunk, etc.* | Sub. plup. | Que j'eusse *bu,* etc. | *That I might have drunk, etc.* |

CONJUGATE IN THE SAME MANNER:

| Reboire | - - - - | *To drink again.* |
|---|---|---|
| Emboire | - - - - | *— imbibe, to coat* (with oil or wax). |

# VERB *CONCLURE*, TO CONCLUDE.

## INFINITIVE MOOD.

| PRESENT. | | PAST. | |
|---|---|---|---|
| Conclu*re*. | *To conclude.* | Avoir *conclu.* | *To have concluded.* |

| PARTICIPLE PRESENT. | | COMP. OF PART. PRESENT. | |
|---|---|---|---|
| Concluant. | *Concluding.* | Ayant *conclu.* | *Having concluded.* |

#### PARTICIPLE PAST.

*Conclu* (m.s.), *conclue* (f.s.), *conclus*, (m.pl.), *conclues*, (f.pl.), *concluded.*

### SIMPLE TENSES.

## INDICATIVE MOOD
### PRESENT.

| | |
|---|---|
| Je conclus. | *I conclude.* |
| Tu conclus. | *thou concludest.* |
| Il conclut. | *he concludes.* |
| Nous concluons. | *we conclude.* |
| Vous concluez. | *you conclude.* |
| Ils concluent. | *they conclude.* |

#### IMPERFECT.

| | |
|---|---|
| Je concluais. | *I was concluding.* |
| Tu concluais. | *thou wast concluding.* |
| Il concluait. | *he was concluding.* |
| Nous concluions. | *we were concluding.* |
| Vous concluiez. | *you were concluding.* |
| Ils concluaient. | *they were concluding.* |

#### PAST DEFINITE.

| | |
|---|---|
| Je *conclus.* | *I concluded.* |
| Tu *conclus.* | *thou concludedst.* |
| Il *conclut.* | *he concluded.* |
| Nous *conclûmes.* | *we concluded.* |
| Vous *conclûtes.* | *you concluded.* |
| Ils *conclurent.* | *they concluded.* |

#### FUTURE.

| | |
|---|---|
| Je conclurai. | *I shall conclude.* |
| Tu concluras. | *thou wilt conclude.* |
| Il conclura. | *he will conclude.* |
| Nous conclurons. | *we shall conclude.* |
| Vous conclurez. | *you will conclude.* |
| Ils concluront. | *they will conclude.* |

## CONDITIONAL MOOD.
### PRESENT.

| | |
|---|---|
| Je conclurais. | *I should conclude.* |
| Tu conclurais. | *thou wouldst conclude.* |
| Il conclurait. | *he would conclude.* |
| Nous conclurions. | *we should conclude.* |
| Vous concluriez. | *you would conclude.* |
| Ils concluraient. | *they would conclude.* |

## IMPERATIVE MOOD.
### PRESENT.

| | | |
|---|---|---|
| Conclus | - | *Conclude (thou).* |
| Qu'il conclue | - | *let him conclude.* |
| Concluons | - | *let us conclude.* |
| Concluez | - | *conclude (you).* |
| Qu'ils concluent | - | *let them conclude.* |

## SUBJUNCTIVE MOOD.
### PRESENT.

| | |
|---|---|
| Que je conclue. | *That I may* |
| Que tu conclues. | *that thou mayest* |
| Qu'il conclue. | *that he may* |
| Que nous concluions. | *that we may* |
| Que vous concluiez. | *that you may* |
| Qu'ils concluent. | *that they may* |

*conclude.*

#### IMPERFECT.

| | |
|---|---|
| Que je *conclusse.* | *That I might* |
| Que tu *conclusses.* | *that thou mightest* |
| Qu'il *conclût.* | *that he might* |
| Que nous *conclussions.* | *that we might* |
| Que vous *conclussiez.* | *that you might* |
| Qu'ils *conclussent.* | *that they might* |

*conclude.*

### COMPOUND TENSES.

| | | | | | |
|---|---|---|---|---|---|
| *Past. ind.* | J'ai *conclu,* etc. | *I have concluded,* etc. | *Cond. past.* | J'aurais *conclu,* etc. | *I should have concluded, etc.* |
| *Plup.* | J'avais *conclu,* etc. | *I had concluded,* etc. | *Sub. past.* | Que j'aie *conclu,* etc. | *that I may have concluded, etc.* |
| *Past. ant.* | J'eus *conclu,* etc. | *I had concluded,* etc. | *Sub. plup.* | Que j'eusse *conclu,* etc. | *that I might have concluded, etc.* |
| *Fut. ant.* | J'aurai *conclu,* etc. | *I shall have concluded, etc.* | | | |

CONJUGATE IN THE SAME MANNER :
Exclure - - - *To exclude.*
Inclure - - - *— include.*

N.B.—*Inclure* is conjugated as *conclure* except in the Past participle, which is : *Inclus* m.s, *Incluse* f.s., *Inclus* m.p. *Incluses* f.p. included.

PLEYBEN CALVARY

QUIMPER, ST. CORENTIN CATHEDRAL

# VERB *CONDUIRE*, to conduct, to lead.

## INFINITIVE MOOD.

| PRESENT. | | PAST. | |
|---|---|---|---|
| Conduire. | To conduct. | Avoir *conduit*. | To have conducted. |
| **PARTICIPLE PRESENT.** | | **COMPOUND OF PARTICIPLE PRESENT.** | |
| Conduisant. | Conducting. | Ayant *conduit* | Having conducted. |

**PARTICIPLE PAST.**
*Conduit* (m.s.), *conduite* (f.s.), *conduits* (m.pl.), *conduites* (f.pl.), conducted.

## SIMPLE TENSES.

### INDICATIVE MOOD.

**PRESENT.**

| Je conduis. | I conduct. |
|---|---|
| Tu conduis. | thou conductest. |
| Il conduit. | he conducts. |
| Nous *conduisons*. | we conduct. |
| Vous *conduisez*, | you conduct. |
| Ils *conduisent*. | they conduct. |

**IMPERFECT.**

| Je *conduisais*. | I was conducting. |
|---|---|
| Tu *conduisais*. | thou wast conducting. |
| Il *conduisait*. | he was conducting. |
| Nous *conduisions*. | we were conducting. |
| Vous *conduisiez*. | you were conducting. |
| Ils *conduisaient*. | they were conducting. |

**PAST DEFINITE.**

| Je *conduisis*. | I conducted. |
|---|---|
| Tu *conduisis*. | thou conductedst. |
| Il *conduisit*. | he conducted. |
| Nous *conduisîmes*. | we conducted. |
| Vous *conduisîtes*. | you conducted. |
| Ils *conduisirent*. | they conducted. |

**FUTURE.**

| Je conduirai. | I shall conduct. |
|---|---|
| Tu couduiras. | thou wilt conduct. |
| Il conduira. | he will conduct. |
| Nous conduirons. | we shall conduct. |
| Vous conduirez. | you will conduct. |
| Ils conduiront. | they will conduct. |

### CONDITIONAL MOOD.

**PRESENT.**

| Je conduirais. | I should conduct. |
|---|---|
| Tu conduirais. | thou wouldst conduct. |
| Il conduirait. | he would conduct. |
| Nous conduirions. | we should conduct. |
| Vous conduiriez. | you would conduct. |
| Ils conduiraient. | they would conduct. |

### IMPERATIVE MOOD.

**PRESENT.**

| Conduis. | Conduct (thou). |
|---|---|
| Qu'il *conduise*. | let him conduct. |
| Conduisons. | let us conduct. |
| Conduisez. | conduct (you). |
| Qu'ils *conduisent*. | let them conduct. |

### SUBJUNCTIVE MOOD.

**PRESENT.**

| Que je *conduise*. | That I may |
|---|---|
| Que tu *conduises*. | that thou mayest |
| Qu'il *conduise*. | that he may |
| Que nous *conduisions*. | that we may |
| Que vous *conduisiez*. | that you may |
| Qu'ils *conduisent*. | that they may |

(conduct.)

**IMPERFECT.**

| Que je *conduisisse*. | That I might |
|---|---|
| Que tu *conduisisses*. | that thou mightest |
| Qu'il *conduisît*. | that he might |
| Que nous *conduisissions*. | that we might |
| Que vous *conduisissiez*. | that you might |
| Qu'ils *conduisissent*. | that they might |

(conduct.)

## COMPOUND TENSES.

| *Past. ind.* | J'ai *conduit*, etc. | I have conducted, etc. |
|---|---|---|
| *Plup.* | J'avais *conduit*, etc. | I had conducted, etc. |
| *Past. ant.* | J'eus *conduit*, etc. | I had conducted, etc. |
| *Fut. ant.* | J'aurai *conduit*, etc. | I shall have conducted, etc. |

| *Cond. past.* | J'aurais *conduit*, etc. | I should have conducted, etc. |
|---|---|---|
| *Sub. past.* | Que j'aie *conduit*, etc. | that I may have conducted. |
| *Sub. plup.* | Que j'eusse *conduit*, etc. | that I might have conducted, etc. |

### CONJUGATE IN THE SAME MANNER.

| | | |
|---|---|---|
| Construire - | To construct. | |
| Cuire - - | — cook, to bake. | |
| Déduire - | — deduct. | |
| Déconstruire | — unbuild. | |
| Détruire - | — destroy. | |
| Éconduire - } | — show out. — refuse, to deny. | |
| Enduire - | — do over, to plaster. | |
| Induire - | — lead, to induce. | |

Instruire - To instruct.
Nuire - { —prejudice, to hurt. Its participle *nui* is invariable.
Introduire. To lead in, to show in, to bring in, to introduce. When referring to persons, *to introduce*, corresponds to the French verb *présenter*.

| Produire | - To produce. |
|---|---|
| Recuire | - — cook again. |
| Reconstruire | —rebuild. |
| Reconduire | —reconduct, to take back. |
| Réduire | - — reduce. |
| Reproduire | — reproduce. |
| Séduire | — seduce. |
| Traduire | - — translate. |

# VERB *CONFIRE*, TO PICKLE, TO PRESERVE.

## INFINITIVE MOOD.

| PRESENT. | | PAST. | |
|---|---|---|---|
| Confi*re*. | *To pickle.* | Avoir *confit.* | *To have pickled.* |
| PARTICIPLE PRESENT. | | COMP. OF PART PRESENT. | |
| Confi*sant.* | *Pickling.* | Ayant *confit.* | *Having pickled.* |

PARTICIPLE PAST.

*Confit* (m.s.), *confite* (f.s.), *confits* (m.pl.), *confites* (f.pl.), *pickled.*

## SIMPLE TENSES.

### INDICATIVE MOOD.

PRESENT.

| Je confis. | *I pickle.* |
|---|---|
| Tu confis. | *thou picklest.* |
| Il confit. | *he pickles.* |
| Nous *confisons.* | *we pickle.* |
| Vous *confisez.* | *you pickle.* |
| Ils *confisent.* | *they pickle.* |

IMPERFECT.

| Je *confisais.* | *I was pickling.* |
|---|---|
| Tu *confisais.* | *thou wast pickling.* |
| Il *confisait.* | *he was pickling.* |
| Nous *confisions.* | *we were pickling.* |
| Vous *confisiez.* | *you were pickling.* |
| Ils *confisaient.* | *they were pickling.* |

PAST DEFINITE.

| Je confis. | *I pickled.* |
|---|---|
| Tu confis. | *thou pickledst.* |
| Il confit. | *he pickled.* |
| Nons confîmes. | *we pickled.* |
| Vous confîtes. | *you pickled.* |
| Ils confirent. | *they pickled.* |

FUTURE.

| Je confirai. | *I shall pickle.* |
|---|---|
| Tu confiras. | *thou wilt pickle.* |
| Il confira. | *he will pickle.* |
| Nous confirons. | *we shall pickle.* |
| Vous confirez. | *you will pickle.* |
| Ils confiront. | *they will pickle.* |

### CONDITIONAL MOOD.

PRESENT.

| Je confirais. | *I should pickle.* |
|---|---|
| Tu confirais. | *thou wouldst pickle.* |
| Il confirait. | *he would pickle.* |
| Nous confirions. | *we should pickle.* |
| Vous confiriez. | *you would pickle.* |
| Ils confiraient. | *they would pickle.* |

### IMPERATIVE MOOD.

PRESENT.

| Confis - - - - | *Pickle (thou).* |
|---|---|
| Qu'il *confise* - - | *let him pickle.* |
| Confisons - - - | *let us pickle.* |
| Confisez - - - | *pickle (you).* |
| Qu'ils *confisent* - | *let them pickle.* |

### SUBJUNCTIVE MOOD.

PRESENT.

| Que je *confise.* | *That I may pickle.* |
|---|---|
| Que tu *confises.* | *that thou mayest pickle.* |
| Qu'il *confise.* | *that he may pickle.* |
| Que nous *confisions.* | *that we may pickle.* |
| Que vous *confisiez.* | *that you may pickle.* |
| Qu'ils *confisent.* | *that they may pickle.* |

IMPERFECT.

| Que je confisse. | *That I might pickle.* |
|---|---|
| Que tu confisses. | *that thou mightest pickle.* |
| Qu'il confît. | *that he might pickle.* |
| Que nous confissions. | *that we might pickle.* |
| Que vous confissiez. | *that you might pickle.* |
| Qu'ils confissent. | *that they might pickle.* |

## COMPOUND TENSES.

| Past ind. | J'ai *confit*, etc. | *I have pickled, etc.* | Cond.past | J'aurais *confit*, etc. | *I should have pickled, etc.* |
|---|---|---|---|---|---|
| Plup. | J'avais *confit*, etc. | *I had pickled, etc.* | Sub. past | Que j'aie con*fit*, etc. | *That I may have pickled, etc.* |
| Past ant. | J'eus *confit*, etc. | *I had pickled, etc.* | Sub. plup. | Que j'eusse con*fit*, etc. | *That I might have pickled, etc.* |
| Fut. ant. | J'aurai *confit*, etc. | *I shall have pickled, etc.* | | | |

CONJUGATE IN THE SAME MANNER :

| Suffire - - - - | *To suffice, to be sufficient.* |
|---|---|
| Circoncire - - - - | *— circumcise.* |
| Déconfire - - - - | *— discomfit, to defeat.* |

N.B.—The past participle *suffire* is : *suffi* (invariable); and that of *circoncire* is : *circoncis* (variable).

110

# VERB *CONNAÎTRE*, TO KNOW.

## INFINITIVE MOOD.

| PRESENT. | | PAST. | |
|---|---|---|---|
| Connaître. | *To know.* | Avoir *connu.* | *To have known.* |
| **PARTICIPLE PRESENT.** | | **COMP. OF PART. PRESENT.** | |
| *Connaissant.* | *Knowing.* | Ayant *connu.* | *Having known.* |

### PARTICIPLE PAST.

*Connu* (m.s.), *connue* (f.s.), *connus* (m.pl.), *connues* (f.pl.), *known.*

## SIMPLE TENSES.

### INDICATIVE MOOD.

#### PRESENT.
| | |
|---|---|
| Je *connais* | *I know.* |
| Tu *connais.* | *thou knowest.* |
| Il *connaît.* | *he knows.* |
| Nous *connaissons.* | *we know.* |
| Vous *connaissez.* | *you know.* |
| Ils *connaissent.* | *they know.* |

#### IMPERFECT.
| | |
|---|---|
| Je *connaissais.* | *I was knowing.* |
| Tu *connaissais.* | *thou wast knowing.* |
| Il *connaissait.* | *he was knowing.* |
| Nous *connaissions.* | *we were knowing.* |
| Vous *connaissiez.* | *you were knowing.* |
| Ils *connaissaient.* | *they were knowing.* |

#### PAST DEFINITE,
| | |
|---|---|
| Je *connus.* | *I knew.* |
| Tu *connus.* | *thou knewest.* |
| Il *connut.* | *he knew.* |
| Nous *connûmes.* | *we knew.* |
| Vous *connûtes.* | *you knew.* |
| Ils *connurent.* | *they knew.* |

#### FUTURE.
| | |
|---|---|
| Je connaîtrai. | *I shall know,* |
| Tu connaîtras. | *thou wilt know.* |
| Il connaîtra. | *he will know.* |
| Nous connaîtrons. | *we shall know.* |
| Vous connaîtrez. | *you will know.* |
| Ils connaîtront. | *they will know.* |

### CONDITIONAL MOOD.

#### PRESENT.
| | |
|---|---|
| Je connaîtrais, | *I should know.* |
| Tu connaîtrais. | *thou wouldst know.* |
| Il connaîtrait. | *he would know.* |
| Nous connaîtrions. | *we should know.* |
| Vous connaîtriez. | *you would know.* |
| Ils connaîtraient. | *they would know.* |

### IMPERATIVE MOOD.

#### PRESENT.
| | |
|---|---|
| Connais - - - | *Know (thou).* |
| Qu'il *connaisse* - | *let him know.* |
| *Connaissons* - - | *let us know.* |
| *Connaissez* - - - | *know (you).* |
| Qu'ils *connaissent* | *let them know.* |

### SUBJUNCTIVE MOOD.

#### PRESENT.
| | |
|---|---|
| Que je *connaisse.* | *That I may know.* |
| Que tu *connaisses.* | *that thou mayest know.* |
| Qu'il *connaisse.* | *that he may know.* |
| Que nous *connaissions.* | *that we may know.* |
| Que vous *connaissiez.* | *that you may know.* |
| Qu'ils *connaissent.* | *that they may know.* |

#### IMPERFECT.
| | |
|---|---|
| Que je *connusse.* | *That I might know.* |
| Que tu *connusses.* | *that thou mightest know.* |
| Qu'il *connût.* | *that he might know.* |
| Que nous *connussions.* | *that we might know.* |
| Que vous *connussiez.* | *that you might know.* |
| Qu'ils *connussent.* | *that they might know.* |

## COMPOUND TENSES.

| | | | | | |
|---|---|---|---|---|---|
| *Past ind.* | J'ai *connu,* etc. | *I have known, etc.* | *Cond. past* | J'aurais *connu,* etc. | *I should have known, etc.* |
| *Plup.* | J'avais *connu,* etc. | *I had known, etc.* | *Sub. past* | Que j'aie *connu,* etc. | *That I may have known, etc.* |
| *Past ant.* | J'eus *connu,* etc. | *I had known, etc.* | *Sub. plup.* | Que j'eusse *connu,* etc. | *That I might have known, etc.* |
| *Fut. ant.* | J'aurai *connu,* etc. | *I shall have known, etc.* | | | |

## CONJUGATE LIKE *CONNAÎTRE:*

| | | | |
|---|---|---|---|
| Apparaître | - - *To appear.* | Paraître - - | *To appear, to look* |
| Comparaître | - - *— appear (before a court).* | Reconnaître - | { *— recognise, to reconnoiter, to know again.* |
| Disparaître | - - *— disappear.* | | |
| Méconnaître | - - *— not to know.* | Reparaître - | *— appear again.* |

N.B.—I. *Apparaître* is conjugated with *avoir* when it expresses an action, and with *être* when a state.
 II. The *i* of *connaître,* and verbs conjugated as *connaître,* preserves the circumflex accent when followed by *t* only.
 III. For the difference between *connaître* and *savoir,* see page 100.
 IV. Se *connaître à or* en—*To be a judge of*—(a connoisseur).

# VERB *COUDRE*, to sew.

## INFINITIVE MOOD.

| PRESENT. | | PAST. | |
|---|---|---|---|
| Coud*re*. | *To sew.* | Avoir *cousu*. | *To have sewed.* |
| **PARTICIPLE PRESENT.** | | **COMPOUND OF PARTICIPLE PRESENT.** | |
| *Cousant*. | *Sewing.* | Ayant *cousu*. | *Having sewed.* |

**PARTICIPLE PAST.**

*Cousu* (m.s.), *cousue* (f.s.), *cousus* (m.pl.), *cousues* (f.pl.), *sewed.*

## SIMPLE TENSES.

### INDICATIVE MOOD.

#### PRESENT.

| | |
|---|---|
| Je couds. | *I sew.* |
| Tu couds. | *thou sewest.* |
| Il coud. | *he sews.* |
| Nous *cousons*. | *we sew.* |
| Vous *cousez*, | *you sew.* |
| Ils *cousent*. | *they sew.* |

#### IMPERFECT.

| | |
|---|---|
| Je *cousais*. | *I was sewing.* |
| Tu *cousais*. | *thou wast sewing.* |
| Il *cousait*. | *he was sewing.* |
| Nous *cousions*. | *we were sewing.* |
| Vous *cousiez*. | *you were sewing.* |
| Ils *cousaient*. | *they were sewing.* |

#### PAST DEFINITE.

| | |
|---|---|
| Je *cousis*. | *I sewed.* |
| Tu *cousis*. | *thou sewedst.* |
| Il *cousit*. | *he sewed.* |
| Nous *cousîmes*. | *we sewed.* |
| Vous *cousîtes*. | *you sewed.* |
| Ils *cousirent*. | *they sewed.* |

#### FUTURE.

| | |
|---|---|
| Je coudrai. | *I shall sew.* |
| Tu coudras. | *thou wilt sew.* |
| Il coudra. | *he will sew.* |
| Nous coudrons. | *we shall sew.* |
| Vous coudrez. | *you will sew.* |
| Ils coudront. | *they will sew.* |

### CONDITIONAL MOOD.

#### PRESENT.

| | |
|---|---|
| Je coudrais. | *I should sew.* |
| Tu coudrais. | *thou wouldst sew.* |
| Il coudrait. | *he would sew.* |
| Nous coudrions. | *we should sew.* |
| Vous coudriez. | *you would sew.* |
| Ils coudraient. | *they would sew.* |

### IMPERATIVE MOOD.

#### PRESENT.

| | |
|---|---|
| Couds - - - | *Sew (thou).* |
| Qu'il *couse* - - | *let him sew.* |
| Cousons - - | *let us sew.* |
| Cousez - - - | *sew (you).* |
| Qu'ils *cousent* - | *let them sew.* |

### SUBJUNCTIVE MOOD.

#### PRESENT.

| | |
|---|---|
| Que je *couse*. | *That I may sew.* |
| Que tu *couses*. | *that thou mayest sew.* |
| Qu'il *couse*. | *that he may sew.* |
| Que nous *cousions*. | *that we may sew.* |
| Que vous *cousiez*. | *that you may sew.* |
| Qu'ils *cousent*. | *that they may sew.* |

#### IMPERFECT.

| | |
|---|---|
| Que je *cousisse*. | *That I might sew.* |
| Que tu *cousisses*. | *that thou mightest sew.* |
| Qu'il *cousît*. | *that he might sew.* |
| Que nous *cousissions*. | *that we might sew.* |
| Que vous *cousissiez*. | *that you might sew.* |
| Qu'ils *cousissent*. | *that they might sew.* |

## COMPOUND TENSES.

| | | | |
|---|---|---|---|
| Past def. | J'ai *cousu*, etc. *I have sewed, etc.* | Cond. past. | J'aurais *cousu*, *I should have* etc. *sewed, etc.* |
| Past ant. | J'eus *cousu*, etc. *I had sewed, etc.* | | |
| Plup. | J'avais *cousu*, etc. *I had sewed, etc.* | Sub. past. | Que j'aie *cousu*, *That I may have* etc. *sewed, etc.* |
| Fut. | J'aurai *cousu*, etc. *I shall have sewed, etc.* | Sub. plup. | Que j'eusse *cousu*, etc. *That I might have sewed, etc.* |

## CONJUGATE LIKE *COUDRE*:

| | | | |
|---|---|---|---|
| Découdre | - - - - | *To unsew.* | Recoudre - - - *To sew again.* |

# VERB *CRAINDRE*, TO FEAR.

## INFINITIVE MOOD.

| | PRESENT. | | PAST. |
|---|---|---|---|
| Craindre. | To fear. | Avoir *craint*. | To have feared. |
| | PARTICIPLE PRESENT. | | COMPOUND OF PARTICIPLE PRESENT. |
| *Craignant*. | Fearing. | Ayant *craint*. | Having feared. |

PARTICIPLE PAST.

*Craint* (m.s.), *crainte* (f.s.),, *craints* (m.pl.), *craintes* (f.pl.), *feared*.

SIMPLE TENSES.

## INDICATIVE MOOD. — CONDITIONAL MOOD.

### PRESENT.
| | | | |
|---|---|---|---|
| Je *crains*. | I fear. | Je craindrais. | I should fear. |
| Tu *crains*. | thou fearest. | Tu craindrais. | thou wouldst fear. |
| Il *craint*. | he fears. | Il craindrait. | he would fear. |
| Nous *craignons*. | we fear. | Nous craindrions. | we should fear |
| Vous *craignez*. | you fear. | Vous craindriez. | you would fear. |
| Ils *craignent*. | they fear. | Ils craindraient. | they would fear. |

### IMPERFECT. — IMPERATIVE MOOD.
PRESENT.
| | | | |
|---|---|---|---|
| Je *craignais*. | I was fearing. | Crains | Fear (thou). |
| Tu *craignais*. | thou wast fearing. | Qu'il *craigne* | let him fear. |
| Il *craignait*. | he was fearing. | Craignons | let us fear. |
| Nous *craignions*. | we were fearing. | Craignez | fear (you). |
| Vous *craigniez*. | you were fearing. | Qu'ils *craignent* | let them fear. |
| Ils *craignaient*. | they were fearing. | | |

### PAST DEFINITE. — SUBJUNCTIVE MOOD.
PRESENT.
| | | | |
|---|---|---|---|
| Je *craignis*. | I feared. | Que je *craigne*. | That I may fear. |
| Tu *craignis*. | thou fearedst. | Que tu *craignes*. | that thou mayest fear. |
| Il *craignit*. | he feared. | Qu'il *craigne*. | that he may fear. |
| Nous *craignîmes*. | we feared. | Que nous *craignions*. | that we may fear. |
| Vous *craignîtes*. | you feared. | Que vous *craigniez*. | that you may fear. |
| Ils *craignirent*. | they feared. | Qu'ils *craignent*. | that they may fear. |

### FUTURE. — IMPERFECT.
| | | | |
|---|---|---|---|
| Je craindrai. | I shall fear. | Que je craignisse. | That I might fear. |
| Tu craindras. | thou wilt fear. | Que tu craignisses. | that thou mightest fear. |
| Il craindra. | he will fear. | Qu'il craignît. | that he might fear. |
| Nous craindrons. | we shall fear. | Que nous craignissions. | that we might fear. |
| Vous craindrez. | you will fear. | Que vous craignissiez. | that you might fear. |
| Ils craindront. | they will fear. | Qu'ils craignissent. | that they might fear. |

## COMPOUND TENSES.

| | | | | |
|---|---|---|---|---|
| Past Ind. | J'ai *craint*, etc. | I have feared, etc. | Cond. past. | J'aurais *craint*, etc. | I should have feared, etc. |
| Plup. | J'avais *craint*, etc. | I had feared, etc. | Sub. pres. | Que j'aie *craint*, etc. | That I may have feared, etc. |
| Past ant. | J'eus *craint*, etc. | I had feared, etc. | Sub. plup. | Que j'eusse *craint*, etc. | That I might have feared, etc. |
| Fut. ant. | J'aurai *craint*, etc. | I shall have feared, etc. | | | |

CONJUGATE IN THE SAME MANNER:
| | | | |
|---|---|---|---|
| Contraindre | To compel. | Plaindre | To pity. |

AND THE FOLLOWING VERBS ENDING IN *eindre*:

| | | | | |
|---|---|---|---|---|
| Astreindre | To compel. | Éteindre | To put out. |
| Atteindre | reach. | Étreindre | clasp, to grasp. |
| Aveindre | take out, to fetch out. | Feindre | feign. |
| Ceindre | gird. | Geindre | moan. |
| Dépeindre | to depict, to describe. | Peindre | paint. |
| Déteindre | take out the colour. | Ratteindre | catch again. |
| Enfreindre | infringe, to transgress. | Repeindre | paint anew. |
| Enceindre | surround. | Restreindre | restrain. |
| Empreindre | impress. | Reteindre | dye again. |
| Épreindre | press, to squeeze out. | Teindre | dye. |

N.B.—The verbs ending by *aindre* or *eindre* preserve the *d* only in the Future and Conditional Present.

# VERB *CROIRE*, TO BELIEVE.

## INFINITIVE MOOD.

| PRESENT. | | PAST. | |
|---|---|---|---|
| Croire. | *To believe.* | Avoir cru. | *To have believed.* |
| **PARTICIPLE PRESENT.** | | **COMP. OF PART. PRESENT.** | |
| Croyant. | *Believing.* | Ayant cru. | *Having believed.* |

### PARTICIPLE PAST.

Cru (m.s.), crue (f.s.), crus (m.pl.), crues (f.pl.), *believed.*

## SIMPLE TENSES.

### INDICATIVE MOOD.

#### PRESENT.

| | |
|---|---|
| Je crois. | *I believe.* |
| Tu crois. | *thou believest.* |
| Il croit. | *he believes.* |
| Nous croyons. | *we believe.* |
| Vous croyez. | *you believe.* |
| Ils croient. | *they believe.* |

#### IMPERFECT.

| | |
|---|---|
| Je croyais. | *I was believing.* |
| Tu croyais. | *thou wast believing,* |
| Il croyait. | *he was believing.* |
| Nous croyions. | *we were believing.* |
| Vous croyiez. | *you were believing.* |
| Ils croyaient. | *they were believing.* |

#### PAST DEFINITE.

| | |
|---|---|
| Je crus. | *I believed.* |
| Tu crus. | *thou believedst.* |
| Il crut. | *he believed.* |
| Nous crûmes. | *we believed.* |
| Vous crûtes. | *you believed.* |
| Ils crurent. | *they believed.* |

#### FUTURE.

| | |
|---|---|
| Je croirai. | *I shall believe.* |
| Tu croiras. | *thou wilt believe.* |
| Il croira. | *he will believe.* |
| Nous croirons. | *we shall believe.* |
| Vous croirez. | *you will believe.* |
| Ils croiront. | *they will believe.* |

### CONDITIONAL MOOD.

#### PRESENT.

| | |
|---|---|
| Je croirais. | *I should believe.* |
| Tu croirais. | *thou wouldst believe.* |
| Il croirait. | *he would believe.* |
| Nous croirions. | *we should believe.* |
| Vous croiriez. | *you would believe.* |
| Ils croiraient. | *they would believe.* |

### IMPERATIVE MOOD.

#### PRESENT.

| | |
|---|---|
| Crois - - - - | *Believe (thou).* |
| Qu'il croie - - - | *let him believe.* |
| Croyons - - - - | *let us believe.* |
| Croyez - - - - | *believe (you).* |
| Qu'ils croient - - | *let them believe.* |

### SUBJUNCTIVE MOOD.

#### PRESENT.

| | |
|---|---|
| Que je croie. | *That I may believe.* |
| Que tu croies. | *that thou mayest believe.* |
| Qu'il croie. | *that he may believe.* |
| Que nous croyions. | *that we may believe.* |
| Que vous croyiez. | *that you may believe.* |
| Qu'ils croient. | *that they may believe.* |

#### IMPERFECT.

| | |
|---|---|
| Que je crusse. | *That I might believe.* |
| Que tu crusses. | *that thou mightest believe.* |
| Qu'il crût. | *that he might believe.* |
| Que nous crussions. | *that we might believe.* |
| Que vous crussiez. | *that you might believe.* |
| Qu'ils crussent. | *that they might believe.* |

## COMPOUND TENSES.

| | | | |
|---|---|---|---|
| Past ind. | J'ai cru, etc. | *I have believed, etc.* | |
| Plup. | J'avais cru, etc. | *I had believed, etc.* | |
| Past ant. | J'eus cru, etc. | *I had believed, etc.* | |
| Fut. ant. | J'aurai cru, etc. | *I shall have believed, etc.* | |
| Cond. past. | J'aurais cru, etc, | *I should have believed, etc.* | |
| Sub. past. | Que j'aie cru, etc. | *That I may have believed, etc.* | |
| Sub. plup. | Que j'eusse cru, etc. | *That I might have believed, etc.* | |

N.B.—The *y* is followed by *i* in the *Imperfect of the Indicative* first and second person plural, and in the *Present of the Subjunctive* first and second person plural, in the verb *Croire*, and also in all verbs in which the *Participle Present* ends by *yant*.

# VERB *CROÎTRE*, TO GROW.

## INFINITIVE MOOD.

| PRESENT. | | PAST. | |
|---|---|---|---|
| Croître. | *To grow.* | Avoir crû. | *To have grown.* |

| PARTICIPLE PRESENT. | | COMP. OF PART. PRESENT. | |
|---|---|---|---|
| Croissant. | *Growing.* | Ayant crû. | *Having grown.* |

### PARTICIPLE PAST.

Crû (m.s.), crûe (f.s.), crûs (m.pl.), crûes (f.pl.), *grown.*

### SIMPLE TENSES.

#### INDICATIVE MOOD.

**PRESENT.**

| Je crois. | *I grow.* |
|---|---|
| Tu crois. | *thou growest.* |
| Il croît. | *he grows.* |
| Nous croissons. | *we grow.* |
| Vous croissez. | *you grow.* |
| Ils croissent. | *they grow.* |

**IMPERFECT.**

| Je croissais. | *I was growing.* |
|---|---|
| Tu croissais. | *thou wast growing.* |
| Il croissait. | *he was growing.* |
| Nous croissions. | *we were growing.* |
| Vous croissiez. | *you were growing.* |
| Ils croissaient. | *they were growing.* |

**PAST DEFINITE.**

| Je crûs. | *I grew.* |
|---|---|
| Tu crûs. | *thou grewest.* |
| Il crût. | *he grew.* |
| Nous crûmes. | *we grew.* |
| Vous crûtes. | *you grew.* |
| Ils crûrent. | *they grew.* |

**FUTURE.**

| Je croîtrai. | *I shall grow.* |
|---|---|
| Tu croîtras. | *thou wilt grow.* |
| Il croîtra. | *he will grow.* |
| Nous croîtrons. | *we shall grow.* |
| Vous croîtrez. | *you will grow.* |
| Ils croîtront. | *they will grow.* |

#### CONDITIONAL MOOD.

**PRESENT.**

| Je croîtrais. | *I should grow.* |
|---|---|
| Tu croîtrais. | *thou wouldst grow.* |
| Il croîtrait. | *he would grow.* |
| Nous croîtrions, | *we should grow.* |
| Vous croîtriez. | *you would grow.* |
| Ils croîtraient. | *they would grow.* |

#### IMPERATIVE MOOD.

**PRESENT.**

| Croîs | - - - - | *Grow (thou).* |
|---|---|---|
| Qu'il croisse | - - - | *let him grow.* |
| Croissons | - - - - | *let us grow.* |
| Croissez | - - - | *grow (you).* |
| Qu'ils croissent | - - | *let them grow.* |

#### SUBJUNCTIVE MOOD.

**PRESENT.**

| Que je croisse. | *That I may grow.* |
|---|---|
| Que tu croisses. | *that thou mayest grow.* |
| Qu'il croisse. | *that he may grow.* |
| Que nous croissions. | *that we may grow.* |
| Que vous croissiez. | *that you may grow.* |
| Qu'ils croissent. | *that they may grow.* |

**IMPERFECT.**

| Que je crûsse. | *That I might grow.* |
|---|---|
| Que tu crûsses. | *that thou mightest grow.* |
| Qu'il crût. | *that he might grow.* |
| Que nous crûssions. | *that we might grow.* |
| Que vous crûssiez. | *that you might grow.* |
| Qu'ils crûssent. | *that they might grow.* |

### COMPOUND TENSES.

| *Past ind.* J'ai crû, etc. | *I have grown, etc.* | *Cond. past.* J'aurais crû, etc. | *I should have grown, etc.* |
|---|---|---|---|
| *Plup.* J'avais crû, etc. | *I had grown, etc.* | *Sub. past.* Que j'aie crû, etc. | *That I may have grown, etc.* |
| *Past ant.* J'eus crû, etc. | *I had grown, etc.* | *Sub. plup.* Que j'eusse crû, etc. | *That I might have grown, etc.* |
| *Fut. ant.* J'aurai crû, etc. | *I shall have grown, etc.* | | |

---

CONJUGATE IN THE SAME MANNER:

| Accroître | - - - - | *To increase.* | Recroître | - - - | *To grow again.* |
|---|---|---|---|---|---|
| Décroître | - - - - | *— decrease.* | | | |

N.B.—I. The verb *croître* is spelt like *croire* in the following tenses:

*Indicative Present* in the three persons singular—*Je crois, tu crois, il croît.*

*Past Definite* throughout the tense—*Je crûs, tu crûs,* etc.

*Imperative,* first person singular—*crois.*

*Imperfect of the Subjunctive* throughout the tense *Que je crûsse, etc.* and Past Participle crû, etc.

When *croître* is spelt as *croire,* a circumflex accent is placed over the *i* or the *u* to distinguish it from *croire,* so: *Je crois* without accent means : *I believe,* and *Je croîs* with accent : *I grow.*

II. The verbs : *Accroître, décroître, recroître,* are conjugated with *avoir* and *être* ; with *avoir* when they express *action,* and with *être* when they mark the result of the *action.*

Ex. : La rivière a décru rapidement. La rivière est beaucoup décrue.

III. The verb *Décroître* preserves the circumflex accent over the *i* in the three persons singular of the Present of the Indicative. *Je décrois, tu décroîs, il décroît,* and in the Imperative *décroîs.*

IV. The Past Participles *accru* and *décru* are written without any circumflex accent, but *recru* takes it in the masculine singular only—*recrû,* m.s., *recrue,* f.s.

# VERB *DIRE*, TO SAY, TO TELL.

## INFINITIVE MOOD.

| PRESENT. | | PAST. |
|---|---|---|
| Dire. | *To say.* | Avoir *dit.* | *To have said.* |
| PARTICIPLE PRESENT. | | COMP. OF PART. PRESENT. |
| Disant. | *Saying.* | Ayant *dit.* | *Having said.* |

PAST PARTICIPLE.
*Dit* (m.s.), *dite* (f.s.), *dits* (m.pl.), *dites* (f.pl.), *said.*

## SIMPLE TENSES.

### INDICATIVE MOOD.

PRESENT.

| Je dis. | *I say.* |
|---|---|
| Tu dis. | *thou sayest.* |
| Il *dit.* | *he says.* |
| Nous *disons.* | *we say.* |
| Vous *dites.* | *you say.* |
| Ils *disent.* | *they say.* |

IMPERFECT.

| Je *disais.* | *I was saying.* |
|---|---|
| Tu *disais.* | *thou wast saying.* |
| Il *disait.* | *he was saying.* |
| Nous *disions.* | *we were saying.* |
| Vous *disiez.* | *you were saying.* |
| Ils *disaient.* | *they were saying.* |

PAST DEFINITE.

| Je *dis.* | *I said.* |
|---|---|
| Tu *dis.* | *thou saidst.* |
| Il *dit.* | *he said.* |
| Nous *dîmes.* | *we said.* |
| Vous *dîtes.* | *you said.* |
| Ils *dirent.* | *they said,* |

FUTURE.

| Je dirai. | *I shall say.* |
|---|---|
| Tu diras. | *thou wilt say.* |
| Il dira. | *he will say.* |
| Nous dirons. | *we shall say.* |
| Vous direz. | *you will say.* |
| Ils diront. | *they will say.* |

### CONDITIONAL MOOD.

PRESENT.

| Je dirais. | *I should say.* |
|---|---|
| Tu dirais. | *thou wouldst say.* |
| Il dirait. | *he would say.* |
| Nous dirions. | *we should say.* |
| Vous diriez. | *you would say.* |
| Ils diraient. | *they would say.* |

### IMPERATIVE MOOD.

PRESENT.

| Dis - - - - - | *Say (thou).* |
|---|---|
| Qu'il *dise* - - - - | *let him say.* |
| Disons - - - - - | *let us say.* |
| Dites - - - - - | *say (you).* |
| Qu'ils *disent* - - - | *let them say.* |

### SUBJUNCTIVE MOOD.

PRESENT.

| Que je *dise.* | *That I may say.* |
|---|---|
| Que tu *dises.* | *that thou mayest say.* |
| Qu'il *dise.* | *that he may say.* |
| Que nous *disions.* | *that we may say.* |
| Que vous *disiez.* | *that you may say.* |
| Qu'ils *disent.* | *that they may say.* |

IMPERFECT.

| Que je *disse.* | *That I might say.* |
|---|---|
| Que tu *disses.* | *that thou mightest say.* |
| Qu'il *dît.* | *that he might say.* |
| Que nous *dissions.* | *that we might say.* |
| Que vous *dissiez.* | *that you might say.* |
| Qu'ils *dissent.* | *that they might say.* |

## COMPOUND TENSES.

| Past. ind, | J'ai *dit,* etc. | *I have said, etc.* | Cond, past. | J'aurais *dit,* etc. | *I should have said, etc.* |
|---|---|---|---|---|---|
| Plup. | J'avais *dit,* etc. | *I had said, etc.* | | | |
| Past ant. | J'eus *dit,* etc. | *I had said, etc.* | Sub. past. | Que j'aie *dit,* etc. | *That I may have said, etc.* |
| Fut. ant. | J'aurai *dit,* etc. | *I shall have said, etc,* | Sub. plup. | Que j'eusse *dit,* etc. | *That I might have said, etc.* |

Redire, *to say again,* is conjugated in the same way.
The following verbs are conjugated like *dire* except in the Present of the Indicative, second person plural, and the Imperative second person plural.

| | | | | | |
|---|---|---|---|---|---|
| Contredire | - - | *To contradict.* | contredisez | | *contredites.* |
| Dédire | - - | *— disown.* | dédisez | | *dédites.* |
| Interdire | - - | *— forbid.* | interdisez | instead of | *interdites.* |
| Médire de | - - | *— slander.* | médisez | | *médites.* |
| Prédire | - - | *— foretell.* | prédisez | | *prédites.* |
| Maudire | - - | *— curse* (See page 120). | | | |

# VERB *ÉCRIRE*, to write.

### INFINITIVE MOOD.

| PRESENT. | | PAST. | |
|---|---|---|---|
| Écrire. | *To write.* | Avoir *écrit.* | *To have written.* |
| **PARTICIPLE PRESENT.** | | **COMPOUND OF PARTICIPLE PRESENT.** | |
| Écrivant. | *Writing.* | Ayant *écrit.* | *Having written.* |

**PARTICIPLE PAST.**

Écrit (m.s.), *écrite* (f.s.). *écrits* (m.pl.), *écrites* (f.pl.), *written.*

## SIMPLE TENSES.

### INDICATIVE MOOD.
#### PRESENT.
| | |
|---|---|
| J'écris. | *I write.* |
| Tu écris. | *thou writest.* |
| Il écrit. | *he writes.* |
| Nous *écrivons.* | *we write.* |
| Vous *écrivez.* | *you write.* |
| Ils *écrivent.* | *they write.* |

#### IMPERFECT.
| | |
|---|---|
| J'*écrivais.* | *I was writing.* |
| Tu *écrivais.* | *thou wast writing.* |
| Il *écrivait.* | *he was writing.* |
| Nous *écrivions.* | *we were writing.* |
| Vous *écriviez.* | *you were writing.* |
| Ils *écrivaient.* | *they were writing.* |

#### PAST DEFINITE.
| | |
|---|---|
| J'*écrivis.* | *I wrote.* |
| Tu *écrivis.* | *thou wrotest.* |
| Il *écrivit.* | *he wrote.* |
| Nous *écrivîmes.* | *we wrote.* |
| Vous *écrivîtes.* | *you wrote.* |
| Ils *écrivirent.* | *they wrote.* |

#### FUTURE.
| | |
|---|---|
| J'écrirai. | *I shall write.* |
| Tu écriras. | *thou wilt write.* |
| Il écrira. | *he will write.* |
| Nous écrirons. | *we shall write.* |
| Vous écrirez. | *you will write.* |
| Ils écriront. | *they will write.* |

### CONDITIONAL MOOD.
#### PRESENT.
| | |
|---|---|
| J'écrirais. | *I should write.* |
| Tu écrirais. | *thou wouldst write.* |
| Il écrirait. | *he would write.* |
| Nous écririons. | *we should write.* |
| Vous écririez. | *you would write.* |
| Ils écriraient. | *they would write.* |

### IMPERATIVE MOOD.
#### PRESENT.
| | | |
|---|---|---|
| Écris | - - | *Write ( thou ).* |
| Qu'il *écrive* | - | *let him write.* |
| Écrivons | - | *let us write.* |
| Écrivez | - - | *write (you).* |
| Qu'ils *écrivent* | - | *let them write.* |

### SUBJUNCTIVE MOOD.
#### PRESENT.
| | |
|---|---|
| Que j'*écrive.* | *That I may write.* |
| Que tu *écrives.* | *that thou mayest write.* |
| Qu'il *écrive.* | *that he may write.* |
| Que nous *écrivions.* | *that we may write.* |
| Que vous *écriviez.* | *that you may write.* |
| Qu'ils *écrivent.* | *that they may write.* |

#### IMPERFECT.
| | |
|---|---|
| Que j'*écrivisse.* | *That I might* |
| Que tu *écrivisses.* | *that thou mightest* |
| Qu'il *écrivît.* | *that he might* |
| Que nous *écrivissions.* | *that we might* |
| Que vous *écrivissiez.* | *that you might* |
| Qu'ils *écrivissent.* | *that they might* |

*write.*

## COMPOUND TENSES.

| | | | | | |
|---|---|---|---|---|---|
| Past ind. | J'ai *écrit*, etc. | *I have written, etc.* | Cond. past. | J'aurais *écrit*, etc. | *I should have written, etc.* |
| Plup. | J'avais *écrit*, etc. | *I had written, etc.* | Sub. past. | Que j'aie *écrit*, etc. | *That I may have written, etc.* |
| Past ant. | J'eus *écrit*, etc. | *I had written, etc.* | | | |
| Fut. ant. | J'aurai *écrit*, etc. | *I shall have written, etc.* | Sub. plup. | Que j'eusse *écrit*, etc. | *That I might have written, etc.* |

### CONJUGATE IN THE SAME MANNER :

| | | | | | |
|---|---|---|---|---|---|
| Circonscrire | - - - | *To circumscribe.* | Proscrire | - - - | *To proscribe.* |
| Décrire | - - - | *— describe.* | Récrire | - - - | *— write again.* |
| Inscrire | - - - | *— inscribe.* | Souscrire | - - - | *— subscribe.* |
| Prescrire | - - - | *— prescribe.* | Transcrire | - - - | *— transcribe* |

# VERB *FAIRE*, TO DO, TO MAKE.

## INFINITIVE MOOD.

| PRESENT. | | PAST. | |
|---|---|---|---|
| Fai*re*. | *To do.* | Avoir *fait*. | *To have done.* |
| **PARTICIPLE PRESENT.** | | **COMPOUND OF PARTICIPLE PRESENT.** | |
| *Faisant.* | *Doing.* | Ayant *fait*. | *Having done.* |

### PARTICIPLE PAST.
*Fait* (m.s.), *faite* (f.s.), *faits* (m.pl.), *faites* (f.pl.), *done.*

### SIMPLE TENSES.

## INDICATIVE MOOD.

### PRESENT.
| | |
|---|---|
| Je fais. | *I do.* |
| Tu fais. | *thou doest.* |
| Il *fait*. | *he does.* |
| Nous *faisons*. | *we do.* |
| Vous *faites*. | *you do.* |
| Ils *font*. | *they do.* |

### IMPERFECT.
| | |
|---|---|
| Je *faisais*. | *I was doing.* |
| Tu *faisais*. | *thou wast doing.* |
| Il *faisait*. | *he was doing.* |
| Nous *faisions*. | *we were doing.* |
| Vous *faisiez*. | *you were doing.* |
| Ils *faisaient*. | *they were doing.* |

### PAST DEFINITE.
| | |
|---|---|
| Je *fis*. | *I did.* |
| Tu *fis*. | *thou didst.* |
| Il *fit*. | *he did.* |
| Nous *fîmes*. | *we did.* |
| Vous *fîtes*. | *you did.* |
| Ils *firent*. | *they did.* |

### FUTURE.
| | |
|---|---|
| Je *ferai*. | *I shall do.* |
| Tu *feras*. | *thou wilt do.* |
| Il *fera*. | *he will do.* |
| Nous *ferons*. | *we shall do.* |
| Vous *ferez*. | *you will do.* |
| Ils *feront*. | *they will do.* |

## CONDITIONAL MOOD.

### PRESENT.
| | |
|---|---|
| Je *ferais*. | *I should do.* |
| Tu *ferais*. | *thou wouldst do.* |
| Il *ferait*. | *he would do.* |
| Nous *ferions*. | *we should do.* |
| Vous *feriez*. | *you would do.* |
| Ils *feraient*. | *they would do.* |

## IMPERATIVE MOOD.
### PRESENT.
| | |
|---|---|
| Fais | *Do (thou).* |
| Qu'il *fasse* | *let him do.* |
| Faisons | *let us do.* |
| Faites | *do (you).* |
| Qu'ils *fassent* | *let them do.* |

## SUBJUNCTIVE MOOD.
### PRESENT.
| | |
|---|---|
| Que je *fasse*. | *That I may do.* |
| Que tu *fasses*. | *that thou mayest do.* |
| Qu'il *fasse*. | *that he may do.* |
| Que nous *fassions*. | *that we may do.* |
| Que vous *fassiez*. | *that you may do.* |
| Qu'ils *fassent*. | *that they may do.* |

### IMPERFECT.
| | |
|---|---|
| Que je *fisse*. | *That I might do.* |
| Que tu *fisses*. | *that thou mightest do.* |
| Qu'il *fît*. | *that he might do.* |
| Que nous *fissions*. | *that we might do.* |
| Que vous *fissiez*. | *that you might do.* |
| Qu'ils *fissent*. | *that they might do.* |

## COMPOUND TENSES.

| | | | | | |
|---|---|---|---|---|---|
| Past. ind. | J'ai *fait*, etc. | *I have done, etc.* | Cond. past. | J'aurais *fait*, etc. | *I should have done, etc.* |
| Plup. | J'avais *fait*, etc. | *I had done, etc.* | | | |
| Past. ant. | J'eus *fait*, etc. | *I had done, etc.* | Sub. past. | Que j'aie *fait*, etc. | *That I may have done, etc.* |
| Fut. ant. | J'aurai *fait*, etc. | *I shall have done, etc.* | Sub. plup. | Que j'eusse *fait*, etc. | *That I might have done, etc.* |

### CONJUGATE LIKE *FAIRE*.

| | | |
|---|---|---|
| Contrefaire | *To counterfeit, to mimic.* | |
| Défaire | *— undo, to defeat.* | |
| Forfaire | *— forfeit.* | |
| Méfaire | *— do harm.* | |
| Parfaire | *To perfect, to complete.* | |
| Refaire | *— do again.* | |
| Redéfaire | *— undo again.* | |
| Satisfaire | *— satisfy.* | |
| Surfaire | *— exact, to overcharge.* | |

In the Future and Conditional Present of *Faire* and its compound, the two letters AI have been changed into E. *Future*—Je ferais, etc. *Conditional*—Je ferais, etc. See above.

# VERB *JOINDRE*, TO JOIN.

## INFINITIVE MOOD.

| PRESENT. | | PAST. | |
|---|---|---|---|
| Joind*re*. | *To join.* | Avoir *joint*. | *To have joined.* |
| PARTICIPLE PRESENT. | | COMP. OF PARTICIPLE PRESENT. | |
| *Joignant*. | *Joining.* | Ayant *joint*. | *Having joined.* |

PARTICIPLE PAST.

*Joint* (m. s.), *jointe* (f. s.), *joints* (m. pl.), *jointes* (f. pl.), *joined.*

## SIMPLE TENSES.

### INDICATIVE MOOD.
#### PRESENT.

| | |
|---|---|
| Je *joins*. | *I join.* |
| Tu *joins*. | *thou joinest.* |
| Il *joint*. | *he joins.* |
| Nous *joignons*. | *we join.* |
| Vous *joignez*. | *you join.* |
| Ils *joignent*. | *they join.* |

#### IMPERFECT

| | |
|---|---|
| Je *joignais*. | *I was joining.* |
| Tu *joignais*. | *thou wast joining.* |
| Il *joignait*. | *he was joining.* |
| Nous *joignions*. | *we were joining.* |
| Vous *joigniez*. | *you were joining.* |
| Ils *joignaient*. | *they were joining.* |

#### PAST DEFINITE.

| | |
|---|---|
| Je *joignis*. | *I joined.* |
| Tu *joignis*. | *thou joined.* |
| Il *joignit*. | *he joined.* |
| Nous *joignîmes*. | *we joined.* |
| Vous *joignîtes*. | *you joined.* |
| Ils *joignirent*. | *they joined.* |

#### FUTURE.

| | |
|---|---|
| Je joindrai. | *I shall join.* |
| Tu joindras. | *thou wilt join.* |
| Il joindra. | *he will join.* |
| Nous joindrons. | *we shall join.* |
| Vous joindrez. | *you will join.* |
| Ils joindront. | *they will join.* |

### CONDITIONAL MOOD.
#### PRESENT.

| | |
|---|---|
| Je joindrais. | *I should join.* |
| Tu joindrais. | *thou wouldst join.* |
| Il joindrait. | *he would join.* |
| Nous joindrions. | *we should join.* |
| Vous joindriez. | *you would join.* |
| Ils joindraient. | *they would join.* |

### IMPERATIVE MOOD.
#### PRESENT.

| | | |
|---|---|---|
| *Joins* - | - - | *Join (thou).* |
| Qu'il *joigne* - | - | *let him join.* |
| *Joignons* | - | *let us join.* |
| *Joignez* - | - - | *join (you).* |
| Qu'ils *joignent* | - | *let them join.* |

### SUBJUNCTIVE MOOD.
#### PRESENT.

| | |
|---|---|
| Que je *joigne*. | *That I may join.* |
| Que tu *joignes*. | *that thou mayest join.* |
| Qu'il *joigne*. | *that he may join.* |
| Que nous *joignions*. | *that we may join.* |
| Que vous *joigniez*. | *that you may join.* |
| Qu'ils *joignent*. | *that they may join.* |

#### IMPERFECT.

| | |
|---|---|
| Que je *joignisse*. | *That I might join.* |
| Que tu *joignisses*. | *that thou mightest join.* |
| Qu'il *joignît*. | *that he might join.* |
| Que nous *joignissions*. | *that we might join.* |
| Que vous *joignissiez*. | *that you might join.* |
| Qu'ils *joignissent*. | *that they might join.* |

## COMPOUND TENSES.

| | | | | | |
|---|---|---|---|---|---|
| *Past ind.* | J'ai *joint*, etc. | *I have joined, etc.* | *Cond. past.* | J'aurais *joint*, etc. | *I should have joined, etc.* |
| *Past ant.* | J'eus *joint*, etc. | *I had joined, etc.* | | | |
| *Plup.* | J'avais *joint*, etc. | *I had joined, etc.* | *Sub. past.* | Que j'aie *joint*, etc. | *That I may have joined, etc.* |
| *Fut. ant.* | J'aurai *joint*, etc. | *I shall have joined, etc.* | *Sub. plup.* | Que j'eusse *joint*, etc. | *That I might have joined, etc.* |

### CONJUGATE LIKE *JOINDRE*:

| | | | |
|---|---|---|---|
| Adjoindre | - - - | *To adjoin.* | |
| Conjoindre | | *— join, to unite.* | |
| Oindre | - - - - | *— anoint.* | |

| | | | |
|---|---|---|---|
| Déjoindre | - - - | *To disjoin.* | |
| Disjoindre | - | *— separate.* | |
| Enjoindre | - - - | *— enjoin.* | |
| Rejoindre | - - - | *— rejoin.* | |

# VERB *LIRE*, TO READ.

## INFINITIVE MOOD.

| PRESENT. | | PAST. | |
|---|---|---|---|
| Lire. | *To read.* | Avoir *lu.* | *To have read.* |
| **PARTICIPLE PRESENT.** | | **COMP. OF PART. PRESENT.** | |
| Lisant. | *Reading.* | Ayant *lu.* | *Having read.* |

### PARTICIPLE PAST.
*Lu* (m.s.), *lue* (f.s.), *lus* (m.pl.), *lues* (f.pl.), *read.*

### SIMPLE TENSES.

#### INDICATIVE MOOD.

**PRESENT.**

| | |
|---|---|
| Je lis. | *I read.* |
| Tu lis. | *thou readest.* |
| Il *lit.* | *he reads.* |
| Nous *lisons.* | *we read.* |
| Vous *lisez.* | *you read.* |
| Ils *lisent.* | *they read.* |

**IMPERFECT.**

| | |
|---|---|
| Je *lisais.* | *I was reading.* |
| Tu *lisais.* | *thou wast reading.* |
| Il *lisait.* | *he was reading.* |
| Nous *lisions.* | *we were reading.* |
| Vous *lisiez.* | *you were reading.* |
| Ils *lisaient.* | *they were reading.* |

**PAST DEFINITE.**

| | |
|---|---|
| Je *lus.* | *I read.* |
| Tu *lus.* | *thou readest.* |
| Il *lut.* | *he read.* |
| Nous *lûmes.* | *we read.* |
| Vous *lûtes.* | *you read.* |
| Ils *lurent.* | *they read.* |

**FUTURE.**

| | |
|---|---|
| Je lirai. | *I shall read.* |
| Tu liras. | *thou wilt read.* |
| Il lira. | *he will read.* |
| Nous lirons. | *we shall read.* |
| Vous lirez. | *you will read.* |
| Ils liront. | *they will read.* |

#### CONDITIONAL MOOD.

**PRESENT.**

| | |
|---|---|
| Je lirais. | *I should read.* |
| Tu lirais. | *thou wouldst read.* |
| Il lirait. | *he would read.* |
| Nous lirions. | *we should read.* |
| Vous liriez. | *you would read.* |
| Ils liraient. | *they would read.* |

#### IMPERATIVE MOOD.

**PRESENT.**

| | |
|---|---|
| Lis - - - | *Read (thou).* |
| Qu'il *lise* - - | *let him read.* |
| *Lisons* - - - | *let us read.* |
| *Lisez* - - - | *read (you).* |
| Qu'ils *lisent* - - | *let them read.* |

#### SUBJUNCTIVE MOOD.

**PRESENT.**

| | |
|---|---|
| Que je *lise.* | *That I may read.* |
| Que tu *lises.* | *that thou mayest read.* |
| Qu'il *lise.* | *that he may read.* |
| Que nous *lisions.* | *that we may read.* |
| Que vous *lisiez.* | *that you may read.* |
| Qu'ils *lisent.* | *that they may read.* |

**IMPERFECT.**

| | |
|---|---|
| Que je *lusse.* | *That I might read.* |
| Que tu *lusses.* | *that thou mightest read.* |
| Qu'il *lût.* | *that he might read.* |
| Que nous *lussions.* | *that we might read.* |
| Que vous *lussiez.* | *that you might read.* |
| Qu'ils *lussent.* | *that they might read.* |

### COMPOUND TENSES.

| | | | |
|---|---|---|---|
| *Past ind.* J'ai *lu,* etc. | *I have read, etc.* | *Cond. past.* J'aurais *lu,* etc. | *I should have read, etc.* |
| *Plup.* J'avais *lu,* etc. | *I had read, etc.* | *Sub. past.* Que j'aie *lu,* etc. | *That I may have read, etc.* |
| *Past ant.* J'eus *lu,* etc. | *I had read, etc.* | | |
| *Fut. ant.* J'aurai *lu,* etc. | *I shall have read, etc.* | *Sub. plup.* Que j'eusse *lu,* etc. | *That I might have read, etc.* |

### CONJUGATE LIKE *LIRE* :

| | | |
|---|---|---|
| Élire - - - - | *To elect.* | Relire - - - *To read again.* |
| Réélire - - - - | *— re-elect.* | Prélire - - - *— read a first time, (print).* |

# VERB *MAUDIRE*, TO CURSE.

## INFINITIVE MOOD.

| PRESENT. | | PAST. | |
|---|---|---|---|
| Maudi*re*. | *To curse.* | Avoir *maudit*. | *To have cursed.* |
| **PARTICIPLE PRESENT.** | | **COMP. OF PART. PRESENT.** | |
| *Maudissant*. | *Cursing.* | Ayant *maudit*. | *Having cursed.* |

### PARTICIPLE PAST.

*Maudit* (m.s.), *maudite* (f.s.), *maudits* (m.pl.), *maudites* (f.pl.), *cursed.*

## SIMPLE TENSES.

### INDICATIVE MOOD.

#### PRESENT.

| | |
|---|---|
| Je maudis. | *I curse.* |
| Tu maudis. | *thou cursest.* |
| Il *maudit*. | *he curses.* |
| Nous *maudissons*. | *we curse.* |
| Vous *maudissez*. | *you curse.* |
| Ils *maudissent*. | *they curse.* |

#### IMPERFECT.

| | |
|---|---|
| Je *maudissais*. | *I was cursing.* |
| Tu *maudissais*. | *thou wast cursing.* |
| Il *maudissait*. | *he was cursing.* |
| Nous *maudissions*. | *we were cursing.* |
| Vous *maudissiez*. | *you were cursing.* |
| Ils *maudissaient*. | *they were cursing.* |

#### PAST DEFINITE.

| | |
|---|---|
| Je maudis. | *I cursed.* |
| Tu maudis. | *thou cursedst.* |
| Il maudit. | *he cursed.* |
| Nous maudîmes. | *we cursed.* |
| Vous maudîtes. | *you cursed.* |
| Ils maudirent. | *they cursed.* |

#### FUTURE.

| | |
|---|---|
| Je maudirai. | *I shall curse.* |
| Tu maudiras. | *thou wilt curse.* |
| Il maudira. | *he will curse.* |
| Nous maudirons. | *we shall curse.* |
| Vous maudirez. | *you will curse.* |
| Ils maudiront. | *they will curse.* |

### CONDITIONAL MOOD.

#### PRESENT.

| | |
|---|---|
| Je maudirais. | *I should curse.* |
| Tu maudirais. | *thou wouldst curse.* |
| Il maudirait. | *he would curse.* |
| Nous maudirions. | *we should curse.* |
| Vous maudiriez. | *you would curse.* |
| Ils maudiraient. | *they would curse.* |

### IMPERATIVE MOOD.

#### PRESENT.

| | |
|---|---|
| Maudis. | *curse* (*thou*). |
| Qu'il *maudisse*. | *let him curse.* |
| *Maudissons*. | *let us curse.* |
| *Maudissez*. | *curse* (*you*). |
| Qu'ils *maudissent*. | *let them curse.* |

### SUBJUNCTIVE MOOD.

#### PRESENT.

| | | |
|---|---|---|
| Que je *maudisse*. | *That I may* | |
| Que tu *maudisses*. | *that thou mayest* | |
| Qu'il *maudisse*. | *that he may* | *curse.* |
| Que nous *maudissions*. | *that we may* | |
| Que vous *maudissiez*. | *that you may* | |
| Qu'ils *maudissent*. | *that they may* | |

#### IMPERFECT.

| | | |
|---|---|---|
| Que je maudisse. | *That I might* | |
| Que tu maudisses. | *that thou mightest* | |
| Qu'il maudît. | *that he might* | *curse.* |
| Que nous maudissions. | *that we might* | |
| Que vous maudissiez. | *that you might* | |
| Qu'ils maudissent. | *that they might* | |

## COMPOUND TENSES.

| | | | |
|---|---|---|---|
| *Past. ind.* | J'ai *maudit*, etc. | *I have cursed,* etc. | |
| *Plup.* | J'avais *maudit*, etc. | *I had cursed, etc.* | |
| *Past. ant.* | J'eus *maudit*, etc. | *I had cursed, etc.* | |
| *Fut. ant.* | J'aurai *maudit*, etc. | *I shall have cursed, etc.* | |

| | | | |
|---|---|---|---|
| *Cond. past.* | J'aurais *maudit*, etc. | *I should have cursed, etc.* | |
| *Sub. past.* | Que j'aie *maudit*, etc. | *that I may have cursed, etc.* | |
| *Sub. plup.* | Que j'eusse *maudit*, etc. | *that I might have cursed, etc.* | |

N.B.—*Maudire* is conjugated like *Dire*, except in the following tenses: Indicative Present: first, second, third person plural—Imperfect—Imperative.—Subjunctive Present, and Participle Present.

# VERB *METTRE*, to put.

## INFINITIVE MOOD.

| PRESENT. | | PAST. | |
|---|---|---|---|
| Mettre. | *To put.* | Avoir *mis.* | *To have put.* |

| PARTICIPLE PRESENT. | | COMP. OF PART. PRESENT. | |
|---|---|---|---|
| Mettant. | *Putting.* | Ayant *mis.* | *Having put.* |

### PARTICIPLE PAST.

*Mis* (m.s.), *mise* (f.s.), *mis* (m.pl.), *mises* (f.pl.), *put.*

### SIMPLE TENSES.

## INDICATIVE MOOD.

### PRESENT.

| | |
|---|---|
| Je *mets.* | *I put.* |
| Tu *mets.* | *thou puttest.* |
| Il *met.* | *he puts.* |
| Nous mettons. | *we put.* |
| Vous mettez. | *you put.* |
| Ils mettent. | *they put.* |

### IMPERFECT.

| | |
|---|---|
| Je mettais. | *I was putting.* |
| Tu mettais. | *thou wast putting.* |
| Il mettait. | *he was putting.* |
| Nous mettions. | *we were putting.* |
| Vous mettiez. | *you were putting.* |
| Ils mettaient. | *they were putting.* |

### PAST DEFINITE.

| | |
|---|---|
| Je *mis.* | *I put.* |
| Tu *mis.* | *thou puttedst.* |
| Il *mit.* | *he put.* |
| Nous *mîmes.* | *we put.* |
| Vous *mîtes.* | *you put.* |
| Ils *mirent.* | *they put.* |

### FUTURE.

| | |
|---|---|
| Je mettrai. | *I shall put.* |
| Tu mettras. | *thou wilt put.* |
| Il mettra. | *he will put.* |
| Nous mettrons. | *we shall put.* |
| Vous mettrez. | *you will put.* |
| Ils mettront. | *they will put.* |

## CONDITIONAL MOOD.

### PRESENT.

| | |
|---|---|
| Je mettrais. | *I should put.* |
| Tu mettrais. | *thou wouldst put.* |
| Il mettrait. | *he would put.* |
| Nous mettrions. | *we should put.* |
| Vous mettriez. | *you would put.* |
| Ils mettraient. | *they would put.* |

## IMPERATIVE MOOD.

### PRESENT.

| | | |
|---|---|---|
| Mets | - | *Put (thou).* |
| Qu'il mette | | *let him put.* |
| Mettons | - | *let us put.* |
| Mettez | · | *put (you).* |
| Qu'ils mettent | - | *let them put.* |

## SUBJUNCTIVE MOOD.

### PRESENT.

| | |
|---|---|
| Que je mette. | *That I may put.* |
| Que tu mettes. | *that thou mayest put.* |
| Qu'il mette. | *that he may put.* |
| Que nous mettions. | *that we may put.* |
| Que vous mettiez. | *that you may put.* |
| Qu'ils mettent. | *that they may put.* |

### IMPERFECT.

| | |
|---|---|
| Que je *misse.* | *That I might put.* |
| Que tu *misses.* | *that thou mightest put.* |
| Qu'il *mît.* | *that he might put.* |
| Que nous *missions.* | *that we might put.* |
| Que vous *missiez.* | *that you might put.* |
| Qu'ils *missent.* | *that they might put.* |

### COMPOUND TENSES.

| | | |
|---|---|---|
| Past ind. | J'ai *mis,* etc. | *I have put, etc.* |
| Plup. | J'avais *mis,* etc. | *I had put, etc.* |
| Past ant. | J'eus *mis,* etc. | *I had put, etc.* |
| Fut. ant. | J'aurai *mis,* etc. | *I shall have put, etc.* |

| | | |
|---|---|---|
| Cond. past. | J'aurais *mis,* etc. | *I should have put, etc.* |
| Sub. past. | Que j'aie *mis,* etc. | *that I may have put, etc.* |
| Sub. plup. | Que j'eusse *mis,* etc. | *that I might have put, etc.* |

### CONJUGATE IN THE SAME MANNER :

| | | | |
|---|---|---|---|
| Admettre | - | - | *To admit.* |
| Commettre | - | - | *— commit.* |
| Compromettre | - | - | *— compromise.* |
| Démettre | - | - | *— dismiss, to dislocate.* |
| Émettre | - | - | *— issue, to emit.* |
| S'entremettre | - | - | *— intervene.* |
| Omettre | - | - | *— omit.* |

| | | | |
|---|---|---|---|
| Permettre | - | - | *To permit.* |
| Promettre | - | - | *— promise.* |
| Réadmettre | - | - | *— re-admit.* |
| Remettre | - | - | *— put again.* |
| Repromettre | - | - | *— promise again.* |
| Soumettre | - | - | *— submit.* |
| Transmettre | - | - | *— transmit.* |

# VERB *MOUDRE*, TO GRIND.

## INFINITIVE MOOD.

| | PRESENT. | | PAST. |
|---|---|---|---|
| Moud*re*. | *To grind.* | Avoir *moulu*. | *To have ground.* |
| | PARTICIPLE PRESENT. | | COMP. OF PART. PRESENT. |
| *Moulant.* | *Grinding.* | Ayant *moulu*. | *Having ground.* |

PARTICIPLE PAST.
*Moulu* (m.s.), *moulue* (f.s.), *moulus* (m.pl.), *moulues* (f.pl.), *ground.*

## SIMPLE TENSES.

### INDICATIVE MOOD.
#### PRESENT.

| | |
|---|---|
| Je mouds. | *I grind.* |
| Tu mouds. | *thou grindest.* |
| Ils moud. | *he grinds.* |
| Nous *moulons*. | *we grind.* |
| Vous *moulez*. | *you grind.* |
| Ils *moulent*. | *they grind.* |

#### IMPERFECT.

| | |
|---|---|
| Je *moulais*. | *I was grinding.* |
| Tu *moulais*. | *thou wast grinding.* |
| Il *moulait*. | *he was grinding.* |
| Nous *moulions*. | *we were grinding.* |
| Vous *mouliez*. | *you were grinding.* |
| Ils *moulaiant*. | *they were grinding.* |

#### PAST DEFINITE.

| | |
|---|---|
| Je *moulus*. | *I ground.* |
| Tu *moulus*. | *thou groundst.* |
| Il *moulut*. | *he ground.* |
| Nous *moulûmes*. | *we ground.* |
| Vous *moulûtes*. | *you ground.* |
| Ils *moulurent*. | *they ground.* |

#### FUTURE.

| | |
|---|---|
| Je moudrai. | *I shall grind.* |
| Tu moudras. | *thou wilt grind.* |
| Il moudra. | *he will grind.* |
| Nous moudrons. | *we shall grind.* |
| Vous moudrez. | *you will grind.* |
| Ils moudront. | *they will grind.* |

### CONDITIONAL MOOD.
#### PRESENT.

| | |
|---|---|
| Je moudrais. | *I should grind.* |
| Tu moudrais. | *thou wouldst grind.* |
| Il moudrait. | *he would grind.* |
| Nous moudrions. | *we should grind.* |
| Vous moudriez. | *you would grind.* |
| Ils moudraient. | *they would grind.* |

### IMPERATIVE MOOD.
#### PRESENT.

| | | |
|---|---|---|
| Mouds | - - | *Grind (thou).* |
| Qu'il *moule* | - | *let him grind.* |
| *Moulons* - | - | *let us grind.* |
| *Moulez* - | - | *grind (you).* |
| Qu'ils *moulent* - | | *let them grind.* |

### SUBJUNCTIVE MOOD.
#### PRESENT.

| | |
|---|---|
| Que je *moule*. | *That I may grind.* |
| Oue tu *moules*. | *that thou mayest grind.* |
| Qu'il *moule*. | *that he may grind.* |
| Que nous *moulions*. | *that we may grind.* |
| Que vous *mouliez*. | *that you may grind.* |
| Qu'ils *moulent*. | *that they may grind.* |

#### IMPERFECT.

| | |
|---|---|
| Que je *moulusse*. | *That I might* |
| Que tu *moulusses*. | *that thou mightest* |
| Qu'il *moulût*. | *that he might* |
| Que nous *moulussions*. | *that we might* |
| Que vous *moulussiez*. | *that you might* |
| Qu'ils *moulussent*. | *that they might* |

*grind.*

## COMPOUND TENSES.

| | | | |
|---|---|---|---|
| *Past ind.* | J'ai *moulu*, etc. | *I have ground,* etc. | |
| *Plup.* | J'avais *moulu*, etc. | *I had ground,* etc. | |
| *Past ant.* | J'eus *moulu*, etc. | *I had ground,* etc. | |
| *Fut. ant.* | J'aurai *moulu*, etc. | *I shall have ground, etc.* | |
| *Cond. past.* | J'aurais *moulu*, etc. | *I should have ground, etc.* | |
| *Sub. past.* | Que j'aie *moulu*, etc. | *that I may have ground, etc.* | |
| *Sub. plup.* | Que j'eusse *moulu*, etc. | *that I might have ground, etc.* | |

CONJUGATE IN THE SAME MANNER :

| | | | |
|---|---|---|---|
| Émoudre | - | *To grind, (knives, razors, etc.)* | Rémoudre - *To grind again, (knives, razors etc.)* |
| Remoudre | - | *— grind again, (corn, etc.)* | |

Observe the difference between *remoudre* and *rémoudre*.

**123**

# VERB *NAÎTRE*, TO BE BORN, TO SPRING.

## INFINITIVE MOOD.

| PRESENT. | | PAST. | |
|---|---|---|---|
| Naître. | *To spring.* | Être né. | *To have sprung.* |

| PARTICIPLE PRESENT. | | COMP. OF PART. PRESENT. | |
|---|---|---|---|
| Naissant. | *Springing.* | Étant né. | *Having sprung.* |

### PARTICIPLE PAST.
*Né* (m.s.), *née* (f.s.), *nés* (m.pl.), *nées* (f.pl.), *sprung.*

## SIMPLE TENSES.

### INDICATIVE MOOD.

**PRESENT.**

| | |
|---|---|
| Je *nais.* | *I spring.* |
| Tu *nais.* | *thou springest.* |
| Il *naît.* | *he springs.* |
| Nous *naissons.* | *we spring.* |
| Vous *naissez.* | *you spring.* |
| Ils *naissent.* | *they spring.* |

**IMPERFECT.**

| | |
|---|---|
| Je *naissais.* | *I was springing.* |
| Tu *naissais.* | *thou wast springing.* |
| Il *naissait.* | *he was springing.* |
| Nous *naissions.* | *we were springing.* |
| Vous *naissiez.* | *you were springing.* |
| Ils *naissaient.* | *they were springing.* |

**PAST DEFINITE.**

| | |
|---|---|
| Je *naquis.* | *I sprung.* |
| Tu *naquis.* | *thou sprungest.* |
| Il *naquit.* | *he sprung.* |
| Nous *naquîmes.* | *we sprung.* |
| Vous *naquîtes.* | *you sprung.* |
| Ils *naquirent.* | *they sprung.* |

**FUTURE.**

| | |
|---|---|
| Je naîtrai. | *I shall spring.* |
| Tu naîtras. | *thou wilt spring.* |
| Il naîtra. | *he will spring.* |
| Nous naîtrons. | *we shall spring.* |
| Vous naîtrez. | *you will spring.* |
| Ils naîtront. | *they will spring.* |

### CONDITIONAL MOOD.

**PRESENT.**

| | |
|---|---|
| Je naîtrais. | *I should spring.* |
| Tu naîtrais. | *thou wouldst spring.* |
| Il naîtrait. | *he would spring.* |
| Nous naîtrions. | *we should spring.* |
| Vous naîtriez. | *you would spring.* |
| Ils naîtraient. | *they would spring.* |

### IMPERATIVE MOOD.

**PRESENT.**

| | |
|---|---|
| Nais - - - | *Spring (thou).* |
| Qu'il *naisse* - - | *let him spring.* |
| Naissons - - | *let us spring.* |
| Naissez - - - | *spring (you).* |
| Qu'ils *naissent* - - | *let them spring.* |

### SUBJUNCTIVE MOOD.

**PRESENT.**

| | | |
|---|---|---|
| Que je *naisse.* | *That I may* | |
| Que tu *naisses.* | *that thou mayest* | |
| Qu'il *naisse.* | *that he may* | *spring.* |
| Que nous *naissions.* | *that we may* | |
| Que vous *naissiez.* | *that you may* | |
| Qu'ils *naissent.* | *that they may* | |

**IMPERFECT.**

| | | |
|---|---|---|
| Que je *naquisse.* | *that I might* | |
| Que tu *naquisses.* | *that thou mightest* | |
| Qu'il *naquît.* | *that he might* | *spring.* |
| Que nous *naquissions.* | *that we might* | |
| Que vous *naquissiez.* | *that you might* | |
| Qu'ils *naquissent.* | *that they might* | |

## COMPOUND TENSES.

| | | | |
|---|---|---|---|
| *Past ind.* Je suis *né,* etc. | *I have sprung,* etc. | *Cond. past.* Je serais *né,* etc. | *I should have sprung,* etc. |
| *Plup.* J'étais *né,* etc. | *I had sprung,* etc. | *Sub. past.* Que je sois *né,* etc. | *that I may have sprung,* etc. |
| *Past ant.* Je fus *né,* etc. | *I had sprung,* etc. | *Sub. plup.* Que je fusse *né,* etc. | *that I might have sprung,* etc. |
| *Fut. ant.* Je serai *né,* etc. | *I shall have sprung,* etc. | | |

CONJUGATE IN THE SAME MANNER :

Renaître - - *To be born again, to spring again.*
Verb *Naître* takes the auxiliary *être* in its compound tenses. *The Participle Past of* Renaître, rené m.s., renée, f.s., is seldom used (Littré's Dict).

# VERB *PLAIRE*, TO PLEASE.

## INFINITIVE MOOD.

| PRESENT. | | PAST. | |
|---|---|---|---|
| Plai*re*. | *To please.* | Avoir *plu*. | *To have pleased.* |
| **PARTICIPLE PRESENT.** | | **COMP. OF PART. PRESENT.** | |
| *Plaisant.* | *Pleasing.* | Ayant *plu*. | *Having pleased.* |

**PARTICIPLE PAST.**

*Plu* (invariable), *pleased.*

## SIMPLE TENSES.

### INDICATIVE MOOD.

#### PRESENT.

| | |
|---|---|
| Je plais. | *I please.* |
| Tu plais. | *thou pleasest.* |
| Il *plaît*. | *he pleases.* |
| Nous *plaisons*. | *we please.* |
| Vous *plaisez*. | *you please.* |
| Ils *plaisent*. | *they please.* |

#### IMPERFECT.

| | |
|---|---|
| Je *plaisais*. | *I was pleasing.* |
| Tu *plaisais*. | *thou wast pleasing.* |
| Il *plaisait*. | *he was pleasing.* |
| Nous *plaisions*. | *we were pleasing.* |
| Vous *plaisiez*. | *you were pleasing.* |
| Ils *plaisaient*. | *they were pleasing.* |

#### PAST DEFINITE.

| | |
|---|---|
| Je *plus*. | *I pleased.* |
| Tu *plus*. | *thou pleasedst.* |
| Il *plut*. | *he pleased.* |
| Nous *plûmes*. | *we pleased.* |
| Vous *plûtes*. | *you pleased.* |
| Ils *plurent*. | *they pleased.* |

#### FUTURE.

| | |
|---|---|
| Je plairai. | *I shall please.* |
| Tu plairas. | *thou wilt please.* |
| Il plaira. | *he will please.* |
| Nous plairons. | *we shall please.* |
| Vous plairez. | *you will please.* |
| Ils plairont. | *they will please.* |

### CONDITIONAL MOOD.

#### PRESENT.

| | |
|---|---|
| Je plairais. | *I should please.* |
| Tu plairais. | *thou wouldst please.* |
| Il plairait. | *he would please.* |
| Nous plairions. | *we should please.* |
| Vous plairiez. | *you would please.* |
| Ils plairaient. | *they would please.* |

### IMPERATIVE MOOD.

#### PRESENT.

| | |
|---|---|
| Plais - - - | *Please (thou).* |
| Qu'il *plaise* - - | *let him please.* |
| Plaisons - - - | *let us please.* |
| Plaisez - - - | *please (you).* |
| Qu'ils *plaisent* - - | *let them please* |

### SUBJUNCTIVE MOOD.

#### PRESENT.

| | |
|---|---|
| Que je *plaise*. | *That I may please.* |
| Que tu *plaises*. | *that thou mayest please.* |
| Qu'il *plaise*. | *that he may please.* |
| Que nous *plaisions*. | *that we may please.* |
| Que vous *plaisiez*. | *that you may please.* |
| Qu'ils *plaisent*. | *that they may please.* |

#### IMPERFECT.

| | |
|---|---|
| Que je *plusse*. | *That I might please.* |
| Que tu *plusses*. | *that thou mightest please.* |
| Qu'il *plût*. | *that he might please.* |
| Que nous *plussions*. | *that we might please.* |
| Que vous *plussiez*. | *that you might please.* |
| Qu'ils *plussent*. | *that they might please.* |

## COMPOUND TENSES.

| | | | | | |
|---|---|---|---|---|---|
| Past def. | J'ai *plu*, etc. | *I have pleased, etc.* | Cond. past. | J'aurais *plu*, etc. | *I should have pleased, etc.* |
| Plup. | J'avais *plu*, etc. | *I had pleased, etc.* | Sub. past. | Que j'aie *plu*, etc. | *That I may have pleased, etc.* |
| Past ant. | J'eus *plu*, etc. | *I had pleased, etc.* | | | |
| Fut. ant. | J'aurai *plu*, etc. | *I shall have pleased, etc.* | Sub. plup. | Que j'eusse *plu*, etc. | *That I might have pleased, etc.* |

CONJUGATE IN THE SAME MANNER:

Déplaire - - - - *To displease.* | Complaire - - - *To please, to humour.*

# VERB *PRENDRE*, TO TAKE.

## INFINITIVE MOOD.

| PRESENT. | | PAST. | |
|---|---|---|---|
| Prend*re*. | *To take.* | Avoir *pris.* | *To have taken.* |
| **PARTICIPLE PRESENT.** | | **COMPOUND OF PARTICIPLE PRESENT.** | |
| *Prenant.* | *Taking.* | Ayant *pris.* | *Having taken.* |

### PARTICIPLE PAST.

*Pris* (m.s.), *prise* (f.s.), *pris* (m.pl.), *prises* (f.pl.), *taken.*

## SIMPLE TENSES.

### INDICATIVE MOOD.

#### PRESENT.

| Je prends. | *I take.* |
|---|---|
| Tu prends. | *thou takest.* |
| Il prend. | *he takes.* |
| Nous *prenons.* | *we take.* |
| Vous *prenez.* | *you take.* |
| Ils *prennent.* | *they take.* |

#### IMPERFECT.

| Je *prenais.* | *I was taking.* |
|---|---|
| Tu *prenais.* | *thou wast taking.* |
| Il *prenait.* | *he was taking.* |
| Nous *prenions.* | *we were taking.* |
| Vous *preniez.* | *you were taking.* |
| Ils *prenaient.* | *they were taking.* |

#### PAST DEFINITE.

| Je *pris.* | *I took.* |
|---|---|
| Tu *pris.* | *thou tookest.* |
| Il *prit.* | *he took.* |
| Nous *prîmes.* | *we took.* |
| Vous *prîtes.* | *you took.* |
| Ils *prirent.* | *they took.* |

#### FUTURE.

| Je prendrai. | *I shall take.* |
|---|---|
| Tu prendras. | *thou wilt take.* |
| Il prendra. | *he will take.* |
| Nous prendrons. | *we shall take.* |
| Vous prendrez. | *you will take.* |
| Ils prendront. | *they will take.* |

### CONDITIONAL MOOD.

#### PRESENT.

| Je prendrais. | *I should take.* |
|---|---|
| Tu prendrais. | *thou wouldst take.* |
| Il prendrait. | *he would take.* |
| Nous prendrions. | *we should take.* |
| Vous prendriez. | *you would take.* |
| Ils prendraient. | *they would take.* |

### IMPERATIVE MOOD.
#### PRESENT.

| Prends - - - | *Take (thou).* |
|---|---|
| Qu'il *prenne* - | . *let him take.* |
| *Prenons* - - | - *let us take.* |
| *Prenez* - - - | *take (you).* |
| Qu'ils *prennent* | - *let them take.* |

### SUBJUNCTIVE MOOD.
#### PRESENT.

| Que je *prenne.* | *That I may take.* |
|---|---|
| Que tu *prennes.* | *that thou mayest take.* |
| Qu'il *prenne.* | *that he may take.* |
| Que nous *prenions.* | *that we may take.* |
| Que vous *preniez.* | *that you may take.* |
| Qu'ils *prennent.* | *that they may take.* |

#### IMPERFECT.

| Que je *prisse.* | *That I might take.* |
|---|---|
| Que tu *prisses.* | *that thou mightest take.* |
| Qu'il *prît.* | *that he might take.* |
| Que nous *prissions.* | *that we might take.* |
| Que vous *prissiez.* | *that you might take.* |
| Qu'ils *prissent.* | *that they might take.* |

## COMPOUND TENSES.

| Past ind. | J'ai *pris,* etc. | *I have taken, etc.* |
|---|---|---|
| Plup. | J'avais *pris,* etc. | *I had taken. etc.* |
| Past ant. | J'eus *pris,* etc. | *I had taken, etc.* |
| Fut. ant. | J'aurai *pris,* etc. | *I shall have taken, etc.* |

| Cond. past. | J'aurais *pris,* etc. | *I should have taken, etc.* |
|---|---|---|
| Sub. past. | Que j'aie *pris,* etc. | *That I may have taken, etc.* |
| Sub. plup. | Que j'eusse *pris,* etc. | *That I might have taken, etc.* |

### CONJUGATE IN THE SAME MANNER:

| Apprendre | - | *To learn.* |
|---|---|---|
| Comprendre | - | *— understand, to comprehend.* |
| Déprendre | - | *— detach, to loosen.* |
| Désapprendre | - | *— to unlearn, to forget.* |

| Entreprendre | - | - | *To undertake.* |
|---|---|---|---|
| Se méprendre | - | - | *— mistake.* |
| Rapprendre | - | - | *— learn again.* |
| Reprendre | - | - | *— retake.* |
| Surprendre | - | - | *— surprise.* |

N.B.—The *n* of the above verbs is doubled, as in *Prendre,* in the following persons: Third person plural of the present of the Indicative; first, second, third person singular, and third person plural of the Subjunctive; and in the Imperative third person singular and third person plural. *That is to say, when* N *comes before the mute terminations* E, ES, ENT.

## VERB *RÉSOUDRE,* TO RESOLVE.

### INFINITIVE MOOD.

| PRESENT. | | PAST. | |
|---|---|---|---|
| Résoud*re.* | *To resolve.* | Avoir *résolu.* | *To have resolved.* |
| PARTICIPLE PRESENT. | | COMP. OF PART. PRESENT. | |
| *Résolvant.* | *Resolving.* | Ayant *résolu.* | *Having resolved.* |

PARTICIPLE PAST.

*Résolu* (m.s.), *résolue* (f.s.), *résolus* (m.pl.), *résolues* (f.pl.), *resolved.*

### SIMPLE TENSES.

#### INDICATIVE MOOD.

##### PRESENT.

| Je *résous.* | *I resolve.* |
|---|---|
| Tu *résous.* | *thou resolvest.* |
| Il *résout.* | *he resolves.* |
| Nous *résolvons.* | *we resolve.* |
| Vous *résolvez.* | *you resolve.* |
| Ils *résolvent.* | *they resolve.* |

##### IMPERFECT.

| Je *résolvais.* | *I was resolving.* |
|---|---|
| Tu *résolvais.* | *thou wast resolving.* |
| Il *résolvait.* | *he was resolving.* |
| Nous *résolvions.* | *we were resolving.* |
| Vous *résolviez.* | *you were resolving.* |
| Ils *résolvaient.* | *they were resolving.* |

##### PAST DEFINITE.

| Je *résolus.* | *I resolved.* |
|---|---|
| Tu *résolus.* | *thou resolvedst.* |
| Il *résolut.* | *he resolved.* |
| Nous *résolûmes.* | *we resolved.* |
| Vous *résolûtes.* | *you resolved.* |
| Ils *résolurent.* | *they resolved.* |

##### FUTURE.

| Je résoudrai. | *I shall resolve.* |
|---|---|
| Tu résoudras. | *thou wilt resolve.* |
| Il résoudra. | *he will resolve.* |
| Nous résoudrons. | *we shall resolve.* |
| Vous résoudrez. | *you will resolve.* |
| Ils résoudront. | *they will resolve.* |

#### CONDITIONAL MOOD.

##### PRESENT.

| Je résoudrais. | *I should resolve.* |
|---|---|
| Tu résoudrais. | *thou wouldst resolve.* |
| Il résoudrait. | *he would resolve.* |
| Nous résoudrions. | *we should resolve.* |
| Vous résoudriez. | *you would resolve.* |
| Ils résoudraient. | *they would resolve.* |

#### IMPERATIVE MOOD.

##### PRESENT.

| Résous | - | - | *Resolve (thou).* |
|---|---|---|---|
| Qu'il *résolve* | | - | *let him resolve.* |
| *Résolvons* | - | - | *let us resolve.* |
| *Résolvez* | - | - | *resolve (you).* |
| Qu'ils *résolvent* | | - | *let them resolve.* |

#### SUBJUNCTIVE MOOD.

##### PRESENT.

| Que je *résolve.* | *That I may resolve.* |
|---|---|
| Que tu *résolves.* | *that thou mayest resolve.* |
| Qu'il *résolve.* | *that he may resolve.* |
| Que nous *résolvions.* | *that we may resolve.* |
| Que vous *résolviez.* | *that you may resolve.* |
| Qu'ils *résolvent.* | *that they may resolve.* |

##### IMPERFECT.

| Que je *résolusse.* | *That I might* |
|---|---|
| Que tu *résolusses.* | *that thou mightest* |
| Qu'il *résolût.* | *that he might* |
| Que nous *résolussions.* | *that we might* |
| Que vous *résolussiez.* | *that you might* |
| Qu'ils *résolussent.* | *that they might* |

*resolve.*

### COMPOUND TENSES.

| Past ind. | J'ai *résolu,* etc. *I have resolved, etc.* | Cond. past. | J'aurais *résolu, I should have re-* |
|---|---|---|---|
| Plup. | J'avais *résolu, I had resolved,* etc. *etc.* | | *solved, etc.* |
| Past ant. | J'eus *résolu,* etc. *I had resolved, etc.* | Sub. past. | Que j'aie *ré- That I may have* solu, etc. *resolved, etc.* |
| Fut. ant. | J'aurai *résolu, I shall have re-* etc. *solved, etc.* | Sub. plup. | Que j'eusse *ré- That I might have* solu, etc. *resolved, etc.* |

N.B,—The verb *Résoudre* has two past participles : *résolu* and *résous.* When *résoudre* means *to determine, to decide,* the participle *résolu* m., *résolue* f., is to be used.
When *résoudre* signifies *to change a thing into another,* its participle is *résous* (and that participle is invariable).
Ex. : *Le froid a résous le brouillard en pluie*—The cold has turned the fog into rain.

## VERB *RIRE*, TO LAUGH.

### INFINITIVE MOOD.

| PRESENT. | | PAST. | |
|---|---|---|---|
| Ri*re*. | *To laugh.* | Avoir *ri*. | *To have laughed.* |
| | PARTICIPLE PRESENT. | | COMP. OF PART. PRESENT. |
| Riant. | *Laughing.* | Ayant *ri*. | *Having laughed.* |

PARTICIPLE PAST.
*Ri* (invariable), *laughed.*

SIMPLE TENSES.

### INDICATIVE MOOD.

**PRESENT.**

| Je ris. | *I laugh.* |
|---|---|
| Tu ris. | *thou laughest.* |
| Il rit. | *he laughs.* |
| Nous rions. | *we laugh.* |
| Vous riez. | *you laugh.* |
| Ils rient. | *they laugh.* |

**IMPERFECT.**

| Je riais. | *I was laughing.* |
|---|---|
| Tu riais. | *thou wast laughing.* |
| Il riait. | *he was laughing.* |
| Nous riions. | *we were laughing.* |
| Vous riiez. | *you were laughing.* |
| Ils riaient. | *they were laughing.* |

**PAST DEFINITE.**

| Je *ris*. | *I laughed.* |
|---|---|
| Tu *ris*. | *thou laughedst.* |
| Il *rit*. | *he laughed.* |
| Nous *rîmes*. | *we laughed.* |
| Vous *rîtes*. | *you laughed.* |
| Ils *rirent*. | *they laughed.* |

**FUTURE.**

| Je rirai. | *I shall laugh.* |
|---|---|
| Tu riras. | *thou wilt laugh.* |
| Il rira. | *he will laugh.* |
| Nous rirons. | *we shall laugh.* |
| Vous rirez. | *you will laugh.* |
| Ils riront. | *they will laugh.* |

### CONDITIONAL MOOD.

**PRESENT.**

| Je rirais. | *I should laugh.* |
|---|---|
| Tu rirais. | *thou wouldst laugh.* |
| Il rirait. | *he would laugh.* |
| Nous ririons. | *we should laugh.* |
| Vous ririez. | *you would laugh.* |
| Ils riraient. | *they would laugh.* |

### IMPERATIVE MOOD.

**PRESENT.**

| Ris | - | - | - | *Laugh (thou).* |
|---|---|---|---|---|
| Qu'il rie | | - | - | *let him laugh.* |
| Rions | - | - | - | *let us laugh.* |
| Riez | - | - | - | *laugh (you).* |
| Qu'ils rient | - | | - | *let them laugh.* |

### SUBJUNCTIVE MOOD.

**PRESENT.**

| Que je rie. | *That I may laugh.* |
|---|---|
| Que tu ries. | *that thou mayest laugh.* |
| Qu'il rie. | *that he may laugh.* |
| Que nous riions. | *that we may laugh.* |
| Que vous riiez. | *that you may laugh.* |
| Qu'ils rient. | *that they may laugh.* |

**IMPERFECT.**

| Que je *risse*. | *That I might* |
|---|---|
| Que tu *risses*. | *that thou mightest* |
| Qu'il *rît*. | *that he might* |
| Que nous *rissions*. | *hat we might* |
| Que vous *rissiez*. | *that you might* |
| Qu'ils *rissent*. | *that they might* |

*laugh.*

### COMPOUND TENSES.

| *Past ind.* | J'ai *ri*, etc. | *I have laughed, etc.* | *Cond. past.* | J'aurais *ri*, etc. | *I should have laughed, etc.* |
|---|---|---|---|---|---|
| *Plup.* | J'avais *ri*, etc. | *I had laughed, etc.* | | | |
| *Past ant.* | J'eus *ri*, etc. | *I had laughed, etc.* | *Sub. past.* | Que j'aie *ri*, etc. | *that I may have laughed, etc.* |
| *Fut. ant.* | J'aurai *ri*, etc. | *I shall have laughed, etc.* | *Sub. plup.* | Que j'eusse *ri*, etc. | *that I might have laughed, etc.* |

N.B.—I. *Se rire de* means *to laugh at, to ridicule. Se rire de* being a pronominal verb, is conjugated with two pronouns: Je me; tu te, etc. Indicative Present: Je me ris de, *I laugh at, I ridicule.* Tu te ris de, *thou laughest at,* etc.
In compound tenses, *Se rire de* is conjugated, being a pronominal verb, with *to be,* être.
*Past Indefinite*—Je me suis ri de, *I have laughed at, I ridiculed.*
II. *Sourire,* to smile, is conjugated like *rire.*
III. *Rire* takes two *i*'s in the Imperfect of the Indicative, first and second person plural, and the *Present of the Subjunctive,* same persons,(see above), and also all verbs in which the Participle Present ends by IANT.

ROUEN, THE GROS HORLOGE CLOCKTOWER

BAYEUX, NOTRE DAME CATHEDRAL

# VERB *SUIVRE*, TO FOLLOW.

## INFINITIVE MOOD.

| PRESENT. | | PAST. | |
|---|---|---|---|
| Suivre. | *To follow.* | Avoir suivi. | *To have followed.* |
| **PARTICIPLE PRESENT.** | | **COMP. OF PART. PRESENT.** | |
| Suivant. | *Following.* | Ayant suivi. | *Having followed.* |

### PARTICIPLE PAST.

*Suivi* (m.s.), *suivie* (f.s.), *suivis* (m.pl.), *suivies* (f.pl.), *followed.*

---

## SIMPLE TENSES.

### INDICATIVE MOOD.

#### PRESENT.

| | |
|---|---|
| Je *suis.* | *I follow.* |
| Tu *suis.* | *thou followest.* |
| Il *suit.* | *he follows.* |
| Nous suivons. | *we follow.* |
| Vous suivez. | *you follow.* |
| Ils suivent. | *they follow.* |

#### IMPERFECT.

| | |
|---|---|
| Je suivais. | *I was following.* |
| Tu suivais. | *thou wast following.* |
| Il suivait. | *he was following.* |
| Nous suivions. | *we were following.* |
| Vous suiviez. | *you were following.* |
| Ils suivaient. | *they were following.* |

#### PAST DEFINITE.

| | |
|---|---|
| Je suivis. | *I followed.* |
| Tu suivis. | *thou followedst.* |
| Il suivit. | *he followed.* |
| Nous suivîmes. | *we followed.* |
| Vous suivîtes. | *you followed.* |
| Ils suivirent. | *they followed.* |

#### FUTURE.

| | |
|---|---|
| Je suivrai. | *I shall follow.* |
| Tu suivras. | *thou wilt follow.* |
| Il suivra. | *he will follow.* |
| Nous suivrons. | *we shall follow.* |
| Vous suivrez. | *you will follow.* |
| Ils suivront. | *they will follow.* |

### CONDITIONAL MOOD.

#### PRESENT.

| | |
|---|---|
| Je suivrais. | *I should follow.* |
| Tu suivrais. | *thou wouldst follow.* |
| Il suivrait. | *he would follow.* |
| Nous suivrions. | *we should follow.* |
| Vous suivriez. | *you would follow.* |
| Ils suivraient. | *they would follow.* |

### IMPERATIVE MOOD.

#### PRESENT.

| | |
|---|---|
| Suis - - - | *Follow* (*thou*). |
| Qu'il suive - - | *let him follow.* |
| Suivons - - - | *let us follow.* |
| Suivez - - - | *follow* (*you*). |
| Qu'ils suivent - - | *let them follow.* |

### SUBJUNCTIVE MOOD.

#### PRESENT.

| | |
|---|---|
| Que je suive. | *That I may* |
| Que tu suives. | *that thou mayest* |
| Qu'il suive. | *that he may* |
| Que nous suivions. | *that we may* |
| Que vous suiviez. | *that you may* |
| Qu'ils suivent. | *that they may* |

} *follow.*

#### IMPERFECT.

| | |
|---|---|
| Que je suivisse. | *That I might* |
| Que tu suivisses. | *that thou mightest* |
| Qu'il suivît. | *that he might* |
| Que nous suivissions. | *that we might* |
| Que vous suivissiez. | *that you might* |
| Qu'ils suivissent. | *that they might* |

} *follow.*

---

## COMPOUND TENSES.

| | | | | | |
|---|---|---|---|---|---|
| Past ind. | J'ai suivi, etc. | *I have followed, etc.* | Cond. past. | J'aurais suivi, etc. | *I should have followed, etc.* |
| Plup. | J'avais suivi, etc. | *I had followed, etc.* | | | |
| Past ant. | J'eus suivi, etc. | *I had followed, etc.* | Sub. past. | Que j'aie suivi, etc. | *That I may have followed, etc.* |
| Fut. ant. | J'aurai suivi, etc. | *I shall have followed, etc.* | Sub. plup. | Que j'eusse suivi, etc. | *That I might have followed, etc.* |

---

CONJUGATE IN THE SAME MANNER:

Poursuivre - - - - *To pursue, to prosecute.*

# VERB *TAIRE* TO CONCEAL, TO KEEP SECRET.

## INFINITIVE MOOD.

| PRESENT. | | PAST. | |
|---|---|---|---|
| Tair*e* | *To conceal.* | Avoir *tu.* | *To have concealed.* |
| **PARTICIPLE PRESENT.** | | **COMP. OF PART. PRESENT.** | |
| *Taisant.* | *Concealing.* | Ayant *tu.* | *Having concealed.* |

### PARTICIPLE PAST.

*Tu* (m.s.), *tue* (f.s.), *tus* (m.pl.), *tues* (f.p.), *concealed.*

## SIMPLE TENSES.

### INDICATIVE MOOD.

#### PRESENT.

| Je tais. | *I conceal.* |
|---|---|
| Tu tais. | *thou concealest.* |
| Il *tait.* | *he conceals.* |
| Nous *taisons.* | *we conceal.* |
| Vous *taisez.* | *you conceal.* |
| Ils *taisent.* | *they conceal.* |

#### IMPERFECT.

| Je *taisais.* | *I was concealing.* |
|---|---|
| Tu *taisais.* | *thou wast concealing.* |
| Il *taisait.* | *he was concealing.* |
| Nous *taisions.* | *we were concealing.* |
| Vous *taisiez.* | *you were concealing.* |
| Ils *taisaient.* | *they were concealing.* |

#### PAST DEFINITE.

| Je *tus.* | *I concealed.* |
|---|---|
| Tu *tus.* | *thou concealedst.* |
| Il *tut.* | *he concealed.* |
| Nous *tûmes.* | *we concealed.* |
| Vous *tûmes.* | *you concealed.* |
| Ils *turent.* | *they concealed.* |

#### FUTURE.

| Je tairai. | *I shall conceal.* |
|---|---|
| Tu tairas. | *thou wilt conceal.* |
| Il taira. | *he will conceal.* |
| Nous tairons. | *we shall conceal.* |
| Vous tairez. | *you will conceal.* |
| Ils tairont. | *they will conceal.* |

### CONDITIONAL MOOD.

#### PRESENT.

| Je tairais. | *I should conceal.* |
|---|---|
| Tu tairais. | *thou wouldst conceal.* |
| Il tairait. | *he would conceal.* |
| Nous tairions. | *we should conceal.* |
| Vous tairiez. | *you would conceal.* |
| Ils tairaient. | *they would conceal.* |

### IMPERATIVE MOOD.

#### PRESENT.

| Tais - | *Conceal (thou).* |
|---|---|
| Qu'il *taise* - | - *let him conceal.* |
| *Taisons* - | - *let us conceal.* |
| *Taisez* - - | - *conceal (you).* |
| Qu'ils *taisent* | - *let them conceal.* |

### SUBJUNCTIVE MOOD.

#### PRESENT.

| Que je *taise.* | *That I may conceal.* |
|---|---|
| Que tu *taises.* | *that thou mayest conceal.* |
| Qu'il *taise.* | *that he may conceal.* |
| Que nous *taisions.* | *that we may conceal.* |
| Que vous *taisiez.* | *that you may conceal.* |
| Qu'ils *taisent.* | *that they may conceal.* |

#### IMPERFECT.

| Que je *tusse.* | *That I might conceal.* |
|---|---|
| Que tu *tusses.* | *that thou mightest conceal.* |
| Qu'il *tût.* | *that he might conceal.* |
| Que nous *tussions.* | *that we might conceal.* |
| Que vous *tussiez.* | *that you might conceal.* |
| Qu'ils *tussent.* | *that they might conceal.* |

## COMPOUND TENSES.

| *Past ind.* | J'ai *tu*, etc. | *I have concealed, etc.* | *Cond. past.* | J'aurais *tu*, etc. | *I should have concealed, etc.* |
|---|---|---|---|---|---|
| *Plup.* | J'avais *tu*, etc. | *I had concealed, etc.* | *Sub. past.* | Que j'aie *tu*, etc. | *That I may have concealed, etc.* |
| *Past ant.* | J'eus *tu*, etc. | *I had concealed, etc,* | | | |
| *Fut. ant.* | J'aurai *tu*, etc. | *I shall have concealed, etc.* | *Sub. plup.* | Que j'eusse *tu*, etc. | *That I might have concealed, etc.* |

**N.B.**—The verb *Se Taire*, To be silent, to hold one's tongue, being pronominal, is conjugated with two pronouns. 
*Indicative Present* { Je me tais, *I am silent, I hold my tongue.* 
{ Tu te tais, etc., *Thou art silent, thou holdest thy tongue.* 
**See the Pronominal verb, page 48.**

# VERB *TRAIRE*, TO MILK.

## INFINITIVE MOOD.

| PRESENT. | | PAST. | |
|---|---|---|---|
| Trai*re* | *To milk.* | Avoir *trait.* | *To have milked.* |

| PARTICIPLE PRESENT. | | COMP. OF PART. PRESENT. | |
|---|---|---|---|
| *Trayant.* | *Milking.* | Ayant *trait.* | *Having milked.* |

PARTICIPLE PAST.

*Trait* (m.s.), *traite* (f.s.), *traits* (m.pl.), *traites* (f.pl.), *milked.*

### SIMPLE TENSES.

#### INDICATIVE MOOD.

PRESENT.

| Je trais. | *I milk.* |
|---|---|
| Tu trais. | *thou milkest.* |
| Il *trait.* | *he milks.* |
| Nous *trayons.* | *we milk.* |
| Vous *trayez.* | *you milk.* |
| Ils *traient.* | *they milk.* |

IMPERFECT.

| Je *trayais.* | *I was milking.* |
|---|---|
| Tu *trayais.* | *thou wast milking.* |
| Il *trayait.* | *he was milking.* |
| Nous *trayions.* | *we were milking.* |
| Vous *trayiez.* | *you were milking.* |
| Ils *trayaient.* | *they were milking.* |

*(No Preterite Definite.)*

FUTURE.

| Je trairai. | *I shall milk.* |
|---|---|
| Tu trairas. | *thou wilt milk.* |
| Il traira. | *he will milk.* |
| Nous trairons. | *we shall milk.* |
| Vous trairez. | *you will milk.* |
| Ils trairont. | *they will milk.* |

#### CONDITIONAL MOOD.

PRESENT.

| Je trairais. | *I should milk.* |
|---|---|
| Tu trairais. | *thou wouldst milk.* |
| Il trairait. | *he would milk.* |
| Nous trairions. | *we should milk.* |
| Vous trairiez. | *you would milk.* |
| Ils trairaient. | *they would milk.* |

#### IMPERATIVE MOOD.

PRESENT.

| Trais - - - | *Milk (thou).* |
|---|---|
| Qu'il *traie* - | *let him milk.* |
| *Trayons* | *let us milk.* |
| *Trayez* - - - | *milk (you).* |
| Qu'ils traient - - | *let them milk.* |

#### SUBJUNCTIVE MOOD.

PRESENT.

| Que je traie. | *That I may milk.* |
|---|---|
| Que tu traies. | *that thou mayest milk.* |
| Qu'il traie. | *that he may milk.* |
| Que nous *trayions.* | *that we may milk.* |
| Que vous *trayiez.* | *that you may milk.* |
| Qu'ils *trayent.* | *that they may milk.* |

*(No Imperfect.)*

### COMPOUND TENSES.

| Past ind. | J'ai *trait*, etc. | *I have milked, etc.* | Cond. past. | J'aurais *trait*, etc. | *I should have milked, etc.* |
|---|---|---|---|---|---|
| Plup. | J'avais *trait*, etc. | *I had milked, etc.* | Sub. past. | Que j'aie *trait*, etc. | *That I may have milked, etc.* |
| Past ant. | J'eus *trait*, etc. | *I had milked, etc.* | Sub. plup. | Que j'eusse *trait*, etc. | *That I might have milked.* |
| Fut. ant. | J'aurai *trait*, etc. | *I shall have milked, etc.* | | | |

CONJUGATE IN THE SAME MANNER:

| Abstraire | - - - - | *To abstract.* | Retraire | - - - | *To redeem an estate (law).* |
|---|---|---|---|---|---|
| Distraire | - - - | *— distract.* | Rentraire - | - - | *—fine draw, to darn.* |
| Extraire | - . - - | *— extract* | Soustraire - | - - | *— subtract.* |

N.B.—According to Littré's Dict. Attraire. *To allure, to entice*, is conjugated like *Traire.*

## VERB *VAINCRE*, TO VANQUISH.

### INFINITIVE MOOD.

| PRESENT. | | PAST. | |
|---|---|---|---|
| Vaincre. | To vanquish. | Avoir vaincu | To have vanquished. |
| **PARTICIPLE PRESENT.** | | **COMP. OF PART PRESENT.** | |
| Vainquant. | Vanquishing. | Ayant vaincu. | Having vanquished. |

#### PARTICIPLE PAST.

Vaincu (m.s.), vaincue (f.s.), vaincus (m.pl.), vaincues (f.pl.), vanquished.

### SIMPLE TENSES.

#### INDICATIVE MOOD.
##### PRESENT.

| Je vaincs. | I vanquish. |
|---|---|
| Tu vaincs. | thou vanquishest. |
| Il vainc. | he vanquishes. |
| Nous vainquons. | we vanquish. |
| Vous vainquez. | you vanquish. |
| Ils vainquent. | they vanquish. |

##### IMPERFECT.

| Je vainquais. | I was vanquishing. |
|---|---|
| Tu vainquais. | thou wast vanquishing. |
| Il vainquait. | he was vanquishing. |
| Nous vainquions. | we were vanquishing. |
| Vous vainquiez. | you were vanquishing. |
| Ils vainquaient. | they were vanquishing. |

##### PAST DEFINITE.

| Je vainquis. | I vanquished. |
|---|---|
| Tu vainquis. | thou vanquishedst. |
| Il vainquit. | he vanquished. |
| Nous vainquîmes. | we vanquished. |
| Vous vainquîtes. | you vanquished. |
| Ils vainquirent. | they vanquished. |

##### FUTURE.

| Je vaincrai. | I shall vanquish. |
|---|---|
| Tu vaincras. | thou wilt vanquish. |
| Il vaincra. | he will vanquish. |
| Nous vaincrons. | we shall vanquish. |
| Vous vaincrez. | you will vanquish. |
| Ils vaincront. | they will vanquish. |

#### CONDITIONAL MOOD
##### PRESENT.

| Je vaincrais. | I should vanquish. |
|---|---|
| Tu vaincrais. | thou wouldst vanquish. |
| Il vaincrait. | he would vanquish. |
| Nous vaincrions. | we should vanquish. |
| Vous vaincriez. | you would vanquish. |
| Ils vaincraient. | they would vanquish. |

#### IMPERATIVE MOOD.
##### PRESENT.

| Vaincs | - - | Vanquish (thou). |
|---|---|---|
| Qu'il vainque | - | let him vanquish. |
| Vainquons | - - | let us vanquish. |
| Vainquez | - - | vanquish (you). |
| Qu'ils vainquent | - | let them vanquish. |

#### SUBJUNCTIVE MOOD.
##### PRESENT.

| Que je vainque. | That I may |
|---|---|
| Que tu vainques. | that thou mayest |
| Qu'il vainque. | that he may |
| Que nous vainquions. | that we may |
| Que vous vainquiez. | that you may |
| Qu'ils vainquent. | that they may |

*vanquish.*

##### IMPERFECT.

| Que je vainquisse. | That I might |
|---|---|
| Que tu vainquisses. | that thou mightest |
| Qu'il vainquît. | that he might |
| Que nous vainquissions. | that we might |
| Que vous vainquissiez. | that you might |
| Qu'ils vainquissent. | that they might |

*vanquish.*

### COMPOUND TENSES.

| *Past def.* | J'ai vaincu, etc. | I have vanquished, etc. | *Cond. past.* | J'aurais vaincu, etc. | I should have vanquished, etc. |
|---|---|---|---|---|---|
| *Plup.* | J'avais vaincu, etc. | I had vanquished, etc. | *Sub. past.* | Que j'aie vaincu, etc. | that I may have vanquished, etc. |
| *Past ant.* | J'eus vaincu, etc. | I had vanquished, etc. | | | |
| *Fut. ant.* | J'aurai vaincu, etc. | I shall have vanquished, etc. | *Sub. plup.* | Que j'eusse vaincu, etc. | that I might have vanquished, etc. |

Convaincre, *To convince*, is conjugated in the same manner.
N.B.—*Vaincre* is seldom used in the *Present* and *Imperfect* of the *Indicative*. (Academy.)

**132**

# VERB *VIVRE*, TO LIVE.

## INFINITIVE MOOD.

| PRESENT. | | PAST. | |
|---|---|---|---|
| Vivre. | *To live.* | Avoir *vécu*. | *To have lived.* |
| **PARTICIPLE PRESENT.** | | **COMP. OF PARTICIPLE PRESENT.** | |
| Vivant | *Living.* | Ayant *vécu*. | *Having lived.* |

**PARTICIPLE PAST.**
*Vécu* (invariable), *lived.*

---

### SIMPLE TENSES.

## INDICATIVE MOOD.

### PRESENT.

| Je *vis*. | *I live.* |
|---|---|
| Tu *vis*. | *thou livest.* |
| Il *vit*. | *he lives.* |
| Nous vivons. | *we live.* |
| Vous vivez. | *you live.* |
| Ils vivent. | *they live.* |

### IMPERFECT.

| Je vivais. | *I was living.* |
|---|---|
| Tu vivais. | *thou wast living.* |
| Il vivait. | *he was living.* |
| Nous vivions. | *we were living.* |
| Vous viviez. | *you were living.* |
| Ils vivaient. | *they were living.* |

### PAST DEFINITE.

| Je *vécus*. | *I lived.* |
|---|---|
| Tu *vécus*. | *thou livedst.* |
| Il *vécut*. | *he lived.* |
| Nous *vécûmes*. | *we lived.* |
| Vous *vécûtes*. | *you lived.* |
| Ils *vécurent*. | *they lived.* |

### FUTURE.

| Je vivrai. | *I shall live.* |
|---|---|
| Tu vivras. | *thou wilt live.* |
| Il vivra. | *he will live.* |
| Nous vivrons. | *we shall live.* |
| Vous vivrez. | *you will live.* |
| Ils vivront. | *they will live.* |

## CONDITIONAL MOOD.

### PRESENT.

| Je vivrais. | *I should live.* |
|---|---|
| Tu vivrais. | *thou wouldst live.* |
| Il vivrait. | *he would live.* |
| Nous vivrions. | *we should live.* |
| Vous vivriez. | *you would live.* |
| Ils vivraient. | *they would live.* |

## IMPERATIVE MOOD.

### PRESENT.

| Vis | - | - | - | *Live (thou).* |
|---|---|---|---|---|
| Qu'il vive | - | | - | *let him live.* |
| Vivons | - | - | | *let us live.* |
| Vivez | - | - | - | *live (you).* |
| Qu'ils vivent | - | | - | *let them live.* |

## SUBJUNCTIVE MOOD.

### PRESENT.

| Que je vive. | *That I may live.* |
|---|---|
| Que tu vives. | *that thou mayest live.* |
| Qu'il vive | *that he may live.* |
| Que nous vivions. | *that we may live.* |
| Que vous viviez. | *that you may live.* |
| Qu'ils vivent. | *that they may live.* |

### IMPERFECT.

| Que je *vécusse*. | *That I might live.* |
|---|---|
| Que tu *vécusses*. | *that thou mightest live.* |
| Qu'il *vécût*. | *that he might live.* |
| Que nous *vécussions*. | *that we might live.* |
| Que vous *vécussiez*. | *that you might live.* |
| Qu'ils *vécussent*. | *that they might live.* |

---

### COMPOUND TENSES.

| Past. ind. | J'ai *vécu*, etc. | *I have lived, etc.* | Cond. past. | J'aurais *vécu*, etc. | *I should have lived, etc.* |
|---|---|---|---|---|---|
| Plup. | J'avais *vécu*, etc. | *I had lived, etc.* | Sub. past. | Que j'aie *vécu*, etc. | *that I may have lived, etc.* |
| Past. ant. | J'eus *vécu*, etc. | *I had lived, etc.* | Sub. plup. | Que j'eusse *vécu*, etc. | *that I might have lived, etc.* |
| Fut. ant. | J'aurai *vécu*, etc. | *I shall have lived, etc.* | | | |

---

CONJUGATE IN THE SAME MANNER:

| Revivre | - | - | - | *To revive.* | Survivre | - | - | - | *To survive.* |
|---|---|---|---|---|---|---|---|---|---|

N.B.—*To live upon* or *on*, is expressed by *Vivre de*.
Je vis de pain, *I live upon bread.* Je vécus de fruit, *I lived on fruit.*

# CHAPTER 9

## Defective Verbs

THE DEFECTIVE VERBS are those which are lacking in some of the moods, tenses or persons.

---

### ACCROIRE, *To make one believe what is not true.*

Verb used only in the *Infinitive present* and with *Faire as an auxiliary.* INFINITIVE *present.* Faire accroire. — *Participle present.* Faisant accroire. — *Participle past.* Fait accroire.

INDICATIVE *Present.* Je fais accroire, tu fais accroire, il fait accroire, etc. (See Faire, page 117).

CONJUGATE LIKE ACCROIRE.—En faire accroire, *To impose upon.*—S'en faire accroire, *To be self-conceited.*

### AOÛTER, *To ripen.*

Verb scarcely used except in the *Past Participle :* Aoûté, m.s. ; Aoûtée, f.s. ;—Ex. : Melon aoûté. (*The* a *is sounded in Aoûter.*)—Acad.

### APPAROIR, *To appear, to be apparent, (a law term.)*

APPAROIR is used only in the *Infinitive present*, and in the third person singular of the *Indicative present.*

Ex. : Faire apparoir, *To show, to make apparent.*—Il appert, *It appears.* (Acad.)

### ATTRAIRE, *To attract, to allure.*

Verb only used in the *Infinitive present :* Attraire.—Ex. : Le sel est bon pour attraire les pigeons. *Salt is good for attracting pigeons.* (Acad.)

N.B.—In Littré's Dict. ATTRAIRE is conjugated like *Traire* (page 130).

### BASTER, *To suffice, (obsolete.)*

Verb used only in some familiar phrases.—Baste *or* Baste pour cela.—*Well ! let it be so.* (Acad.)

### BRAIRE, *To bray.*

The following tenses and persons are used only : (Acad.) INDICATIVE *Present.*—Il brait, ils braient.—*Future.* Il braira, ils brairont.

CONDITIONAL *Present.*—Il brairait, ils brairaient.

N.B.—*The following tenses according to Littré's Dict. could be employed.* INDICATIVE *Present.* Je brais, tu brais, il brait ; nous brayons, vous brayez, ils braient. *Imperfect.* Il brayait.—*Future.* Je brairai, tu brairas, il braira ; nous brairons, vous brairez, ils brairont. CONDITIONAL *Present.* Je brairais, tu brairais, il brairait, etc. *Compound Tenses. Past definite.* Il a brait. *Pluperfect.* Il avait brait, etc.

## BROUIR, *To blight, to blast, to dry up.*

INFINITIVE *Present.* Brouir.—*Participle present.* Brouissant.—*Participle past.* Broui, m.s., brouie, f.s.

INDICATIVE *Present.* Il brouit, ils brouissent.—*Imperfect.* Il brouissait, ils brouissaient, etc. BROUIR is conjugated like *Finir* but used only in the third persons of each tenses (Bescherelle's Dict.)

## BRUIRE, *To rustle, to rattle.*

Verb used only in the following tenses : INDICATIVE *Present.* Il bruit.—*Imperfect.* Il bruissait, ils bruissaient.—(Acad.)

In Littré's Dict. BRUIRE is conjugated as follows : INFINITITE *Present.* Bruire.— *Participle present.* Bruyant.—*Participle past.* Bruit. INDICATIVE *Present.* Je bruis, tu bruis, il bruit. *(No plural).* *Imperfect.* Je bruyais, tu bruyais, etc.—*Future.* Je bruirai, tu bruiras, il bruira, etc.

CONDITIONAL *Present.* Je bruirais, tu bruirais, il bruirait, etc. COMPOUND TENSES.— *Past indefinite.* Il a bruit, etc.

N.B.—I. Some writers have used the following forms for the *Imperfect of the Indicative.* Je bruissais, tu bruissais, il bruissait, etc., and for the *Subjunctive present.* Que je bruisse, que tu bruisses, qu'il bruisse ; que nous bruissions, que vous bruissiez, qu'ils bruissent.

II. The *Participle present.* BRUISSANT is also used by some grammarians.

## CHALOIR, *To matter, to be important.*

Verb used impersonally, and only in this phrase : Il ne m'en chaut, *No matter.*—(Acad.)

N.B.—The following tenses could be used, according to Littré's Dict. : *Future.* Il chaudra. —CONDITIONAL *Present.* Il chaudrait.—SUBJUNCTIVE *Present.* Qu'il chaille.—INFINITIVE *Present.* Chaloir, as in *Il ne peut* CHALOIR. *Il ne doit* CHALOIR.

## CHANCIR, *To get mouldy.*

INFINITIVE *Present.* Chancir.—*Participle present.* Chancissant.—*Participle past.* Chanci, m.s., chancie, f.s.

INDICATIVE *Present.* Il chancit, ils chancissent.—*Imperfect.* Il chancissait, ils chancissaient.

N.B.—CHANCIR is conjugated like *Finir*, but used only in the third persons.—*The Academy says Chancir is getting obsolete.*

## CHAUVIR, *To prick up* (*the ears.*)

According to the Academy, CHAUVIR is used only in the phrase : *Chauvir des oreilles*, in speaking of horses and mules. Ex. : *Ce cheval chauvit des oreilles*, but the conjugation of the verb is not given.

In Littré's Dict., CHAUVIR is conjugated as follows : INDICATIVE *Present.* Je chauvis, tu chauvis, il chauvit ; nous chauvons, vous chauvez, ils chauvent.—*Imperfect.* Je chauvais, tu chauvais, etc.—*Past Definite.* Je chauvis, tu chauvis, etc.—*Future.* Je chauvirai, tu chauviras, il chauvira, etc.

CONDITIONAL *Present.* Je chauvirais, tu chauvirais, il chauvirait, etc.

N.B.—In Bescherelle's Dict. of the French Verbs, CHAUVIR is conjugated like *Finir*, but used only in the *third persons.* INDICATIVE *Present.* Il chauvit, ils chauvissent, etc.—(See Finir, page 23).

## CHOIR, *To fall, to tumble.*

Verb used only in the INFINITIVE *Present.* Choir,—and in the *Past participle.* Chu, m.s., chue, f.s.—It is conjugated with Être.—Acad.

N.B.—In Littré's Dict. the following tenses are given : INDICATIVE *Present.* Je chois, tu chois, il choit (*No plural*).—*Future.* Je choirai, etc., or je cherrai, etc.

## CLORE, *To close, to shut.*

Verb used only in the following tenses : INDICATIVE *Present.* Je clos, tu clos, il clôt (*No plural*).—*Future.* Je clorai, tu cloras, etc.—CONDITIONAL *Present.* Je clorais, tu clorais, il clorait, etc.—(Acad.) *The compound tenses are used, and formed with* AVOIR. *Past indefinite.* J'ai clos, tu as clos, etc.

N.B.—*To the above tenses the following could be added* (*Littré's Dict.*) : INDICATIVE *Present.* Nous closons, vous closez.—*Imperfect.* Je closais, etc.—*Past definite.* Je closis, tu closis, etc.—SUBJUNCTIVE *Imperfect.* Que je closisse, etc.

## COMPAROIR, *To appear, (a law term.)*

Verb used only in the INFINITIVE *Present* : Être assigné à comparoir, *To be summoned to appear.*—It is obsolete and replaced by *comparaître.* (Acad.)

## SE CONDOULOIR, *To condole.*

Old Verb used in the *Infinitive present :* Se condouloir avec quelqu'un, *To sympathize with someone.*—(Acad.)

## COURRE, (Ancient form of the Infinitive *Courir*), *To run.*

It is used only as a hunting term, and means to pursue.—Ex. : *Courre le cerf, le lièvre, le daim.*—(Acad.)

## DÉCHOIR, *To decay, to fall off, to decline,*

INFINITIVE *Present.* Déchoir.—*No Participle present.*—*Participle past.* Déchu, m.s. déchue, f.s.

INDICATIVE *Present.* Je déchois, tu déchois, il déchoit ; nous déchoyons, vous déchoyez, ils déchoient.—*No Imperfect.*—*Past definite.* Je déchus, tu déchus, il déchut ; nous déchûmes, vous déchûtes, ils déchurent.—*Future.* Je décherrai, tu décherras, il décherra ; nous décherrons, vous décherrez, ils décherront.

CONDITIONAL *Present.* Je décherrais, tu décherrais, etc.—*No Imperative.*

SUBJUNCTIVE *Present.* Que je déchoie, que tu déchoies, qu'il déchoie ; que nous déchoyions, que vous déchoyiez, qu'ils déchoient.—*Imperfect.* Que je déchusse, que tu déchusses, qu'il déchût ; que nous déchussions, que vous déchussiez, qu'ils déchussent.—(Acad.)

N.B.—I. In Littré's Dict. we find : *Il déchet* (3rd pers. sing. of the Pres. of Ind.)—*Future.* Je déchoirai, tu déchoiras, etc.—CONDITIONAL *Present.* Je déchoirais, tu déchoirais, etc. —*Imperative.* Déchois, déchoyons, déchoyez.

II. DÉCHOIR is conjugated with *avoir* and *être* ; with *avoir* if action is meant, and with *être* to express the result of the action.—Ex. ; Depuis ce moment il a déchu de jour en jour.— Il y a longtemps qu'ils sont déchus de ces privilèges.

## DÉCLORE, *To unclose, to open.*

INFINITIVE *Present.* Déclore.—*No Participle present.*—*Participle past.*—Déclos, m.s., déclose, f.s.

INDICATIVE *Present.* Je déclos, tu déclos, il déclôt (*no plural*).—*Future.* Je déclorai, tu décloras, etc.—CONDITIONAL. Je déclorais, tu déclorais, etc.

SUBJUNCTIVE *Present.* Que je déclose, que tu décloses, qu'il déclose ; que nous déclosions, que vous déclosiez, qu'ils déclosent.—(Littré's Dict.)

N.B.—In the Dict. of the Acad. Déclore is not conjugated.

## DÉCROIRE, *To disbelieve.*

Verb used only in this phrase : *Je ne crois, ni ne décrois*—(Acad.), I neither believe nor disbelieve.

## DÉFAILLIR, *To faint, to fail, to grow weak.*

INDICATIVE *Present.* (*No singular*) Nous défaillons, vous défaillez, ils défaillent.—*Imperfect.* Je défaillais, tu défaillais, etc.—*Past definite.* Je défaillis, tu défaillis, il défaillit ; nous défaillîmes, vous défaillîtes, ils défaillirent.—*Past indefinite.* J'ai défailli, etc.
INFINITIVE *Present.* Défaillir.—*No Participle present.*—*Participle past.* Défailli, m.s., défaillie, f.s.
N.B.—I. The Academy says that, besides the above tenses, the following have been used sometimes : INDICATIVE *Present.* Je défaus, tu défaus, il défaut.—*Future.* Je défaudrai, tu défaudras, etc.—CONDITIONAL *Present.* Je défaudrais, tu défaudrais, etc.—SUBJUNCTIVE *Present.* Que je défaille, que tu défailles, etc.—*Imperfect.* Que je défaillisse, que tu défaillisses, etc.
II. The *Participle present*, défaillant (often used adjectively), is found in Littré's Dict.

## DÉMOUVOIR, *To make one desist, (a law term.)*

Verb used mostly in the INFINITIVE *Present.* Rien ne l'a pu démouvoir.—(Littré's Dict.)

## DÉPOURVOIR, *To unprovide, to deprive.*

Verb used in the INFINITIVE *Present.* Dépourvoir, and in the *Past definite.* Je dépourvus, tu dépourvus, il dépourvut ; nous dépourvûmes, vous dépourvûtes, ils dépourvurent.—(Acad.)
N.B.—In Littré's Dict., *Dépourvoir* is conjugated like Pourvoir (page 98).

## SE DOULOIR, *To complain, to grieve, (obsolete.)*

Verb used only in the INFINITIVE *Present.* On l'entendit *se douloir.*

## ÉCLORE, *To be hatched, to blow, to open.*

INFINITIVE *Present.* Éclore.—*No participle present.*—*Participle past.* Éclos, m.s., éclose, f.s.
INDICATIVE *Present.* J'éclos, tu éclos, *il éclôt*, nous éclosons, vous éclosez, *ils éclosent.*—*Imperfect.* J'éclosais, tu éclosais, etc.—*No Past definite.*—*Future.* J'éclôrai, tu éclôras, *il éclôra*, nous éclôrons, vous éclôrez, *ils éclôront.*
CONDITIONAL *Present.* J'éclôrais, tu éclôrais, *il éclôrait*, nous éclôrions, vous éclôriez, *ils éclôraient—no Imperative.*
SUBJUNCTIVE *Present.* Que j'éclose, que tu écloses, *qu'il éclose*, que nous éclosions, que vous éclosiez, *qu'ils éclosent.* *The compound tenses are formed with être.* (Littré's Dict.)
N.B.—The persons *in italics*, are the only ones given by the Academy.

## ÉBOUILLIR, *To boil away.*

Verb conjugated like *bouillir*, seldom used but in the *Infinitive present*, ÉBOUILLIER and in the *Past participle* : Ébouilli, m.s. Ébouillie, f.s.—The compound tenses are formed with *être.*

## ÉCHOIR, *To fall, to expire, to be due.*

INFINITIVE *Present.* Échoir.—*Participle present.* Échéant—*Participle past.* Échu, m.s. ; Échue, f.s.
INDICATIVE *Present.* Il échoit or il échet, ils échoient.—*No Imperfect. Past definite.* J'échus, tu échus, il échut, nous échûmes, vous échûtes, ils échurent.—*Future.* J'écherrai, tu écherras, etc.—*Conditional present.* J'écherrais, tu écherrais, etc.

No Subjunctive *Present.—Imperfect.* Que j'échusse, que tu échusses, qu'il échut, que nous échussions, que vous échussiez, qu'ils échussent.—Échoir *takes être in its compound tenses* (Acad.)

In Littré's Dict.—Échoir is conjugated in the third *Persons only* and as follows :—
Indicative *Present.*—Il échoit or il échet—ils échaient or ils échéent.—*Imperfect.* Il échoyait, ils échoyaient.—*Past definite.* Il échut, ils échurent.—*Future.* Il écherra or échoira, ils écherront or échoiront.

Conditional *Present.*—Il écherrait or échoirait ; ils écherraient or échoiraient.—Subjunc-tive *Present.*—Qu'il échoie, qu'ils échoient.—*Imperfect.* Qu'il échût, qu'ils échussent.—*Participle present.* échéant.—*Participle past.* Échu m.s ; Échue, f.s.

Compound tenses.—*Past indef.* Il est échu, ils sont échus, etc.

N.B.—*Avoir échu, is said of the day on which a payment falls due.*—Mon billet a échu le 30 du mois dernier ; il y a un mois qu'il est échu.

## S'EMBOIRE, *To get dull, (Paint.)*

Infinitive *Present.* S'Emboire.—*Participle present.* S'embuvant.—*Participle past.* Embu, m.s. ; embue, f.s. Indicative *Present.* Il s'emboit, ils s'emboivent, etc.

N.B. I. S'Emboire is conjugated like *Boire* page 106, but used only in the 3rd persons.
II. Emboire, *to imbibe,to soak in*—is used in each person and conjugated like Boire.

## ENCLORE, *To enclose, to close in, to fence.*

Enclore, is conjugated like clore (page 135.) Academy—In Litttré's Dict. it is conjugated as follows :—
Infinitive *Present,* Enclore.—*Participle present,* Enclosant.—*Participle past.* Enclos, m.s. ; Enclose, f.s.

Indicative *Present.*—J'enclos, tu enclos, il enclôt, nous enclosons,, vous enclosez, ils enclosent. *Imperfect.* J'enclosais, tu enclosais, etc.—*No Past definite.*—*Future.* J'enclorai, tu encloras, etc.

Conditional *Present.*—J'enclorais, tu enclorais, etc.—*Imperative.* Enclos, enclosons enclosez.

Subjunctive *Present.*—Que j'enclose, que tu encloses, etc. *No Imperfect.*

## FAILLIR, *To fail, to err, to come short, etc.*

Infinitive *Present.*—Faillir.—*Participle present.* Faillant. *Participle past.* Failli. m.s. , faillie, f.s.

Indicative *Present*—Je faux, tu faux, il faut ; nous faillons, vous faillez, ils faillent. *Imperfect.* Je faillais, tu faillais, etc.—*Past definite.* Je faillis, tu faillis, il faillit ; nous faillîmes, vous faillîtes, ils faillirent.—*Future.* Je faudrai, tu faudras, etc.

Conditional *Present.* Je faudrais, tu faudrais, etc.—Compound Tenses. J'ai failli, etc.—J'avais failli, etc. Many of the above tenses, says the Academy, are not used.

N.B.—I.—In Littré's Dict. we find the following remarks on the verb Faillir : The three persons singular of the *Present of the Ind.,* the *Future* and *Conditional* are becoming obsolete.
II. Some grammarians conjugate *Faillir* in the sense of to fail (in trade), to become *bankrupt,* as the regular verb, Finir, (Page 23.)

## FÉRIR, *To strike.*

Verb used only in the *Infinitive present,* and in this phrase : Sans coup férir, *without striking a blow.*
The *Past participle* ı Féru, m s., férue, f.s. ; *Wounded, struck* is employed by veterinary surgeons. *Ce cheval a le tendon féru.*

## FORCLORE, *To foreclose, (a law term.)*

Verb used only in the *Infinitive present,* Forclore, and the *Past participle* : Forclos, m.s. ; forclose, f.s. Ex : Il s'est laissé forclore.—Il a été forclos.—(Acad.)

## FORFAIRE, *To forfeit, to fail, to transgress.*

It is used only in the *Infinitive present* and the compound tenses which are formed with avoir.—*Infinitive present,* Forfaire.—*Past participle,* Forfait. (Laveaux). In Littré's Dict. Forfaire is conjugated like *Faire,* page 117.

## FRIRE, *To fry.*

INFINITIVE *Present,* Frire.—*No Participle present.*—*Participle past.* Frit, m.s. ; Frite, f.s.

INDICATIVE *Present,* Je fris, tu fris, il frit. *No plural. No Imperfect. No Past definite.*—*Future,* Je frirai, tu friras, il frira ; nous frirons, vous frirez, ils friront.

CONDITIONAL *Present,* Je frirais, tu frirais, etc.—*Imperative,* Fris.—COMPOUND TENSES. J'ai frit.—J'avais frit.—J'eus frit, etc.

N.B.—To supply the persons and tenses which are wanting, we employ *Faire,* prefixed to the *Infinitive* Frire. *Indicative present.* (Plural), Nous faisons frire, vous faites frire, ils font frire.—*Imperfect.* Je faisais frire, etc.—(Acad.)

## GÉSIR, *To lie (ill, dead, overthrown.)*

Verb used in the following tenses. INDICATIVE *Present,* Il gît, nous gisons, vous gisez, ils gisent.—*Imperfect,* Je gisais, tu gisais, etc.—*Participle present* Gisant ; some grammarians write Gissant.—(Acad.)

N.B.—*Ci-gît*—Here lies—*is the ordinary form by which an epitaph is begun.*

## HONNIR, *to dishonour, to disgrace.*

It is conjugated like FINIR, page 23, but is getting obsolete. *Honni soit qui mal y pense.* Evil be to him that evil thinks.

## IMBOIRE, *To imbue, (obsolete.)*

The *Past participle* remains only of this verb : *Imbu,* m.s. ; *Imbue,* f.s. Imbued, impressed. (Acad.)

N.B.—In Littré's Dict. Imboire is conjugated like Boire. (Page 106).

## ISSIR, *To descend, to spring from, (obsolete.)*

Verb used only in the *Past participle* ; Issu, m.s., Issue, f.s.

## JAILLIR, *To spout out.*

Verb conjugated like FINIR, but used only in the third persons of each tense. (Bescherelle's Dict.)

## LUIRE, *To shine.*

INFINITIVE *Present.* Luire.—*Participle present,* Luisant.—*Participle past.* Lui, (invariable).

INDICATIVE *Present* Je luis, tu luis, il luit, nous luisons, vous luisez, ils luisent. *Imperfect.* Je luisais, tu luisais, il luisait, nous luisions, vous luisiez, ils luisaient. No *Preterite. Future.* Je luirai, tu luiras, etc.

CONDITIONAL *Present.* Je luirais, tu luirais, etc. *Imperative,* Luis, luisons, luisez.

SUBJUNCTIVE *Present.* Que je luise, que tu luises, qu'il luise, que nous luisions, que vous luisiez, qu'ils luisent. —*No Imperfect.*—(Acad).

## MÉCROIRE, *To disbelieve.*

Verb used only in this *proverbial phrase* : Il est dangereux de croire et de mécroire.—(Acad.)

N.B.—In Littré's Dict. Mécroire is conjugated like Croire (page 113).

# MÉFAIRE, *To do evil, harm.*

**Verb scarcely used.**—(Acad.)—*Méfaire* is conjugated like *Faire*, and employed only in the INFINITIVE *Present*: *Méfaire*, and the *Participle past*, *Méfait*. It takes the auxiliary verb AVOIR, it is used only in the jocular or familiar style.—(Laveaux.)

# MALFAIRE, *To do evil.*

Verb used in the *Infinitive present* only—Ex:: être inclin à malfaire.—Il ne se plait qu'à malfaire.

N.B.—MALFAIRE, according to Leveaux and Littré, could be used in the Past Participle: *Malfait*—and in the compound tenses: Il a malfait—Ils ont malfait, etc.

# MESSEOIR, *To be unbecoming—not to become.*

MESSOIR is not used in the Infinitive Present, it is conjugated as Seoir, page 141.—(Acad.) In Littré's Dict. *Messeoir* has the following tenses: INDICATIVE *Present.* Je messieds, tu messieds, il messied; nous messeyons, vous messeyez, ils messeyent.—*Imperfect.* Je messayais, tu messayais, etc.—*Future.* Je messiérai, tu messiéras, il messiéra, etc.—CONDITIONAL *Present.* Je messiérais, tu messiérais, etc.

SUBJUNCTIVE *Present.* Que je messeye, que tu messeyes, qu'ils messeye, que nous messeyions, que vous messeyiez, qu'ils messeyient.

INFINITIVE *Present.* Messeoir. *Participle present.* Messéant. *No Participle past*, therefore no compound tenses.

# SE MOURIR, *To be dying, expiring.*

SE MOURIR, is seldom used, except in the *Indicative Present.* Je me meurs, tu te meurs, etc., and in the Imperfect. Je me mourais, tu te mourais, etc. (Acad.) See Mourir, page 84.

# OCCIRE, *To kill, (obsolete.)*

INFINITIVE *Present.* Occire.—*Participle present.* Occisant.—*Participle past.* Occis, m.s.; Occisse, f.s.—.INDICATIVE *present..* J'occis, tu occis, etc. See *Confire* for the other tenses, page 109.

N.B.—*Occire is used only in the familiar language or by archaism.* (Littré.)

# OUIR, *To hear.*

INFINITIVE *Present.* Ouir.—*Participle present*, Oyant.—*Participle past.* Ouï, m.s.; ouïe, f.s. INDICATIVE *Present.* J'ois, tu oit, il oit; nous oyons, vous oyez, ils oyent.—*Imperfect* J'oyais, tu oyais, etc.—*Past definite.* J'ouïs, tu ouïs, il ouït, nous ouïmes, vous ouïtes, ils ouïrent.— *Future* J'oirai, tu oiras, etc.—CONDITIONAL. J'oirais, tu oirais, etc.—*Imperative.* Oyons, oyez. SUBJUNCTIVE *Present.* Que j'oie, or que j'oye, etc. *Imperfect.* Que j'ouïsse, que tu ouïsses, etc. COMPOUND TENSES: *Past definite.* J'ai ouï, tu as ouï, etc.

N.B.—I. The verb *Ouir* is seldom used, except in the *Compound tenses* and the *Infinitive present.*—(Acad.)

II. The other tenses are employed in the jocular style, except, the *Past definite* and the *Imperfect* (Sub.)—(Littré.)

# PAÎTRE, *To graze.*

INFINITIVE *Present.* Paître.—*Participle present.* Paissant.—*Participle past.* Pu, (no feminine). INDICATIVE *Present.* Je pais, tu pais, il paît; nous paissons, vous paissez, ils paissent.— *Imperfect.* Je paissais, tu paissais, etc. *No Past definite.*—*Future.* Je paîtrai, tu paîtras, il paîtra, nous paîtrons, vous paîtrez, ils paîtront.

CONDITIONAL *Present.* Je paîtrais, tu paîtrais, il paîtrait, nous paîtrions, vous paîtriez, ils paîtraient.—*Imperative.* Pais, paissons, paissez.

SUBJUNCTIVE *Present.* Que je paisse, que tu paisses, qu'il paisse, que nous paissions, que vous paissiez, qu'ils paissent. *No Imperfect.*

N.B—I. The *Past Participle*, PU, is only used as a term of falconry.—Acad.

II. Repaître is conjugated like *Paître* and has besides the *Past definite ;* Je repus, tu repus, il reput, nous repûmes, vous repûtes, ils repurent ; and the *Imperfect* of the Sub., Que je repusse, que tu repusses, etc.

## PARFAIRE, *To complete, to finish.*

Verb used only in the *Infinitive Present :* Parfaire, and in the *Participle past*, Parfait. It takes the auxiliary : Avoir. (Laveaux).
N.B. —Parfaire is conjugated like Faire, but scarcely used. (Acad.).

## PARTIR, *To part, to divide.*

Verb seldom used, except in the *Infinitive Present*, and in this proverbial phrase : Avoir maille à *partir* avec quelqu'un. *To have a crow to pluck with anyone.*
N.B.—The *Participle past* Parti, m.s., Partie, f.s., is only employed in heraldry expressions.

## POINDRE, *To sting, to dawn, to break, to peep.*

Poindre, to sting, is seldom used, except in some familiar phrases : *Quel taon vous point ?*
Poindre, to dawn, etc., is employed in the Infinitive Present *Poindre*, and the Future, Je poindrai, tu poindras, il poindra, etc.—(Acad.)
N.B.—In Littré's Dict. *Poindre* is conjugated like *Joindre* (page 118).

## PROMOUVOIR, *To promote, (raise to dignity).*

Promouvoir is used only in the Infinitive Present : *Promouvoir*, and in the Past Participle : *Promu*, m.s. ; *Promue*, f.s. ; the Compound tenses are formed with *Avoir :* J'ai promu, etc.—(Acad.)
N.B.—*Promouvoir* is conjugated like *Mouvoir* (page 97.)—(Littré).

## PUER, *To stink, to smell strong.*

Puer is conjugated like *Parler*, and used in the following tenses : *Infinitive present.* Puer.— *Participle Present.* Puant.—*No Participle past.*—Indicative *Present.* Je pue, tu pues, etc.— *Imperfect.* Je puais, tu puais, etc.—*Future.*—Je puerai, tu pueras, etc.—Conditional *Present.* Je puerais, tu puerais, etc.—(Acad.).
N.B.—The *Past definite.* Je puai, etc.—*The Imperfect ( Sub. )* Que je puasasse, and the *Compound tenses :* Past Indefinite. J'ai pué, etc., could be used.—(Littré).

## QUERIR, *To fetch.*

Verb used only in the *Infinitive present.* Querir, and with the verbs :—*Aller, Venir, Envoyer.*—Ex. : Allez querir. Go and fetch. (It is getting obsolete).—(Acad.)
N.B.—I. Allez chercher—envoyons chercher, etc., are now used instead of : *Allez querir*, etc.
II. Laveaux writes querir, with an acute accent : Quérir.

## RAIRE or RÉER, *To bellow, (like a stag.)*

Infinitive *Present.* Raire.—*Participle present.* Rayant.—*Participle past.* Rait.
Indicative *Present.* Je rais, tu rais, il rait ; nous rayons, vous rayez, ils raient.—*Imperfect.* Je rayais, tu rayais, etc.—*Future.* Je rairai, tu rairas, etc.—*Subjunctive present.* Que je raie, que tu raies, qu'il raie, que nous rayions, que vous rayiez, qu'ils raient.
Réer.—Indicative *Present.* Je rée, tu rées, etc.—*Imperfect.* Je réais, tu réais, etc.— *Future.* Je rérai, tu réras, etc.—Subjunctive *present.* Que je rée, que tu rées, etc.—*Imperfect.* Que je réasse, que tu réasses, etc. *Participle present.* Réant. *Participle past.* Réé—(Littré's Dict.).
N.B.—Raire is not conjugated in the Dict. of the French Academy.

## RAVOIR, *To get again.*

Verb used only in the *Infinitive present.* Ravoir, (Acad.)—The *Future.* Je raurai, tu rauras, etc., and the *Conditional Present.* Je raurais, tu raurais, etc., could be employed.—(Littré).

## RECHOIR, *To fall again, to relapse, (obsolete).*

It is used only in the *Infinitive Present*, Rechoir, and the *Past Participle*, Rechu, m.s. ; rechue, f.s.—(Acad.)

## RECLURE, *To shut up.*

Verb used only in the *Infinitive Present*, Reclure, the *Past Participle*, Reclus, m.s. ; recluse, f.s. and the *Compound tenses :* J'ai reclus, J'avais reclus, etc.,—(Littré's Dict.).

## RELUIRE, *To shine, to glitter.*

RELUIRE is conjugated like *Luire.* (See page 138).

## REPAÎTRE, *To feed.*

Verb conjugated like *Paître.* (See page 139).

## SAILLIR, *To gush, to gush out, to break forth.*

Verb conjugated like *Finir,* but used only in the *Infinitive* and the third persons of some tenses.—(Acad.)—In the Grammaire des Grammaires, by Girault-Duvivier, *Saillir,* is conjugated in the third persons of each tense and the *Infinitive.*

## SAILLIR, *To project, to stand out.*

INFINITIVE *Present.* Saillir.—*Participle present.*—Saillant.—*Participle past.* Sailli, m.s. ; Saillie, f.s.
INDICATIVE *Present.* Il saille, ils saillent.—*Imperfect.* Il saillait, ils saillaient.—*Past definite.* Il saillit, ils saillirent.—*Future.* Il saillera, ils sailleront.—CONDITIONAL *Present.* Il saillerait, ils sailleraient.
SUBJUNCTIVE *Present.* Qu'il saille, qu'ils saillent.—*Imperfect.* Qu'il saillît, qu'ils saillissent. COMPOUND TENSES : *Past definite,* Il a sailli, ils ont sailli, etc.—(Bescherelle's Dict.).

## SEMONDRE, *To invite (to a ceremony), (obsolete).*

Verb used only in the *Infinitive present :* Semondre.—(Acad).
N.B.—The singular of the INDICATIVE *Present.* Je semons, tu semons, il semond.—The *Imperfect.* Je semonnais, tu semonnais, etc.—The *Future.* Je semondrai, tu semondras, etc., and the CONDITIONAL *present.* Je semondrais, tu semondrais, could be used.—(Littré's Dict.).

## SEOIR, *To sit, to be seated.*

The *Participle present :* Séant, and the *Past participle.* Sis, m.s., Sise, f.s., are used only.—(Acad.).
In Littré's Dict. SEOIR is conjugated as follows : INDICATIVE *Present.* Je sieds, tu sieds, il sied, nous seyons, vous seyez, ils seient.—*Imperative.* Sieds-toi, seyons-nous, seyez-vous.—*The participles* as above.
N.B.—The Participles : *Séant* and *Sis* are used in law and mean : Sitting—and situated.

## SEOIR, *To fit, to become, to suit.*

INDICATIVE *Present.* Il sied, ils siéent.—*Imperfect.* Il seyait, ils seyaient.—*Future.* Il siéra, ils siéront.—CONDITIONAL *Present.* Il siérait, ils siéraient.— SUBJUNCTIVE *Present.* Qu'il siée, qu'ils siéent.—*Participle present.* Seyant or Séant.—*Participle past.* Sis.
N.B.—I. The Past Participle *Sis* is not used in that sense.—(Littré's Dict.).
II. The persons in italics, in the above verbs, are the only ones given by the Academy.

## SOUDRE, *To solve (obsolete).*

Verb used only in the *Infinitive present :* Soudre, un problème.—(Acad.). The verb Résoudre, page 126, is now employed instead.

## SOURDRE, *To spring out, to gush forth.*

The *Present of the Infinitive* SOURDRE, and the third persons of the *Present of the Indicative* are used : Il sourd, ils sourdent.—(Acad.)

In Littré's Dict. the following tenses are given : *Indicative present.* Il sourd, ils sourdent.— *Imperfect.* Il sourdait, ils sourdaient. *Past definite.* Il sourdit, ils sourdirent. *Future.* Il sourdra, ils sourdront.

CONDITIONAL *Present.* Il sourdrait, ils sourdraient. SUBJUNCTIVE *Present.* Qu'il sourde, qu'ils sourdent. *Imperfect.* Qu'il sourdît, qu'ils sourdissent.

*Participle present.* Sourdant. (No Participle Past).

## SOULOIR, *To be wont, accustomed (obsolete).*

The *Imperfect :* Je soulais, tu soulais, etc., are the only forms used and these even seldom.—
(Acad.)

## SURGIR, *To land, to reach (a haven).*

The *Infinitive present* :  *Surgir,* is only used.—*Surgir au port.*—(Acad.)

## SURGIR, *To arise, to spring up, to start up.*

Verb conjugated like *Finir* and used nearly in all the tenses, but only in the third persons.—
(Poitevin.)

The tenses mostly employed are : The *Indicative present.* Il surgit, ils surgissent. *Imperfect.* Il surgissait, ils surgissaient—*Past definite,* il surgit, ils surgirent. *Future.* Il surgira, ils surgiront. *Conditional present.* Il surgirait, ils surgiraient. *Participle present.* Surgissant.

## TISTRE, *To weave (obsolete).*

*Tistre* is used only in the compound tenses with its Past Participle, *tissu,* m.s., *tissue,* f.s. ; it is conjugated with *Avoir.*

*Past definite.* J'ai tissu, tu as tissu, il a tissu, etc.

# A COMPLETE LIST OF IRREGULAR AND DEFECTIVE VERBS,

## AND VERBS WITH PECULIAR SPELLINGS.

EIFFEL TOWER, PARIS

VENUS DE MILO,  LOUVRE

# 146

CHATEAU DE CHAUMONT, LOIRE VALLEY